A Place of Refuge

AN EXPERIMENT IN COMMUNAL LIVING

THE STORY OF WINDSOR HILL WOOD

Tobias Jones

Quercus

First published in Great Britain in 2015 by

Quercus Publishing Ltd
Carmelite House
50 Victoria Embankment
London EC4Y 0DZ

An Hachette UK company

A CIP catalogue record for this book is available
from the British Library

HB ISBN 9781848662483
ExTP ISBN 9781848662490
EBOOK ISBN 9781848667907

10 9 8 7 6 5 4 3 2 1

Typeset by Hewer Text UK Ltd, Edinburgh
Printed and bound in Great Britain, by Clays Ltd, St Ives plc

This book is dedicated to
Dennis and Mary Massey.
With love and gratitude.

Author's Note

I've walked an extremely fine line in these pages between authenticity and confidentiality. Nothing here has been invented or fictionalized. The stories and situations in these pages are all true. But whilst I have attempted to be faithful to the people who lived with us, at the same time I have tried to render them unrecognizable. I have changed minor details and the names of almost everyone except my own family and the livestock. I have also blended certain events, backgrounds and traits so that although someone might recognize themselves or a certain individual from a particular detail, some of the incidents in these pages did not involve the person they think they have recognized. I have done this to avoid rather than cause offence, and so that no one can read this book and say, 'That's me'; but I appreciate that this may cause confusion for the people concerned. I have also frequently felt obliged to draw a veil over events and conversations for the sake of confidentiality. I leave it to both the reader, and our guests, to decide if I have strayed too far either side of that fine line.

Preface

'I went to the woods because I wished to live deliberately, to front only the essential facts of life . . . and not,
when I came to die, discover that I had not lived'
                                    –Henry David Thoreau

This book is the story of a woodland sanctuary in Somerset. My
wife, Francesca, and I set it up with the sole purpose of offering
refuge to people going through a period of crisis in their lives. We
hoped to emulate a community we knew down in Dorset, a place
that was a haven for those struggling with addiction, bereavement,
separation, depression, penury, eating disorders, homelessness,
PTSD and all the other ailments, illnesses and misfortunes that
beset us in life.

It's over five years now since we came to live in the woods, and
in that time there have been so many mishaps and miracles, so
many characters and escapades, that it seems a lifetime ago.
Those years have been gruelling, exhilarating, exhausting, uplifting, exciting, depressing, joyful, rewarding and, always,
eye-opening. The learning curve has been so steep that it has
often seemed almost vertical. Human nature is constantly fascinating, and over the years we've seen all sorts, from the very
admirable to the far less so. When you have an open-door policy,

the whole spectrum of humanity will roll up: rough diamonds and smooth talkers, the overbearing and the underwhelming. We've had fantasists and fundamentalists, seekers and plain attention-seekers, wanderers and wayfarers, hippies, heroes, dreamers, diggers, flakes and, sometimes, saviours. Normally, once guests have been with us for a day or two, our children give them a nickname: we've had Roadkill Kev, Inappropriate Ian, Trevor Whatever, Mary Poppins, The Busker, Marshmellow, Virginia Creeper, and many more – from a one-legged Dane wearing half a pair of leopard-skin tights to a seven-foot cross-dresser called Simone. We've had well over a hundred strangers living in our woodland shelter, some staying for just one night, but most for many months and a few for more than a year.

There have been many misconceptions about what we're doing, so it's probably as well to dispel some myths at the start. I was born and brought up in Somerset; this wasn't some urbanite's romantic escape to an idealized countryside. If anything, it was the opposite: an attempt to help people put an end to incessant escapism. I've often thought that modern life is rootless, non-committal and excitedly distracted by fleeting highs, and that part of an individual's healing is about discovering rootedness, commitment and stability. In that sense, Francesca and I never felt we were retreating from the so-called 'real world' but engaging with it more deeply: all sorts of people – troubled soldiers, ex-offenders, victims of abuse, sex-workers, and so on – came to live with us and gave us insights into what life can really be like. We weren't living in some protective bubble, trying to shut something out, but actually throwing our doors wide open. We weren't living out some fantasy but trying to avoid fantasies.

Nor were we looking for a better quality of life. It's true that we yearned for an existence with more rugged simplicity and stillness, but the notion that living communally with tough, wounded characters could increase our comfort or quiet is pretty laughable. Quite often, visitors would look round the woods on a sunny June afternoon and comment on how peaceful it was, and how it must be wonderful to be so far away from the stresses of the city. I was usually pleased that they noticed some serenity but would try to explain that peace is exceptionally hard work, and that the pressures of farming and forestry can equal any anxiety generated by the city.

People generally assumed that we were vegan eco-warriors who home-schooled our kids in an off-grid yurt. It's true that we lived for years without a TV or a dishwasher and that we heat our home, and its water, with wood; it's true that we're concerned about the provenance of what we eat and produce a large proportion of our own food. We avoid noisy machinery as much as possible. But we live in an ordinary house made of bricks and mortar. Our kids go to local schools. We're concerned about sustainability, but as much about the financial, emotional and psychological sort as the environmental. We're not obsessed with self-sufficiency, and are far more interested in interdependency than independence, more attracted by interaction than isolation.

Another misconception is that Francesca and I are nobly helping the needy. It might be the case, I hope, that we're reasonably generous, but we've received as much as we've given. It's one of the mind-blowing aspects of open-door living that more is gifted than stolen, more offered than filched. I've attempted, in this book, to offer a corrective to the popular, bucolic image of communal living – where people hug in flower meadows and strum guitars around campfires – so I've never hidden the fact that it can be demanding, challenging and, occasionally, infuriating. But we've been extremely blessed by our guests over the years, and we've always made it clear that they're helping us as much as the other way round. There's no way we could, by ourselves, manage a ten-acre woodland, look after pigs, sheep, chickens, bees, a polytunnel, a glasshouse, raised beds, an orchard and children, as well as doing the cooking, cleaning, shopping and all the rest. Part of someone's recovery is that they realize they're indispensable: they're needed, not needy, they're caring, not cared for. There's never a sense here that Francesca and I are the strong staff and that our guests are the wobbly clients. We are, I hope, well qualified to do what we're doing, but we've always made it clear that we're not professionals and have no medical or counselling backgrounds. If anything, what we do is deliberately anti-professional because we feel, like George Bernard Shaw, that professionalism is sometimes a conspiracy against the laity. We opened our house to those in crisis not because of a feeling of superiority, but because of identification. We've had quite a few crises ourselves: we could only afford to do this in the first place because of bereavements of our own, and I had a 'lost year' a long time ago that I've never forgotten.

Another common misunderstanding arises from the clichés and preconceptions about communalism. The concept is either demonized or idealized. We all know enough about Jim Jones and Georgetown, David Koresh and Waco, or Osho and Rajneeshpuram, to be aware that communities can often go slowly, but seriously, berserk. When individuals submit completely to a messianic leader, 'community' bleeds into 'cult', a place of slavish obedience and, often, of suicide and murder. That, perhaps, is why the notion of a 'commune' is held so low in the public esteem. Communes are considered to be conceited ghettoes. They are, it's thought, places where like-minded lemmings gather to create homogenous groups that are at best doolally, at worst dangerous. If you're in any doubt as to how bad the reputation of communalism is, try telling your next-door neighbour that you're about to start up a community on the other side of their wall. Unless you're very lucky, their eyes will widen as they take a step away from you, all the while imagining dropouts, drugs and sexual deviancy.

Yet at the same time 'community' has become one of the buzzwords of the political lexicon, offered as a soothing balm for the sores of contemporary life. Each time a village shop, a post office or a pub closes, each time there's an iconic crime, robbery or riot, we're told that lack of community is the cause. With the revelation (in both the 2001 and 2011 censuses) that 34 per cent of households contain only a single inhabitant, and with parts of the country struggling with mass immigration and a dwindling sense of identity, everyone seems to mourn the loss of 'community'. It's a word deployed to describe both a new kind of policeman (the 'community support officer') and a renamed quango (half of the 'Housing Corporation' has become the 'Homes and Communities Agency'). People use 'community' to describe a workforce, or a religious group, or a bunch of people connected online who have never met. It's a word that has become almost completely meaningless.

Our small community is neither a closed cult nor a loose label. But, beyond that, it's extremely difficult to explain quite what it is. We don't even really know what to call it ourselves: 'commune' sounds too hippie or dated, 'community' sounds like half a village and 'fellowship' is, for some, overly religious. We sometimes call it – rather a mouthful – an 'extended household', because it's first and foremost a family home where we lay half a dozen extra places at the table and provide half a dozen extra beds.

We're doing it because we believe that communalism can be an antidote to many of the sadnesses and sorrows of modern life. Not just addiction, say, or homelessness, but also the issues that lie behind those more explicit ones; problems like loneliness or simply dismay at modern life. Communal living offers the chance to find belonging instead of rootlessness, commitment in place of impermanence, and purpose rather than despair. It allows a deeply satisfying, paradoxical combination of anarchism and traditionalism, of counter-culturalism and conservationism. Communal living has invariably been a form of resistance or defiance, a way to set yourself apart and offer a coherent, hard-lived critique of the so-called 'real world': from the Diggers (the agrarian socialists of the seventeenth century) to the Doukhobors (the persecuted, spiritual pacifists of Imperial Russia), any conscious congregation of humans living deliberately beyond the norms of society has been an act of dissent. But it's also trad-itional because in living together and learning ancient crafts, you necessarily draw on centuries of accumulated wisdom and borrow from ancestors' ingenuity and sagacity. Communal living, it seems to me, is an alliance with the past to critique the present in the hope of a better future. That's one of its great attractions: a community is a gathering not just of people but of generations, a way to pass the torch from one age to the next.

In contrast, I've often thought that the nuclear family is a prob-lematic way to live. I'm not even sure that it's a natural way to bring up children. That view might be the result of spending so much time in southern Europe, where – along with much of the rest of the world – families are often 'extended' and various rela-tives and different generations live side by side. In Italy it gives society a predictability and stability and means that, for better or worse, the social fabric is still tightly knit. My own parents were fairly unorthodox in having an open house, usually letting people stay for weeks or months and even inviting them along on family holidays. The memories of that exciting family home where intriguing people rolled up doubtless planted a seed and made the leap to full-blooded communalism far easier. Over the years I began to feel that the nuclear family is like a fortress. Home is no longer the place where charity begins but the castle with a metaphorical moat that holds the big, bad world at bay. And the idealization of the 'perfect family' causes melancholy not just for those who aren't part of one (and, let's be honest, who is?) but also for those who have a fairly happy family yet still feel that something's missing. A nuclear family can sometimes be, I think, claustrophobic, frantic and defensive.

That said, I can understand why a family might be defensive. It's a dangerous world, and young children deserve protection. Inevitably, when people hear of our woodland sanctuary, the first thing they ask about is our three children, about whether it's wise to expose them to all sorts of obvious and less obvious threats. Over the years, we've had to be pretty shrewd to ward off some insidious dangers. But the many advantages to our children of a place like this are another reason why we're doing it in the first place. We noticed when we were travelling around various communities before setting up this refuge that the children who had grown up in radical, open-door groups were remarkably mature, eloquent and unfazed by the most weird or eccentric arrival. They were non-judgemental, but at the same time they were able to make some fairly sound judgements and appeared less susceptible to the seductions of drink, drugs and other temptations. A lot of the children we met didn't discriminate against people, but they were discriminating in the old sense of being discerning. They had enjoyed pretty idyllic childhoods but were streetwise too. That, we thought, was how we wanted our children to grow up. It's been an extremely delicate balancing act and there have been moments in which we've been very concerned about our kids. Not just because of the scariest possibilities but also because of the constant emotional turbulence created by distressed and disturbed guests. I've got to admit that after five years of living like this I can certainly see the attractions of being a nuclear family again. But we still believe it's been great for our children: they share every meal with half a dozen others – recently arrived strangers or long-term guests – which gives them first-hand experience of the wonders and excitements, and the dangers and deceits, of life.

About ten years ago I wrote a book called *Utopian Dreams* (to which this book is, I suppose, the hard-bitten response, a sort of 'Utopian Realities'). *Utopian Dreams* was a quest to find the ideal way in which human beings might share their lives, money, meals, possessions and ideals. We visited and stayed in dozens of different communities both in Britain and Italy and were fortunate to find, in an isolated hamlet near the Dorset coast, a community called Pilsdon. Founded by a maverick Anglican priest and his wife in 1958, it's a working farm that welcomes life's walking wounded and those on the margins of society: anyone bruised and bloodied by bad luck or bad judgement. Twenty to thirty people live there, working the land and reflecting on their lives. There's something about the rhythm of life that feels healthy and wholesome: there is hay to cut, there are cows to milk, logs to split, vegetable beds to weed. It's exceptionally hard work, but somehow relaxing too. The mix of people living there at any one time sounds like an explosive cocktail of characters and yet it's hard not to be blown away by the gentleness of the place. Although everyone is united by some kind of sorrow, it's surprisingly cheerful, with a lot of banter and laughter. Nobody, I thought, felt like a 'charity case', even though people were working at gradually putting their lives back together. There's a monastic simplicity there, with the day punctuated by bells for meals or for prayer. Its compassion is contagious. It's a place where they believe in the survival of the weakest.

Pilsdon's founders, Percy Smith and his wife, Gaynor, had been inspired to start the community by the example of Nicholas Ferrar, the founder of Little Gidding in the seventeenth century. It was Little Gidding, of course, that inspired T. S. Eliot to write his famous poem of the same name, one of the *Four Quartets*. Ferrar himself had been persuaded to start his unusual household by the radical monasticism of the early Church. Throughout the twentieth century people did something similar, gathering together to work the land and offer hospitality to those in need: in Nomadelfia in Tuscany, at the Community of the Ark in southern France, as well as at the Bruderhof, L'Arche, Emmaus and Camphill communities. If you sit at the dining table at some of those places, the chances are you'll be sharing the meal with all sorts: perhaps an asylum seeker, an ex-offender, a jam-maker from round the corner, a recovering addict or a wayfarer. You may well be sitting between a bricklayer and a bishop. There are very few places in Britain where you get that degree of inclusiveness and variety.

There was something about Pilsdon and comparable communities that seemed ancient but also visionary. They offered a way of life that was 'so old that it looks like new'. That was what, probably, attracted us to Pilsdon and to similar shelters. They were low-tech, sometimes deliberately Luddite, yet appeared strangely futuristic, because they were surviving with very little, and that, after this age of abundance, is what the future might be like.

Ten years on, I'm not sure I agree with all the conclusions of *Utopian Dreams*. I'm distrustful of any theorizing or pontificating about communalism. The 'crooked timber' of humanity is so tricky to work with that each edifice will have its own strengths and weaknesses, its own idiosyncratic twists and knots and unusual grains. But writing that book introduced Francesca and me to a way of life that was breathtaking. It was anarchic and unconventional but also peaceful and creative. Over the years we kept going back to Pilsdon. I became a trustee there. We saw close up many of the classic issues with which all communities have to grapple: leadership, finances, boundaries, privacy, rules, inclusion, exclusion and, of course, the washing-up.

We felt a very strong vocation to emulate Pilsdon. It wasn't the stereotypical calling you might see in a film, with a booming voice or a bolt of lightning from the sky. But it was nonetheless a very precise summons, an insistent suggestion that we were expected to do something similar: to turn the Sermon on the Mount into a manifesto for life. Now, I know that I risk forfeiting the sympathy of the vast majority of readers if I confess a religious inspiration behind what we're doing. And I know too that, over the years, many potential guests have been put off by our description of 'traditional Christian hospitality'. But at Windsor Hill Wood actions are more important than beliefs, the fruits more important than the roots. We've had guests who are Muslim, Bahá'í, Hindu, Jewish, Christian, pagan, agnostic and, most commonly, atheist. Very rarely has anyone complained about our inspiration being from the gospels. We happily, though actually fairly rarely, talk about religion, but when we do it's never with the intention of proselytizing. We don't need to because those who live here already believe in what we're doing. They understand it; they get it. And we share so much in our life together – money, silence, food, work, and so on – that the beliefs we don't share are less divisive than they are intriguing.

We wanted the refuge to be a woodland rather than traditional agricultural land for a variety of reasons, mainly, I suppose, because there's something primitive and pleasing about living surrounded by trees. They make you feel cherished by giving you strong columns, speckled ceilings and floral carpets. They provide such an efficient shelter that even in the strongest rainfall you barely get wet if the tree is in leaf. They offer shade in summer and a windbreak in winter. The rustle of leaves in the summer is not unlike the soporific sound of breakers on the sand. The solidity and longevity of trees offer reassurance and rootedness; they offer continuity amidst the chaos of communal living. They have strength but flexibility; they're immobile objects that sway easily in the wind. They're full of energy but also stillness. It's hard to think of a better counsel for human behaviour.

But as well as all that dreamy stuff there were practical reasons for looking for a woodland. I'm a (very amateur) green woodworker, using pole lathes, chisels and axes, so I liked the idea of sourcing wood from our own backyard. And I relished the chance to share quiet carpentry with people in a period of recovery because I was convinced of its therapeutic value. There's something forgiving about working with wood: almost any mistake can be contained, accepted or corrected. It requires precision and concentration but also gives you an opportunity, when you're doing something laborious, for mental freewheeling. It allows you to focus on the minutiae and, whilst you're at it, to discern the bigger picture in your life. I had a suspicion that many people miss manual labour, the kind that is creative and communal. Basic carpentry, I thought, would provide it. A woodland, moreover, would allow us to meet our own fuel needs, as well as giving us free building materials for sheds and barns and the like.

The last reason we decided to embark on the project was the

fact that my day job is slightly unusual: being a writer requires, I think, a lot of time away from the desk. I often find that decent ideas come when I'm chopping wood or doing some carpentry. Personally, I can't write for more than three or four hours a day: not because of stamina but because I simply haven't enough to say to the world and, even if I did, I'm not sure the world would want to listen. Managing a woodland refuge was intended to be the opposite of my writing life. One occupation was solitary, cerebral, vaguely solipsistic and definitely sedentary; the other was social, physical, altruistic and outdoors. The two jobs would dovetail well, I thought, and the contrast would make each an attractive escape from the other, just as, historically, monasteries have always combined manual and cultural labours.

I never expected to write a book about the project. Managing the woodland was the antidote to my writing, not an extension of it. But over the years, as sad, amusing and sometimes mysterious things happened, people kept saying, 'You've got to write a book about this one day.' I wrote a column about our project for the *Observer* for six months, and that period proved that there was a large readership yearning to know about the nitty-gritty of communal living. And as the years went by I realized how many people longed to do something similar but didn't know how. A vast number of questers sought us out and asked advice about how to create their own shelter or refuge. In a way, this book is the guide I wish we had had when we started out and I hope it will serve as one to others who share our calling.

The psychiatrist and Holocaust survivor Viktor Frankl once wrote that 'success, like happiness, cannot be pursued; it must ensue.' I've often thought that the same could be said of a sense of community: it only ensues. It's not enough to long for social or communal cohesion. It comes only in the wake of a greater purpose. In our case, that purpose was offering refuge to people undergoing a period of crisis in their lives. We would offer people a peaceful place where there was a lot of work and a lot of rest. Through all the tough times of our first five years, the simplicity of that vision has never changed.

But when I think back to the beginning of our communal adventure, we were rather wet behind the ears. We were naive and trusting. I have, I think, the dangerous virtue of always seeing the best in people. Looking back, it would have been better, sometimes, to perceive the worst in them too. Many people took us for a ride. Plenty of things went missing. More than a few of our guests fell off the wagon fairly spectacularly. People who weren't at peace with themselves made sure no one else could be at peace either. Slowly, our initial enthusiasm and idealism gave way to a wistful weariness. We were, for long periods, on the brink of nervous exhaustion, compassion fatigue and financial ruin.

It took years to understand how to build and sustain our community, and there were many rows and tears along the way. There were, inevitably, arguments about the washing-up and the workload, about money and leadership. Sometimes, it felt like being stuck in a lift with the same people day after day. Or it was like Christmas every day, with the same excitement and laughter, tension and arguments. If the narrative that follows feels a bit chaotic or contradictory, it's because our tiny community itself was, at times, pretty chaotic and contradictory. There was no smooth, linear progression. If we learned lessons, we quickly discovered we needed to learn new ones. One visitor described our lifestyle as 'the storm before the storm'. But we did, slowly, figure out what we were doing, and something wonderful started to happen. It just began to work. Around the huge chestnut table we had made there would often be ten or twelve people. On any one occasion there might be a monosyllabic man with a long beard, a talkative divorcee, a bipolar teenager, a thin, nervous addict in recovery, our three kids, my wife, me and a couple of others. We had created a micro-community and, quite often, it really was enchanting. Someone would roll up and teach our children the harmonica. Another person would make pink elder-flower cordial. Someone would weave a basket out of the willow we'd just coppiced. We would swap stories around the stove. Having thrown our doors wide open, amazing gifts started to arrive: someone gave us a camper van, a woman donated half a tonne of pig food. Gifts just kept coming: everything from a truck load of pallets to surplus camping gear. We were breeding pigs, chickens and sheep, planting an orchard, coppicing hazel and willow, keeping bees, heating the house and water with wood, sculpting a cob oven, converting outbuildings, making chairs and creating our own charcoal. We were surviving together in the egg-shaped hollow of an old quarry, gradually turning a brown-field, post-industrial site into a working woodland. We began to see the essential facts of life that Thoreau alluded to in *Life in the Woods*, and we'll never, as he warned, regret that we haven't lived.

Year One

'All good men love an axe'
– John Stewart Collis

We liked the name: Rock House. It sounded solid, a place with proper foundations. The name came from the fact that it was the old quarry-master's house, where rocks were sorted and accounts settled. It was at the end of a bumpy track – the end, quite literally, of the road. There was a small stream to the left of the drive which then bent round in front of the house. The house itself must have been mid-Victorian. It had a diminutive fireplace in every room. It wasn't large at all – just a kitchen and a sitting room downstairs, and three petite bedrooms upstairs – but it had a large annexe nearby, and in between was a rustic infill: a spacious room with thick beams, a large wood-burner and huge glass doors that looked out on to the woods. Our predecessors had called it the garden room, so we called it that too. It was the sort of room that made you feel as if you were still outdoors.

Outside, there were two sheds, a workshop, a greenhouse and a couple more stone outbuildings. Behind the workshop, up a gentle slope, was a small meadow of long grass and wild flowers. The rest of the ten-acre site was a combination of woodland and clearings. Being an old quarry, it was all cradled in an area the shape of cupped hands. So although there was no great view, the place felt completely protected and sheltered. The steep sides of the quarry were scree and stone, but even they were covered with trees.

It felt as if nature were slowly but surely taking back the land. If you kicked the ground as you walked around, you would scuff up nothing more than a gravel pit. But it was now disguised by a colourful carpet: there were wild strawberry plants all over the woods; their little serrated leaves covered the gravel and throughout the early summer they produced tiny red berries no bigger than a child's fingernail. There were the yellow-and-red curves of bird's foot trefoil, the hairy purple of heal-all.

The woodland was a mixture of native broadleaves: ash, oak, hawthorn, hazel and a lot of goat willow, also known as sallow. None of it had ever been planted. It had merely colonized the quarry over the previous four or five decades through natural regeneration. That meant that there were often trees so close together you couldn't walk between them. Some had even twisted into each other, so that a sycamore and an ash, or a hazel and an oak, seemed to be growing from the same stem. It was a dense, dark place, occasionally feeling more like a swamp: the trunks were covered with dripping moss or clothed in ivy and old man's beard. Ferns uncurled on the ground, spreading out in all directions like party blowouts. It was a young, scrawny, completely unmanaged woodland. None of the trees was so mature that you couldn't encircle it with two hands.

We quickly realized that this was no bluebell-carpeted, ancient woodland. The site, like many abandoned quarries, had been used as a tip. Poking out between the moss and ferns were car bumpers, rusting prams, broken bricks, gnarls of concrete, smashed bathroom suites, bits of engines, plastic buckets and rusting beer cans.

As we got more used to it, we could recognize, under the ivy, the shape of the tippings, like moguls on a ski slope: rounded humps of unwanted waste and debris that, however overgrown, looked unnatural somehow, too angular or unlikely. Soon after we moved in, I went out foraging for food and saw quite a few tall, thinnish fungi. I turned to the field guide, enthused that I was manfully about to provide my family with the natural gifts of the soil . . . only to read that the shaggy-inkcap mushroom usually grows by the side of roads and on rubbish tips.

So the land wasn't, clearly, virgin territory but a scarred brownfield site. Because of the quarrying, it wasn't flat but had plateaus and dips and, all over the place, ruined buildings. There were walls in the middle of the woodland, steps and sidings and tunnels where you least expected them. There were even one or two caves, almost vertical fissures in the rock that went far deeper than the eye could see. With its huge boulders and ubiquitous gravel, it felt a bit like those 1970s sci-fi sets made of polystyrene.

Nor was it in the most salubrious part of Somerset. It was just outside Shepton Mallet, a town with its fair share of social deprivation and rural poverty. It had been dominated until its recent closure by a lifers' prison with stern walls and barred windows. The town used to be known for its breweries, and there's still a cider factory here, with its iconic Babycham fawn outside. Half the premises on the single high street stand empty, unable to compete with the chains and supermarkets of the trading estates. One of the remaining shops – a friendly ironmonger – is called 'Dredge and Male', a name that sounds a bit like 'Drudge and Bloke'. This, it's clear, isn't a particularly glamorous part of the world.

But communities rarely occur in Georgian mansions or Palladian villas. Because they're usually started by people who

have more ideals than money, they take root in discarded or deso-
late spaces. Slab City in the States, an old barracks in the Colorado
Desert, is just the most famous example of a community emerging on 'the abandoned places of Empire'. I quite liked the fact that
our beautiful woodland was a brownfield site; that after being a
quarry it had clearly been used as a dump for the rubbish people
didn't want. We could use stuff labelled 'rubbish' by the less
resourceful. Any time we were short of money we collected some
of the metal and got twenty or thirty quid for it. And I liked the
fact that nature was rapidly reclaiming the post-industrial landscape: that what was little more than a gravel pit for fly-tippers was
being changed into a far more rewarding kind of wilderness.

We were fond of the town too. It seemed like a land of the
underdog, a place of derelict buildings, abandoned quarries and
disused viaducts. Once you got away from the high street, there
were many narrow alleys and surprising footpaths. It has, I'm
told, more listed buildings than the nearby, and far smarter, city
of Wells. Like many slightly deprived towns, Shepton is a warm
and welcoming place. Because there's a lot of social, and afford-
able, housing, it has – by Somerset standards – a surprising ethnic
diversity. And the surrounding countryside is remarkable. The
rolling hills and windswept plateaus of the Mendips, overlooking
the levels, are stunning. There's something earthy and honest
about Somerset. It's a place where environmentalism – care for
the soil, for wildlife and livestock – isn't a fashion but, for many,
a traditional way of life. Somerset is arguably one of the centres of
English alternative living, a place of rugged hippies and agricultural idealists, the home not only of the Glastonbury Festival but
also of the Green Scythe Fair and plenty of deep ecologists (environmental philosophers). This was the county where I grew up
and I was absurdly content to return.

It sometimes felt, that first summer, as if we were in one of those Disney films where a character finds themselves deep in the wood surrounded by hundreds of animals. There were rabbits calmly bouncing around the clearing outside our house that would occasionally stop to sit and nibble before bouncing some more. Quite often, there would be roe deer too. The beautiful, lean beasts would saunter up to our front door to look inside at the human imposters. We began to recognize their light-brown bodies watching us nonchalantly from between the trees and the way they would suddenly bound away, scampering and jumping at the first hint of danger. The noises, too, were wonderful: the drilling of a woodpecker, the hooting of wood pigeons, the various whistles and warblings of dozens of others. At dusk you could see the playful waddle of badgers as they cautiously emerged from their setts. At night it became even noisier: great shrieks and squawks and scratchings.

There were only four of us to begin with. Francesca, my wife, is from Parma in northern Italy. She's the opposite of the stereotype of the boisterous Italian: self-contained and self-controlled, she seems to have a Zen-like detachment that some people mistake for aloofness. But she can be short with nonsense and hot air, a quality that would come in useful. She has a look that can stop people in their tracks. She's usually the one who tempers my idealism with realism, chuckling when I come up with a crazy plan. 'Are you mad?' is one of her most frequent questions to me. She's a very generous and wise judge of character, and has a great sense of the absurd, often getting the giggles when she's done or seen something ridiculous.

Francesca always insisted that Windsor Hill Wood had to be first and foremost a family home, not an institution. She had sensed a lack of homeliness in many of the communities we had seen, a feeling that nobody cared much because those communities belonged to everyone and to no one. She wanted our home, as much as the woodland and its guests, to be cared for, for it to feel like a homestead, not an asylum. I think many visitors here, expecting a disorderly or down-at-heel place, were surprised to see some Italian panache amidst the simplicity. It was Fra who made the place stylish and warm. She cared about towels and sheets, candles and tablecloths, not because of bourgeois petty-mindedness but because they were signs of hospitality, all part of a visual presentation of ordered generosity. She was also in the midst of life and death. She had recently lost her father, and was still grieving for him, and for the fact that she hadn't, until the final days, been in Italy when he was dying. She was also pregnant with our third child.

Our first, Benedetta, was called Benny by everyone. Ever since birth, Benny had been full of grit. She had learned to speak extremely early, and it was invariably to assert herself. 'Hear me,' she would say, like a town crier, when she wanted an audience. She was a toddler's parody of a diva: demanding, ebullient and incredibly determined. When Emma, her younger sister, came into the room crying, Benny would follow quickly behind, saying, 'I didn't kick her.' Aged four at the beginning of our communal experiment, Benny could already hold her own in any conversation with an adult. She would talk knowingly about an agapanthus or the vegetable she called 'Swiss charge'. It might have been her Italian heritage, but she was obsessed by clothes, usually wearing pantomime frocks from the dressing-up drawer. She loved making things, especially a mess. She could get through miles of sticky tape as she created a pretend robot or a microphone. She made up songs and dance routines that usually involved her getting a fit of giggles when she tried to perform them. She was just at that age when her curly blonde hair was going darker and straighter. Her chunky toddler's frame was becoming slim and lithe.

Emma was two. She had huge eyes that were green-brown, and many freckles across her nose and cheeks. She looked Italian and was still muddling up both languages, talking lovingly about 'Cinderbella' and watering plants with what she called an 'acqua can'. She was extremely good-natured but an absolute drama queen, wailing, 'Blood everywhere!' if she got the tiniest scratch. She too was aspiring to appear grown-up, sitting with her legs crossed and saying, 'Look, I'm swapping my legs.'

In those first few months, we laid some solid foundations. We made vegetable beds and fruit cages and, since my old man was an experienced beekeeper, got a couple of beehives. Friends and I constructed a big tree-house on a three-stemmed sycamore overhanging a bank, so that it felt much higher than it really was. We agreed a decent management plan for the woodland with the Forestry Commission. We installed a wood-fired boiler in a large kennel at the back of the house, which we used to heat our home and its water. There was a real satisfaction in using a fuel that we had personally felled, cross-cut, split, stacked, stored, loaded and lit ourselves. It made us appreciate the warmth more, and made us more cautious about just whacking up the thermostat or leaving doors and windows wide open. As a writer, it felt great to produce another, much more literal, kind of hot air.

Whilst Benny was at school, Emma and I would pootle around outside: we got two goslings and Emma used to bend down in the grass and hand-feed them. We got four chickens and built a small coop. We decided against fencing them in, and just let them wander around wherever they wanted. Emma named one, rather surreally, 'Fluffy Blue Pencil'. They would strut around the site, scratching out a dust bath and perching on any chair or branch they could find. The house was rather overrun with mice, so a neighbour gave us a kitten to deal with the problem.

But those months were slightly eerie. We were at the end of a long, bumpy track, surrounded more by wild animals than human beings. Looking at the enormity of the task ahead, I began to wonder whether we hadn't bitten off more than we could chew. Ten acres sounded great on paper, but on the ground there was so much to do. On the one hand I couldn't wait to get started, but on the other I was paralysed by the enormity of the task. A couple of wise back-to-the-landers we knew had urged us to do very little for the first year: 'Just watch the four seasons in situ,' they said, 'and only then decide where to plant and thin, where to put the livestock and orchard, and so on.' And when Leonardo was born shortly after we moved in, I was happy simply to be a dad, and postponed for a few more months the task of setting up a small community. Having waited years to get started, we were waiting once more: walking and watching, and waking at night to the sound of the human dawn chorus.

Another piece of advice we were given was to think big but start small. The first bit was far easier than the second. It meant that, to begin with, we just laid one extra place at the table. It was more frightening to think small. It felt less impressive, more of a test. But if we couldn't live with one person, we would obviously struggle with half a dozen. We made the best room in the house available: the annexe, with its old beams, a gallery, large sash windows and its own bathroom. Many people had heard of what we were up to – either through word of mouth or the odd inter-view or article – and there was a steady trickle of visitors. Most were day-trippers and weekenders, intrigued to look round and see what was going on.

We were still explaining, rather than realizing, our vision and it often felt we had many of the disadvantages of an open house – people rolling up unannounced wanting to be shown round – and few of the advantages that came with people sharing the load. There was Isobel, a Pilates teacher in her flowing gown with its flamboyant purple hem; an eighty-year-old geologist interested in the quarry; a woman struggling with her own strict community; a young mother who had split from her husband; a student with mild existential confusion. There was Alex, a guy referred from social services who was sleeping rough and was a compulsive sniffer, constantly snorting, as if trying to clear his mind. He would stutter too, like an engine that wouldn't start. There was Arnold, a chap who had checked himself out of a psychiatric hospital and giggled as he told us the paranoid reasons why he had stopped taking his meds. Some stayed a few nights, but none for more than a week. It was sometimes hard to know why they turned up at all. A few were scouting for a solution to their housing problem, or looking for work, or wanting advice about how to do something similar.

We were still unsure of so many things. At that stage, we were simply a family home and we didn't have any legal structure. Windsor Hill Wood was not a charity, or a social enterprise, or a community interest company, or anything else. I could tell visitors all our theories about communal living, but it was still just chatter. We hadn't decided how long people could stay, or on what terms. Our aim was to resolve those issues in conversation with guests, not impose them from the outset. We wanted to let the place evolve naturally and allow those questions to get settled in due course. That's the way I've always worked, whether it's on books, with groups or in classes: it's inefficient and painful, but it allows order to emerge, slowly, from chaos. Years later, it made the place surprisingly stable, I think, because every good idea was absorbed and accepted. Everyone who came was able to contribute their ideas, and that made them feel part of the place, an integral component. But back then, at the outset, it made people think we were underprepared, if not in fact rather capricious.

Of those who shared their ideas about how the place should work, some were aggressively forthright, others simply asked suggestive questions. But it did mean that over those first twelve months we took some key decisions that have never really changed. We knew we had to become a dry house, meaning there would be no alcohol on site. I had volunteered at a couple of recovery communities where people who lived in dry houses were still allowed to get hammered off site, and it made recovery very difficult. If we were serious about helping people battle addiction, we knew there could be no alcohol off site either, meaning none of us could head out, have a drink and then roll up back here. The same went for all non-prescribed drugs. The third golden rule was no physical or verbal violence.

Being a drink- and drug-free house also, I think, sent out a message to everyone who suspected we were whimsical hippies or junkies: this was a serious and safe place. All communities require that something be relinquished. It was one of the first questions I used to ask myself when I visited places: what are they giving up, what are they sacrificing? To us, alcohol seemed a small sacrifice, missed more, if anything, in food than in a glass.

There were other important resolutions. We decided to run a common purse to pay for food, each person contributing thirty quid a week, and kids paying half. It meant nobody had their own shelf in the fridge or the larder. All food was communal, and people could eat whatever they wanted. As we were beginning to have people with eating disorders spending time with us, we all ate together, sharing every meal and making it clear that attendance wasn't optional. Apart from that contribution, however, we decided we would never charge rent. There were two main reasons: we had seen, in many communities, that people paying rent are, understandably, reluctant to do communal work as they feel they've already paid up; and we wanted to make Windsor Hill Wood as accessible as possible. We had visited plenty of well-heeled places, full of wealthy visitors and with a slightly exclusive atmosphere. We wanted somewhere that was open to those who had nothing, and we created a hardship fund so that people unable to pay for food could still stay with us.

It became clear, pretty early on, that quite a few locals had already become heavily reliant on us. There was a lad in his twenties called Max who slept in a caravan on wasteland nearby and often spent most of the day with us. He was a big, loping man, over six foot tall, with curly hair and mutton-chop sideburns. He had Asperger's, and his ruddy face and red eyes suggested he enjoyed too much cider and spliff. He spoke slowly, narrowing his eyes in concentration as he tried to say the simplest things. One night Max was happily sitting beside the fire, and making no move to go. Fra told him it was 9 p.m. and that we were shutting up. Max looked at her and then at the ground, turning his head sideways as if studying a really complex issue.

'But what,' he said in a rich Somerset accent, 'if I need some cheese?'

The last word was drawn out, and we couldn't help laughing. It was as if he were a human mouse and we were the only dairy operation in Somerset. It became one of those phrases which Fra and I repeated to each other occasionally to remind ourselves that we couldn't meet everyone's needs at all hours of the day and night.

The 9 p.m. watershed became a lifeline for us as we came to understand the importance of privacy. We decided that anyone not living here had to be off site by that time, and that no one would ever go in anyone else's room without permission. Everyone had their own sanctuary. There was a door they could shut. Likewise, guests would never come upstairs into the children's rooms. Francesca and I also decided that we would close the door to our side of the house at 9 p.m. Over the years it was one of the things that kept us sane. If there was an emergency, obviously, people were welcome, but apart from that it was a rigid, vital boundary that meant we always had somewhere to which we could retreat after a chaotic, exhausting day.

It's autumn now. The last orange beech leaves are clinging to the thin branches. All other leaves have fallen and the woodland looks suddenly sparse and bare. In the summer you can scarcely see more than a few metres in each direction, so dense are the leaves, bushes and brambles. At this time of year, though, you can see straight through the columns of trunks to far beyond. The ground is sodden, squelching each time you sink a boot. The gales have torn down dead branches which now lie on the woodland floor, gradually rotting. The birds, almost invisible all summer, are our neighbours again, standing like commas on the naked branches. The deer are conspicuous too, staring at you boldly through the trunks until they bounce skittishly away. The chickens look drenched in the rain: they appear half their size as they gather under the coop like damp mops. The woodpiles seem to have always been there: the long trunks are mottled with white fungi and spongy moss. We need to bring them under cover now and let them season in the dry. The place feels forlorn and dank somehow, mourning the loss of the summer, with all its energy and warmth. The glittering frosts and glamorous snow still feel far away, so we light bonfires instead to mark a baptism in the pond, and All Souls' Day, and the autumn equinox. Emma calls them 'bumfires', which makes us laugh. Tools emerge as the undergrowth gives up its hidden gifts: rusty pliers, long-lost trowels, an old sledgehammer. Everything seems to be receding – including my patience with people who don't put tools away.

I spend one blissful afternoon in the autumn sunshine collecting hazelnuts with Benny. We have already seen quite a few hollow shells on the ground and realize we need to harvest fast if we are going to beat the squirrels to the rest. We stand beneath the branches on the fringes of the wood, looking upwards for those familiar clusters in their characteristic green hats. The hazel gets its name from the Anglo-Saxon *haesel*, meaning 'cap'.

Always a bit of a bruiser, Benny gleefully pulls down the branches with a long stick and yanks off the nuts. Doubles and trebles are most common, but occasionally there's a foursome. We compete to see who can spot the largest clusters.

The hazel used to be a vital part of the woodland economy, coppiced to make baskets and hurdles, thatching spars and sticks, charcoal and faggots. But now it's invariably overgrown and overlooked. It's more a shrub than a tree and it has none of the magnificence of an elderly oak or a sturdy beech. And yet hazel was, for the ancients, one of the most important trees, thought to promote healing and wisdom.

There's a lot of lore around the tree: that carrying a double hazelnut in your pocket prevents toothache; that hazel twigs used for divining should be cut on Midsummer's Eve; that entwined in a horse's harness they keep it from being enchanted by the fairies; and that positioning the tree's catkins (also known as lamb's tails) around the kitchen fireplace at lambing time helps keep the births trouble-free. Both Mercury and Hermes had staffs of hazel, and pilgrims were so attached to their hazel staffs that they were often buried with them.

Within an hour Benny and I have harvested almost a kilo of nuts. We go back inside, proudly showing everyone our collection. Benny enjoys the noisy revelation of cracking them open, whilst I put my hands around the shells to stop them ricocheting all over the kitchen. Once open, some yield huge, pointy white nuts, more milky and soft than you would expect. Others have only a tiny white drop in them, as if the nut never quite knew it was supposed to grow.

We find a recipe for hazelnut bread and try it out. Emma and Fra go out to get an egg from the chickens whilst we reduce the nuts to a creamy dust and mix it with self-raising flour; then we add some salt, some sugar and the egg, beaten in milk. It's a fairly basic recipe, but we chuck it in the oven and wait half an hour.

The result is surprising: probably because of the egg and sugar, it tastes more like cake than bread. We offer it to the sophisticated Italian palate of my wife, whose gives the judgement *insipido* (the much-repeated Italian phrase meaning 'not enough salt or flavour').

'But,' asks Benny, who has an allergy to nuts and thinks she's missing out on their mystical properties, 'do you feel any wiser?'

The most important job we did that first year was to create the chapel. There was a sturdy stone outbuilding a hundred yards from the house that we had been told was 'the explosives chamber'. It was, apparently, where they kept the explosives for the quarry. Since those days, a vaguely ecclesiastical stone window, perhaps pilfered from a church ruin somewhere, had been cemented in. The explosives chamber was little more than a shed full of the accumulated junk from previous owners: old sinks, broken tiles, rusty bikes and wonky ladders. We used it to store chicken feed, so it was covered in chicken shit too, as the free-range birds would wander in and out to pick up the scraps. The place felt decidedly solid, but humble.

A friend and I had felled an ugly Lawson's cypress and planked it up into four-inch slabs with a guest from Warminster. We carried three of them into the explosives chamber, setting each one on two upturned tree stumps. The three 'pews' were then arranged in a small horseshoe around a table with a candle and a rusty cowbell. Calling that rustic arrangement a chapel sounded fairly presumptuous, and we toyed with other, less religious descriptions: 'the Meditation Room' or 'the Quiet Space'. I particularly liked 'House of Silence', as one of our models for an inclusive, sacred space was the House of Silence at Neve Shalom, also known as Wahat al-Salam (which mean, in Hebrew and Arabic respectively, 'oasis of peace'). It's a village in Israel that tries to usher in 'peace, equality and understanding' between Arabs and Jews. But everyone here in Somerset, from committed Christians to convinced atheists, thought those fluffy labels rather absurd, and insisted that we stop bending over backwards to be ecumenical and just call the chapel a flipping chapel. So that's what we've stuck with. We meet for a quarter of an hour's silence at 7.30 a.m., the same at 12.30 p.m. before lunch, and for compline – the lullaby of the liturgy – at 9.15 p.m. Nobody is obliged to come. But what was obvious almost immediately was that many of our guests were yearning for silence. Not everyone came, of course, but plenty did. Differences became irrelevant in the periods of silence. As Pierre Lacout, a Carmelite monk turned Quaker once wrote, 'Words scatter, silence gathers together.'

That first year was the calm before the storm, and from then on our woodland community would often be extremely noisy or turbulent, so busy that it felt as if a flock of birds were pecking at you, constantly wanting a piece of you. There were always demands, questions and accusations. But the discipline of observing even those very short periods of silence gave us an internal redoubt to which we could retreat. It was a way to put some distance between ourselves and the unremitting disturbance. It meant we weren't always buffeted and bruised. It gave us a background silence to the day, offering equilibrium and stillness in a place that was often neither stable nor calm.

It also changed, very subtly, the way we spoke. After those short, elective silences, the tongue started to seem extremely powerful, so easily able to wound. For the first time in my life I began to be reticent rather than loquacious. I enjoyed rereading the chapter 'On Being Taciturn' in *The Rule of St Benedict*, and began to understand why even the kindest people in the communities we had visited seemed to be a bit gruff or self-contained. Keeping my counsel became a way to maintain a degree of distance, or precious privacy, in what was often a pretty claustrophobic setting.

Many guests, though, couldn't face it. Some came and found it, paradoxically, too traumatic or noisy, as if the quiet were a dangerous vacuum filled by the voices in their heads or the diversions in their hands. They were so used to distraction and movement and restlessness that really stopping threw them. They didn't know how to sit still, to listen to their breathing or the sound of the wood pigeons. The quietness could be unsettling for many, even rather frightening. One woman said she couldn't sit still for that long. Another guest came and spent the whole time desperate for distraction, constantly looking at the screen of her mobile phone.

'I find it unnerving,' she said to me afterwards.

'What's unnerving?' I wondered.

'The way you all sit there in a trance, not saying anything.' She looked at the chickens that were pecking the ground around her ankles and shrugged.

'I thought you were entranced too,' I said.

'Wasn't. I was checking my phone.'

She left soon afterwards.

That autumn a burly man called Crisp came to stay. I had met him a year before in a woodland I was visiting, and we had laughed a lot together. He looked like he had walked out of an Amish community, with his big beard, wide braces over a woolly jumper and a backpack full of axes and knives. An itinerant carver, he had a 'pedlar's licence' that allowed him to sit on any street corner and carve away whilst trying to make a few sales. He was an artisan obsessed by wood, picking up bits along canal footpaths, in inner cities or from ancient copses where he kipped at night. He would talk about wooden objects being able to 'spread the love' in the world.

Crisp was one of the most charismatic and unusual men I had met for years. Everyone who came here was enchanted by his eccentric appearance and by his obsession with wood. He could make anyone laugh and was able to discuss ancient tools and techniques for hours. He seemed to have stepped out from another time, a distant era when a wandering woodsman was nothing unusual. People were instinctively drawn to this romantic, playful pauper with his cheeky smile and flirtatious quips. He loved teaching and would show the kids tricks that would invariably leave them wide-eyed and shouting, 'Again! Again!' His catchphrase, repeated each time there was a mini-disaster, was simple: 'Everything's going to be fine.'

By his presence alone he made the place feel like a working woodland, a place of slow labour from a bygone era. He had a big heart and an even bigger appetite: 'Sweet,' he would say as he piled food on to his plate. He would 'water down' a double chocolate cake with double cream. He liked to drink pints of coffee throughout the day. Unlike many recovering alcoholics who had been through a twelve-step programme, he hadn't discovered his 'higher power' – he was an adamant atheist – but he always joined us in the chapel for our periods of silence.

Crisp put his finger on what, I suppose, had always attracted me to wood as a material: it's so simple, so common and democratic. It's not exclusive, like silver or steel, or even ceramics. Anyone can find it and work it. He would sit on the floor for hours each day, creating a pile of shavings that fell on to his Buddha-like stomach and the floor all around him. With a few deft cuts, he could whittle a branch into a smooth, slim implement: a spoon, or a butter knife, or a spatula. He would hold the bowl of a spoon in one hand and the handle against his chest as he drew the knife over it, changing the shape in a matter of minutes. He would look at it, turn it round, and go back to carving. There were always shavings, like a young girl's blonde ringlets, attached to his clothes. When he put someone's initials on a piece, he did it by hand with a pick-knife, creating an immaculate bevel and extravagant serifs. Each night Crisp pulled on his woolly hat and headed out under the stars. He was more at home in the woods. He used to string up a tarp between a couple of ash trees and kip out there.

It was soon obvious that we needed to create more accommodation, so Crisp and I decided to convert an old railway building in the woods into a hut where he could sleep in more comfort. It wasn't beautiful – a concrete block two and a half metres by three, with no floor and no ceiling. There were four large ash trees growing in the middle of it and dozens of others nearby: some fallen and rotting, resting on the thick walls; others growing through what would be the window and the door. It took many weeks to turn it into a monastic cell. We felled the trees, put on a turf roof, fitted a window and a new wooden floor. Everything, of course, took longer and cost double what we had expected. It had been dark and cold out there and every day one of us would say, 'Oh', as we realized with horror that we'd been screwing something in back to front or upside down or hadn't thought about something incredibly obvious.

'It's like watching monkeys use tools for the first time,' Crisp joked one day as he watched me struggle to hang the door.

By then it was almost finished and beginning to look beautiful: unexpectedly cosy and rustic. There was no electricity in the woods, which was fine: we had an old paraffin lamp and a lot of candles. But it needed warmth. So we went to a nearby reclamation centre and picked up a stove. It was tiny and cylindrical, but wonderfully efficient. It burnt twigs and sticks which you fed in vertically and it gave off great heat and had space for a kettle on top. Someone donated several metal drainpipes, and a local forge outside Wells put a couple of kinks in them to get the flue out of the wall. We put a cowl on top and suddenly the concrete ruin looked like a rustic retreat: a grassy roof, smoke puffing out of the black flue, a window facing south over the elders and cherries. The warm, welcoming cabin looked like a mini-monument to self-reliance. We decided to make a sign for the place, so planked up a bit of ash and painted it black, then carved out letters which looked, in contrast, creamy: 'The Abode'.

Even then, at the very start, we were beginning to feel slightly overwhelmed by visitors. Since I had started writing a column about Windsor Hill Wood, twenty or thirty people a week were getting in touch, eager to come down and see what was going on. If we weren't careful we could spend our entire time making tea and chit-chatting round the fire. We were having to down tools every time a new arrival turned up wanting to be shown round. So we decided to designate a regular day of the week as a 'volunteer day'. It suited us to have one day in which to concentrate all the visitors, and they too preferred it that way. Most came here not because they wanted a cuppa but because they wanted to get their hands dirty. They wanted to do, as much as see, something. We chose Wednesday because it wouldn't attract weekenders but instead those needing a bit of company or purpose, probably the unemployed and the retired. In return for lots of tea, biscuits, soup and homemade bread, people could come and look round and muck in. It kept our project rooted in the local community too. We were receiving emails from all around the world, and we had had guests from Germany, Israel, Sri Lanka, Pakistan and, obviously, Italy. We enjoyed that multicultural feel but were keen also to serve those within a few miles. Over the course of the next few months, volunteer day really took off as we built up a network of regular, local volunteers. Some were hardy and handy, able to do all sorts of tasks, and others were more like tender outpatients, visiting for the companionship and informal counselling. We had everything from teenagers who had dropped out of school to bereaved widows. Often they had nothing in common, but they would find themselves side by side as they chopped logs.

One of the first people to come to our volunteer day was a former school caretaker called Tony. In his sixties, with white hair, he would arrive in workman's trousers with a car boot full of supplies for us: tools he thought we needed, and a dozen doughnuts for tea break. Tony soon became a legendary figure to everyone here: perhaps because he had once been a social worker, or because he had suffered real sorrow himself, he was able to empathize with all our guests. He would listen and crack jokes and side with the underdog. When I was feeling down he would tell me a quip he had heard on the radio: 'Just because I've been blessed with empathy, it doesn't mean I have to put up with everyone's shit.' Every time I went to the nearby town where he lived, I heard stories about Tony's generosity. On Wednesdays it usually looked like he wasn't doing much: he would stand around and chat, then have a cuppa, look at a job and scratch his head. He would come in for lunch and make everyone laugh and then sit around having more tea, and we all began to wonder when he was going to finish the log store or fix the tap. But then, in a short burst he would do the job far more professionally and cleverly than we could have managed in a fortnight. He was a great teacher, too, unobtrusively introducing us to better ways of using tools and slowly bringing us better bits of kit in return for firewood. There were times, however, when he would be thrown by the chaos and noise. We began to joke that he was our budgie: he wouldn't keel over like the bird in the mines, but if things were too cramped or disturbed he would drive off and we'd know something was amiss. He never left here without forgetting something, so often we would see him over the weekend as he returned to pick up a drill or tape measure, and he would stop and have yet another cup of tea and make us laugh again.

We now had a good crew. There was a festival organizer known locally as Maggie Purple, a woman who called a spade an effing spade and seemed to know everyone in Somerset. There was a woman struggling with an eating disorder, a recently divorced mum, a priest, a pensioner, a landscape gardener called Alan who didn't have much work on, one of the regulars from the AA meeting, and so on. There was a woman from near Yeovil whose partner had set up a fairly well-known community long ago. He visited one Wednesday and wistfully told me what had gone on there: 'A man would show up with his wife and kids and dog and guitar and then leave a year later with just the guitar . . .'

With this regular workforce, a lot was getting done. The size of the small meadow had doubled as people hacked back brambles and small hawthorns. There were large log stores, stacked high with split logs. We used to boil water for tea in the fire pit and we all smelled of woodsmoke. The children seemed to be relishing the fun too. Benny told me proudly that she had helped Alan with the 'grouching'.

'You've been grouching?' I frowned, wondering if this was a new word for being miffed.

Alan came back behind her and held up the grouting float. He smiled and mouthed 'grouting'.

There were plenty of amusing misunderstandings like that. The kids were still young enough that they mixed up words and made us laugh.

'We've been doing some ogre with Helen,' they told us proudly one afternoon.

'Ogre?' Fra asked.

'You know, ogre,' Benny shouted, stretching.

'Eh?'

Benny knelt down on the floor and leant backwards until her shoulder blades were touching the ground. It took us a few tries to work out she meant yoga.

The kids confused visitors, and vice versa, and the misunderstandings were often the result of them having watched too many animated films. One new visitor told us she thought our children must be very devout. We were, even then, used to people projecting their own assumptions on to us – people often thought we must be fanatics, or fundamentalists, or incredibly pious – but the idea that our kids were devout didn't quite ring true.

'But she keeps running up to me,' Karen said, 'and bowing, putting her fist in her palm and saying, "Inner peace."'

We laughed. 'It's just a line,' Fra said, 'from *Kung Fu Panda*.'

'Oh,' Karen said, 'I thought that was something, you know, that you guys did . . .'

I needed to create an office where I could write, and there was a rickety shed outside the house that had a floor made of rotten boards resting on bricks. Whichever way you stepped, something wobbled or broke. We decided to make a new floor out of cob. I had seen pictures of earthen floors in books, and they always looked rich and warm, like a cross between terracotta and leather. The advantage was that we could source almost all the materials – clay, manure and straw – from within a mile or two.

Alan and I pulled up the old boards and bricks and pickaxed down an inch or two. We put in a damp-proof course and laid a sub-floor of gravel, something which, in this abandoned quarry, was in rich supply. The floor was about fifteen square metres, so it took an hour or two to wheelbarrow the gravel back and forth. Then we mixed the ingredients and admired the sludge's appearance: it was a bit like a gritty chocolate, a deep brown with specks and strips of yellow. We slopped it on to the floor and trowelled it out. Very soon everything was covered in mud, with spades and walls and ladders coated in wet slurry.

Karen was just out of rehab and told us her theory that getting dirty is an integral part of staying clean. 'Where I did my rehab, we all did hours of gardening every day,' she said.

'Teaches humility,' Alan said. '"Humility" has the same root as "humus". It's about being grounded.'

We stuck at it all day until, finally, we had only one small area left.

'Where are the kids?' asked Alan. 'We need them to chuck in a coin for future archaeologists.'

I called over Benny and Emma and told them to go and get a coin each from their piggy banks.

'Why?' Benny demanded, her hands on her hips. 'That's my money.'

'I'll do it,' said Emma, racing off to her bedroom. So of course Benny went too, barging her younger sister out of the way as she overtook.

They both came back with a ten-pence coin. They kissed them and squeezed them in their palms, and then chucked them into the mix.

We didn't worry about getting the surface perfect just then. We let it harden for a week or two, before dampening it slightly and doing the final skim. An earthen floor is so forgiving that if anything goes wrong you can just add a bit or take some away. It cracked slightly as it dried, so needed some more of the mixture here and there. Then we sealed it with beeswax from our hives, both girls joining me on hands and knees as we rubbed it to a lovely sheen.

The shed also needed a new roof, and we decided to do it the hard way. Instead of a simple corrugated iron or felt roof, we wanted to do a living one full of sedum and wild flowers. Having soil above your head offers great insulation, against both cold and noise. The building blends beautifully into the natural background and, instead of removing an area for wildlife, there's another large playground for it.

We laid a large heavy-duty membrane called EPDM over the sloping plywood and then protected it with a layer of carpet offcuts. For the drainage layer we used Leca, a lightweight expanded clay aggregate, because it is, as the name suggests, incredibly light. It's basically a lot of holey pebbles. On top of that went some landscape fabric so that the rainwater, not the soil, would drain away. We decided to do a sedum rather than a turf roof because it requires less soil and is therefore less heavy. It takes a lot of barrows to get even a few inches of soil spread over fifteen square metres and getting it up there is a back-breaking job in itself. You can either chuck it up with a shovel or have someone up on the roof yanking up bucket after bucket.

Various other people came and had a laugh as, once again, we lugged wet mud around. Others looked after the children, helping them make a den and light a fire nearby. We put in thyme, sedum, sempervivum, arabis, campanula, lychnis, silene, lewisia and dianthus. We also grabbed random plants that were growing in walls and gutters around the place and put them in: aubrietia and forget-me-nots. Part of the joy of a living roof is that, even when you've finished your work, you've no idea what it will eventually look like. It will almost certainly surprise you as it changes with the seasons. It looked fairly sparse once we had done it, just a few dozen small plants sitting in a large, sloping bed of mud, but by spring it had become a tapestry of colours, a profusion of tiny flowers and chubby foliage.

To begin with I had been a bit embarrassed about all these people coming and helping out at what was our family home. I wondered if we were exploiting their generosity, perhaps, or their goodwill. I worried about asking people to weed our garden or sort out our plumbing; surely they had enough to worry about in their own lives and homes. We were always open about everything we were thinking or doing and so one volunteer day I expressed my anxiety. The assembled volunteers reassured me immediately. 'I love coming here,' one said. 'It's the highlight of my week.' Everyone seemed perfectly happy with the arrangement and, as months passed, I thought less about it, not least because it was already beginning to feel as if it wasn't just our place any more. It was growing; more people were coming to stay. The family home had become an extended household.

Crisp slept in the Abode, so the spare room was free for another guest. It meant that, instead of three adults, there were now four. And as people were often prepared to camp in the bell tent, it was not uncommon to have five or six adults, plus the three kids, all living here. From having just one guest at a time, we suddenly had a micro-community. I remember looking at the eight people round the table one lunchtime and realizing that it had begun, like a party you've been planning that's now in full swing and there's not much more you can do to control what happens. We weren't in charge any longer. Things were happening beyond our control, which is how it should be. It was exciting and slightly nerve-wracking.

Another change was that we started to receive a few significant donations. A couple we barely knew gave us the entire contents of a cottage they were selling in Scotland. We had, until then, been desperately short of basics, such as blankets, bedside tables, laundry baskets, and all the rest. Suddenly, we had everything we needed: wardrobes, linen, cutlery, kettles, armchairs, shelves. It meant not only that I wasn't constantly having to fork out for furniture but also that half the stuff in the house and the outbuildings didn't belong to us. It was a subtle but very beneficial shift: we could accept that the place wasn't entirely ours now. We still cared for everything, but as stewards, not landlords. And it seemed, too, as if people were looking out for us, caring about what happened here. A local man gave us a large woodburner. Small amounts of money began to arrive in the post: a tenner, twenty quid. Someone who had won sixty quid on the lottery sent it our way. People gave us saplings, a luxury hamper, sheep fleeces. Perhaps because we were a dry house, people didn't know what to bring us when they rolled up, so we were always getting surprises: chocolates, cakes, tents. Someone who had lost his father donated the contents of his dad's impressive shed, complete with pliers, spanners, sockets, saws, and so on. The place was feeling full. The generosity of strangers didn't only help in practical ways, it also meant that we felt not isolated but somehow held. People we had never met cared about this project and wanted to contribute to it.

A man called Marty arrived from the Midlands. He said his life felt like it was at an end: he had recently retired and had no direction. The woman he loved had moved abroad, living their shared dream with somebody else. He was lonely, depressed and drinking too much.

Over the next few weeks he told us bits of his story. He had set up a small commune in Scotland in the sixties, before busking his way around Europe. Marty was a brilliant guitarist, the kind that picked more than he strummed. He loved the Mediterranean, especially Italy and Greece, and had enjoyed a successful career as a head teacher and university lecturer.

It was clear that Marty would be a big asset. He was well read but was a listener; as you spoke, he would quietly throw out his palm to you to show he was hearing what you were saying and was understanding. He was witty, but never unkind, more amused by human folly and by his own forgetfulness. Marty couldn't hear very well, and he seemed a bit like the grandfather this place needed. He didn't shave or cut his hair whilst he was with us, so developed a long grey beard and straggly hair. He smoked Golden Virginia all day, which turned the centre of his white moustache yellow. Marty looked like a hobo, which was partly deliberate: he was visibly on the side of the troubled wanderers who came through. He started playing Goebel Reeves' 'Hobo's Lullaby', his rich voice stilling the whole garden room.

The children, of course, loved him. He taught them songs, like 'The Cruel Sister', and he always managed to calm baby Leo by letting him play with his green-and-gold pouch of tobacco. The tobacco became such a comfort blanket that once, when we found ourselves in the supermarket with Leo wailing so much we didn't know what to do, we went up to the tobacco counter and asked if he could cuddle some Golden Virginia. He immediately quietened down, much to the amusement of the salesperson.

'It reminds him of his grandfather,' I explained, trying to keep it simple.

'He's not our grandfather,' Benny said, standing on tiptoes. 'He's an old man who lives on our commune.'

Another guest was called Bill. He had glasses with lenses so thick that his eyes were magnified. His matt-black hair looked unwashed and his tracksuit was too big for him. He was from South Wales and had a strong accent. There was something not quite right about him. He carried his stuff around in two greying plastic bags that looked as if he'd been using them for years. One was so torn it left a trail of tissues and chewing gum in its wake. Bill was in his forties and said he was living with his mother, but it looked more like he had been sleeping rough, or pretty close to it. But, back then, we didn't probe too deeply, didn't ask many questions. Perhaps we felt it would be prying, or impolite, or something. We just took people in, and if they said they needed somewhere to stay we gave them a bed.

Many people who came resented the fact that they had ended up here, the same way a patient can resent a hospital. Even in those exciting early days, it was clear that resentment was going to be a problem. It's that corrosive, corrupting feeling of not having enough, or of doing too much, a feeling that one has been slighted or ignored and needs revenge. As someone once said, 'Resentment is like taking poison and waiting for the other person to die.'

There's always a lot to feel resentful about. Some people here have more money, more time, or more sleep, than others. Some are more healthy and active, others more ailing, more contemplative. Equality is a mirage we talk about but never actually find. It's not even the big things that cause resentment but the little things. Who's taken the scissors and not put them back? Who turned the dial on the toaster so the bread's now burnt?

We're not all seething here. There's a lot of love and laughter. But sometimes there is this resentment bubbling below and I often wonder how to defuse it. The principal way, I suppose, is to have a very clear common purpose so that we're all pulling in the same direction rather than one against the other. It might be my imagination, but I certainly sense that resentment recedes when we have a new guest who needs our help. It's as if the lost scissors no longer matter because we've all got to serve someone who is struggling with life.

It helps, as well, that no one here appears to bottle much up. There's no sulking. We're pretty blunt, and things get raised, contradicted, debated and, usually, sorted out. Until, that is, the next issue arises. Sitting regularly in the chapel, side by side and in silence, also helps somehow. It lets peace come between you. And a serious understanding of forgiveness goes a long way.

But by far the best vaccine against the poison of resentment is gratitude. Before every meal we give thanks, and everyone chips in. For some people, it's grace; for others, it's just a verbalization of gratitude, a timely reminder of all the things that are going right.

'What are we giving thanks for?' I ask.

'Whoever hung out my laundry,' says Marty.

I catch his eye and point at Karen, who smiles at him.

'And the person who emptied the compost bin,' Crisp says.

'For germination.'

'And for clutch slave cylinders,' says Bill.

The other problem here is that those who aren't feeling resentful about doing too much feel guilty that they're not doing enough. I joke that no one need feel guilty unless I tell them to, but there's still an uneasiness about sitting round the fire enjoying a good book whilst others are laying the table or washing up. There's so much to do that it's hard to know when it's legitimate to relax and switch off. Crisp had lived in institutions much of his life and was good at the basics of rotas.

'There's no point cooking lunch every day,' he said. 'We'll just have bread and cheese at midday.'

Francesca and I nodded. 'OK.'

'It's hard work to keep things simple,' Crisp continued, 'but it's more efficient, it makes life easy. So if there are half a dozen adults around, we'll each cook once a week. Sunday evening we'll eat leftovers.'

We nodded again and shrugged, happy to share the burden at last.

'We need –' Crisp was taking command – 'someone on duty each week, someone who will feed all the animals, look after the boiler and cook Sunday lunch. The person on duty will cook soup on volunteer day too. Got it? We'll rotate it.'

It was good to have someone organizing us all. I wanted to enable more than lead, and sat back as Crisp gave out orders. As well as working all day on Wednesdays, we decided we would work together on whatever needed doing on Monday, Tuesday and Thursday mornings, from nine to one, with a tea break in the middle. It meant that there was a good balance between work and relaxation, with people able to do their own thing in the afternoons, and on Friday, Saturday and Sunday.

It's spring and the bare trees are slowly coming into leaf. The hazel leaves look dark red as they unfold. The tiny oak ones seem almost purple, the ruddy colour of a newborn baby. The white sprays of the wayfaring tree look like elderflowers from a distance, but have a rather putrid scent. The hawthorn offers white clouds amongst the pale greens of the goat willow. The concertinaed leaves of lady's mantle are bunched like molehills around the place. There are tiny wild flowers all over the woodland floor: ivy-leaved toadflax, its petite purple-and-white petals looking like a rotund stick-man; the yellow dead nettle, its flowers an open mouth with a curling tongue. There are rare oxlips and cowslips, soapworts and the exquisite Solomon's seal, with its paired flowers hanging from the long stems like cherries.

There's a rhythm to the place now. It seems to be working. Everyone knows what's happening when, and things get sorted without cajoling or reminding. Bells ring a few times through the day for chapel or food. Nobody does it all, but it all gets done. Someone feeds the animals, keeps us warm, goes shopping, does the cooking. That clear timetable means that you rarely have to tap someone on the shoulder and remind them of what needs doing.

The more clarity there was about duties and obligations, the more relaxed everyone became. If you knew it wasn't your turn, you could freewheel. The structure seemed to suit the sort of people who came here. Many were trying to emerge from chaotic lives and needed some sort of timetable. They seemed to yearn for rituals or regularity, to feel the rise and fall of the day. People were empowered by having roles. On one occasion I offered to help Bill clean out the chickens, and he was quite cross, because that was his role in this woodland. He found it rewarding rather than tedious.

There was a drawback to the rotas though. They began to make what was always a family home feel a bit like an institution. Crisp wanted a rota for every chore in the house, whereas Francesca wanted space for spontaneity and goodwill as well as obligation.

'The washing-up just won't get done unless there's a rota,' said Crisp, getting irate.

'It will,' said Fra calmly, 'if there's enough kindness. If you only do jobs because it's your turn, there's not much love involved.'

'Love? Nobody washes up with love.'

The friction produced a bit of heat, and you could sense the central ideological difference between the two. Crisp was cynical, convinced that people only ever looked out for themselves. He wanted a timetable so that the instinctively selfish couldn't get away without doing their share. Fra wanted a family home where we anticipated and met each other's needs without having a laminated roster for doing so. I, inevitably, was with Fra. When there's space for goodwill, you're often surprised by other people's kindnesses. You're making an omelette and discover that someone else has brought in the eggs from the coop; you're cooking and someone has laid the table; you relax after cooking and realize that someone else has washed up; you want to flop on the sofa and find that someone has lit a fire. In any kind of communal life, it's easy to see only the negatives: 'Someone has got mud everywhere' or 'Someone hasn't put the tape measure back where it belongs.' The joy of sharing labour is that 'someone' becomes a positive, the invisible hand becomes a source of great help rather than great irritation. So we left washing-up outside the rotas, trusting in goodwill and good sense.

In April we got a call from Pilsdon, the community that was very much the model for what we were trying to do at Windsor Hill Wood.

'Want any pigs?' Jack asked. We had wanted to get pigs for ages but hadn't got round to it. Francesca's from Parma and I had always been keen on the idea of trying to produce Parma ham in Somerset. We especially liked the idea of getting our pigs from Pilsdon. It was a bit like an Everton fan sourcing his garden turf from Goodison Park.

So Crisp and I put a tarpaulin in the back of the car and drove south towards Bridport. Pilsdon looked the same as ever – although the people change, the place always has a familiar feel. On the north side of the large manor house is a courtyard with sheep, ducks and calves grazing in the middle. The pigs were on the far side, next to the old barn. We got quite a shock when we saw them. We were expecting cute little piglets the size of a young baby. These beasts were already large and muscular.

It was an unusual litter: a mixture of Berkshire, Saddleback and Tamworth. We marked four gilts – females that have never been pregnant – that we liked the look of and then had to tag them before taking them off the farm. They writhed and kicked furiously as we tried to pick them up and punch the herd tag between the veins of their ears. The squeal of a scared weaner is deafening. We put down straw on the tarp in the boot and tied bits of wood behind the headrests to stop the beasts taking over the wheel on the way back.

We went and had a cup of tea in the community's sunlit common room. There's a huge fireplace, a wall of mullioned windows facing south towards the sea – and loads of armchairs, sofas and slices of toast. I chatted with a few old friends and after tea a small crowd gathered in the courtyard to watch the amusing spectacle of us trying to get the pigs into the back of the car. It was a bit like the chicken-chasing scene in *Rocky*: we pursued them around the pen, grabbing any bit of them we could and plonking them in the boot of the car, shutting it before we tried to get the next one.

As we were standing by the car chatting, Jack took me aside. He's a kind, gruff man, in his late seventies, I guess.

'A word of advice,' he said, leading me away from the others. 'I've heard what you're doing up there. Sounds good –' he gave me a hard stare – 'but always put your marriage first.'

I nodded, wondering why he was saying this.

'Don't let it destroy you both,' he said, looking at me through his wiry eyebrows. 'Put your marriage first. Look after each other.'

Of all the advice we were given in those early days, that was what we came back to again and again. If we weren't okay ourselves, there wouldn't be a family home around which to build a community.

The drive to Windsor Hill Wood was fairly pungent. As soon

as we were back, we reversed up to the little top field, then a grassy meadow, and lifted the pigs over the electric fencing. Once again, they writhed and screamed in our grasp. The poor weaners seemed terrified and lay on top of each other in a far corner. When one dared to wander around it got a shock from the fencing and squealed in terror. We filled the ark with straw but still the beautiful beasts were huddling in the corner.

Over the next few days, everything changed. They let us get close to them and, having jumped and twitched every time we patted them, they now seemed to enjoy being stroked and scratched. They ran towards us, since they knew we usually brought food: either pignuts or windfall fruit. The girls and the guests came up with incongruous names: Annabelle, Princess, Harriet Pig Pog and Ginger. Quite often we went up there just to admire them, and they sprinted up to us – a hilarious sight – and started nuzzling our ankles as if demanding grub. Within a few days the field had gone from green to brown. They ploughed and fertilized large areas, but it didn't smell too much. It just looked like a pig field.

Quite often, they would escape. My heart would sink when someone, usually Benny, shouted, 'Pig!' whilst pointing at the clearing in front of our house. The animals could turn our only patch of grass into mud within minutes. Using their snouts as an incredible plough to turn the turf, they would grunt and groan as they snuffled for anything to eat. Getting them back in was always difficult as they wouldn't want to pass over the electric fence. You could switch it off and lay a tarp over it, but they knew it was still there and would go into reverse pretty quickly. Pushing a pig that doesn't want to move is like trying to fell a tree with your bare hands. It might sway a bit if you're lucky, but nothing more.

* * *

It's now May, nine months since we opened our doors, and Crisp and I are slowly getting a great workshop up and running in a garage by the greenhouse. There are two pole lathes, a few axe blocks, some workbenches, a couple of shave horses, a froe, a drawknife, various adzes and axes, some jigs and some beetles (a sort of caveman's mallet, whose name, if you're interested, derives from the Old Norse for 'cock'). Everything here is handmade rather than industrial. Instead of huge metal casings, you can see rough-hewn wood, beautiful bark, thick planks and cleft legs.

We spend a happy hour in the woods looking for the perfect pole for one of the lathes. Until now I've been using a bungee suspended from the rafters, but Crisp is ideologically opposed to manufactured elasticity. We find a twenty-foot pole of ash, about two or three inches in diameter at the base, and feed it through one of paneless windows at the back of the garage. The end of the pole is attached by a nylon cord to a treadle on the floor and it has sufficient elasticity to spring up and down, rotating the object you're turning between two centres.

Like all green woodwork, the joy of it is the simplicity: no dust, no noise, no danger. You don't have to wear a mask or goggles or shoo out the kids. It's the kind of activity that promotes companionship because it's quiet and you can chat whilst you're working away. The energy comes from your foot not the national grid, and as you turn a chair spindle you can hear the birdsong. The means, the making, is as beautiful as the end, the object. You're always in control: relying just on yourself and a few edge tools. As you see ribbons of beige or ochre wood circling to the floor, it's hard not to be hypnotized and find yourself entering a blissful, calm, creative zone. For a place like this, where we hope people will work but also find some serenity, that's a great side effect.

Most green woodworkers don't use sandpaper since it detracts from the originality of the artisan's craft. Why smooth everything down when the beauty is in the skill and uniqueness of the cut? It would be like toning down the colours of an old master to make everything grey. Some people use scrapers made out of old saws to take off a few rogue fibres, but someone who's skilled enough should be able to boss them with his blade, not scrape them into submission. There are various degrees of compromise with modernity. Some puritans might be appalled at the idea, but we use tenoners – effectively, giant pencil sharpeners – which fit on the end of a power drill and really speed up production.

We're beginning to experiment with products that we give, or sell, to visitors: bread boards, spoons, bowls, rattles, stools, ladles, egg cups, boxes, goblets, rounders bats, and so on. Quite often they go wrong and end up as kindling, but we've got the beginnings of a cottage industry and are working out how to make rustic objects that are useful to us or to others. The workshop becomes a hub, as much a common room as the garden room. We have a chiminea someone donated that keeps a kettle on the go, so there's always tea. The fire is fed from the rug of shavings that covers the floor. It makes a soft crunch as you walk around until someone sweeps it all up to get the kettle boiling.

Karen is trying to carve a spatula for her mother's birthday.

'It looks more like a cricket bat,' Bill jokes.

Crisp is sitting on the shave horse, playing the same song on his guitar that he's been trying to learn for the last three months. Marty's sitting on the other shave horse, pulling the drawknife towards his torso as he shapes a spatula. Bill says he reckons we're all going to become millionaires through selling bird boxes.

I often wondered whether, paradoxically, what we were doing was manageable because we *weren't* all friends, or at least not to start off with. It meant that expectations weren't high, and disappointments weren't so great. We had never assumed it would be wonderful, and we weren't shocked when strange antics emerged. We had always imagined our hospitality was the old-fashioned sort that meant welcoming not friends, but instead strangers or even enemies (both 'guest' and 'hostile' have the same etymological root). It was an obligation, even a sacred act, rather than a bit of fun, and perhaps because of that our tolerance was pretty high. We liked the fact that this way of life felt like a form of resistance, a way not of reinforcing social hierarchies and enmities but of undermining them.

I spent a lot of time wondering about hospitality, and watching what happened here. In many languages, the words for 'host' and 'guest' are the same or are somehow interchangeable. I was often a bit anxious about being the host, but frequently I found myself sitting down as someone else ladled out the soup or welcomed a new arrival. There was a sudden, and surprising, equality and a melting away of ownership. Our home became someone else's as they started saying 'our this' and 'our that'. That reciprocity made it clear that our guests were giving us a gift, as much as the other way round. In offering refuge, we were also being granted it; in sharing sustenance, we were being sustained.

But the words 'host' and 'guest' are also linked to sacrifice (*hostia*), and it quickly became clear how many sacrifices we had to make. For years, I had written about living simply. Although I hadn't taken a vow of poverty, I admired the asceticism of monastic life. But the practice was so much harder than the theory. I realized how devoted I still was to objects. Perhaps because we lived so frugally, the things we had acquired over the years were cherished and loved. They were the little objects that reminded us of friends or holidays. Those small, beautiful pieces were strangely intimate tokens of taste, or treasured contributors to comfort. Far more than I ever realized, they were a part of who we were, as much as our own memories and dreams. And now it had become a free-for-all. It was all shared, and I was struggling. I had no beef about sharing things; I just wanted them to be loved and cared for. But most people living here were slightly scatty or chaotic, struggling to look after themselves let alone for random objects to which they had no attachment.

So our favourite things were getting broken or borrowed. Nothing valuable, but a mud-brown sugar bowl by an Ayrshire potter I used to know, a blue-and-yellow salt dish, the oil jug from Venice with its filigree spout. I found a handwritten note on the broken jug saying, 'It just fell apart in me hands,' which made us smile and has become a catchphrase we use every time something breaks. CDs and books went missing. People wore my clothes, not because they went through drawers but because any boots, jumpers, coats or slippers lying around got picked up and used and then, often, forgotten somewhere. Nothing was mine any more: bicycle, torch, blanket – all were borrowed, broken or abandoned outside in the rain. The strangest stuff was taken: not just cash, but duvets and the last set of keys to the camper van.

I had a strange but seemingly effective way of dealing with these losses. I claimed one yellow mug as mine and told everyone that it was the only thing in the house I wouldn't share. I didn't, I said melodramatically, ever want other people to use it. It was the only way I could stay sane, I joked. And they seemed to get it. No one ever used it. Sometimes, a new person would arrive and inadvertently pick it up, and everyone would look at me nervously, expecting me to object. I would say nothing but was amazed how peeved I felt at this unconscious effrontery. It's only a mug, I told myself, but my sadness at the presumption, at the invasion and the soiling, was beyond rational. That one mug had become the sole focus of my sense of ownership and personal sanctity. I could cope with almost everything if people respected that one small symbol.

There were more serious sacrifices. We really struggled with the lack of hygiene. It was obvious that those going through a dark place in their lives didn't find it easy to take care of themselves; and that recovering addicts who battled to stay clean metaphorically found it hard to do so literally. The smell of unwashed bodies was tough, especially at mealtimes. I would say something to someone and hear the water running a little later, but it didn't seem to make much difference. Hands weren't washed. Soiled loo roll was left not in the loo but on the bathroom floor. We kept trying to talk about hygiene, but it didn't seem to sink in. Someone borrowed Karen's razor and toothbrush, which was bad enough in itself, but we knew one of our guests had Hepatitis C, so it was pretty serious. Loose pills were left lying around and, with Leo now crawling and putting anything he could find into his mouth, it worried us. There was an infestation of rats in the kitchen because one of our guests had been adamant, for weeks, that it was morally wrong to kill them. The problem had grown worse every week until I put my foot down and dealt with things my way.

One woman's feet were so putrid it was hard to eat in the same room as her. You needed to open the windows of whatever room she had been in. Part of the problem was how to talk about hygiene in such a way that it made people feel worthy, not worthless. With Hayley, the only solution we could find was the old-fashioned one of washing and oiling her feet every other day. I had expected it to be grim or embarrassingly intimate, but it was neither. We were drawn together as she revealed her sore soles. Inevitably, Benny joined in and made it fun.

'What are you doing?' she asked me.

'Just washing Hayley's feet.'

Benny watched for a while. 'Do you want me to paint your nails?' she asked.

'Sure.'

'What colour?'

It could have been solemn or embarrassing, but it became a game as Benny played the beautician.

The hardest aspect of offering hospitality wasn't that our belongings were out in the open but that our failings were too. It's easy to be perfect in solitude, the same way it's simple for a manuscript to be immaculate when it exists only in your mind. Once everything's out there, though, in the midst of people, perfection is impossible. In a community, there's nowhere to hide. A mirror is held right to your face and shows you how irrationally, angrily, impetuously and thoughtlessly you act. I didn't really mind so much that our little souvenirs of life were being broken or borrowed; I was frustrated by dubious standards of hygiene, but it wasn't the end of the world – but I really minded that I wasn't as serene as I thought I was. When I found loose pills lying around and thought Leo was at risk, I didn't display the evenness of temper I imagined I possessed. I could be surprisingly patient with other people's faults, but I was fed up with seeing my own so frequently. That was the aspect of hospitality I found hardest: not living with strangers' foibles but being forced to witness my own. It required a sort of 'inner hospitality', learning to recognize and accommodate my own weaknesses.

Over time, I realized that it was easier to accommodate people who were openly cynical, who really didn't like the idea of communal living, than the idealists who thought it was a dream.

The idealists would usually be disappointed, whereas the sceptic might be surprised. Fiona was, at least on the surface, one of the idealists. Bill had gone to the shops one day and never come back, and Fiona had moved into his room. A large middle-aged lady, she was blonde and always adorned with colourful beads, scarves and jewellery. She had a deep, husky sort of voice, and I got the impression that she was a lonely woman. She had clearly found consolation in alternative ideas, adopting every wacky New Age notion out there. I had a suspicion that there wasn't really much need for her to come to us. She described a vaguely unpleasant situation at home, saying she had to move out because of troubling energies there, but I guessed that the real reason she was here was that we were only a short hop from Glastonbury. Any time the words 'chakra', 'transcendental' or 'Zen' came up in conversation, she would always say, 'Oh, wow!' with wonder in her voice. Little Emma started imitating her and, because she was only just three and there was no malice to the mimicry, we all laughed openly as she toddled around in the clearing going, 'Oh, wow!' in just the same way as Fiona.

I always informed people about the 9 p.m. boundary, telling them that it was when we retreated to our side of the house. I joked that I would treat anyone like a burglar if they ever came in after the watershed. That brief privacy before collapsing into bed was precious. Everyone knew about it and everyone had been extremely respectful of it.

So it was a real surprise when, one evening, we heard someone clattering around outside our snug. I waited a few minutes, in case it was someone popping in to put something away. But the noise continued and I got up to investigate. There was Fiona, singing cheerfully to herself with her head on her right shoulder as she read the vertical spines of the books. There was something about that nonchalant nosiness that really irked me. It felt like an invasion, or an intrusion: it was as if someone had walked into your bedroom when you were asleep and had started riffling through your drawers. I brusquely told her it was after nine o'clock and that she could come back and look for books in the morning. I checked that she knew about the 9 p.m. thing.

'I thought that was a flexible boundary,' she said, looking hurt.

I got the impression there wasn't any boundary that she didn't think was flexible. By being wafty, she thought she could avoid any lines, clarity or rules. She didn't get it, and the next day accused me of being abusive towards her: 'I'm a vulnerable woman and I can't cope with that sort of abuse.'

'Abuse' was one of those emotive words that people would sometimes pull on me when I reiterated the rules. I knew it was an attempt to turn the tables and make me appear in the wrong. It was a game I didn't play. There wasn't a table to turn. With Fiona, I simply restated the boundary and told her I expected her to respect it. She walked off, muttering to herself about bad energy fields.

Only a few days later, something equally irksome happened. We had a communal computer in the garden room, behind a large wooden post. Fra was sitting there one day, trying to find a last-minute birthday present for a friend, when Fiona strode up.

'I was on there.'

Fra was too shocked to say anything.

'Can you get off, please,' Fiona went on.

'I thought you were in the bath,' Fra said quietly.

'I was, but I was halfway through something.' Fiona was trying to sit down, and if Fra hadn't moved, she would have been sat on. Fra retreated, coming to find me to express her consternation.

A few days later it got worse. It was a period in which Leo

wasn't sleeping much at night, so you would wake up in the morning feeling hollow, like you'd hardly had any rest. One night, at half past two, he was wailing, and I took the easy option and went downstairs to warm up some milk for him. The lights were on everywhere and it felt incredibly warm. I saw an electric heater on at full blast in the garden room and lights on in the corridor and the bathroom. I knocked on the bathroom door and heard some slow splashing.

'What?' a voice said.

'Who's that?' I asked.

'Fiona.'

'What's going on?'

'I must have fallen asleep,' she said.

'It's the middle of the night and all the lights are on. There's an electric heater on in the middle of a woodland.'

'What?' she said, as if she didn't get it.

I went into her room and there was another heater there too, going full blast. The room felt like a sauna.

'We heat this whole house with wood,' I growled, 'and you're consuming colossal quantities of electricity to heat two empty rooms in the middle of the night.'

I was more livid than I had ever been since we started this project. I knew what this would cost, and that it had probably been going on for weeks.

'Where the fuck did these heaters come from anyway?' I muttered under my breath.

'I manifested them,' she said proudly, appearing behind me in a couple of towels. She had used that phrase before to suggest that the universe would grant her wishes because she was so in tune with its cosmic vibes.

'You had better manifest some money pretty quickly.'

'What's the problem?' she asked calmly again, as if she couldn't understand the commotion. 'They're my heaters, I can use them.'

'Who pays the bills?'

She frowned innocently, as if I were just another dull realist she had transcended long ago.

I grabbed both heaters and took them away. I couldn't get back to sleep that night but sat there cuddling Leo, who had crashed out after his slug of warm milk. I was so pissed off, with myself as much as with Fiona. We had naively thought we could offer shelter to people and that our guests would respond with reciprocal thoughtfulness and gratitude. But more and more we found ourselves living with people who took everything they could without any idea of where it was coming from. Fiona genuinely didn't seem to understand that bills had to be paid, or that Fra and I were the only ones paying them. She was gone before breakfast. She had sought out Marty, blagging a lift and fifty quid, which she said she needed for the train to London. Marty never saw his money again but a couple of days later we saw Fiona, of course, in Glastonbury. Shortly afterwards, we received an electricity bill that was three hundred quid higher than the previous ones.

It was high summer now. Benny had finished her first year at school and spent her days swinging on the old tyre that hung from the beech tree, watching for the next arrival. We were such a small operation that even just one new person, staying for a few weeks, could rock the boat. We didn't seem to have any shock absorbers or emotional airbags. There wasn't the space, there weren't the numbers, to allow arrivals to be integrated slowly and gradually ushered into the way of things. They arrived right at the centre, with all their troubles and grief, and we all felt the effects.

What often happened was that someone came to us in such

desperation that they would openly talk about their intimate or profound crises. After a few weeks, though, it was almost as if they felt a little embarrassed at having shared that much information. Once they had been here a while – once they had caught up on sleep, made friends, started eating properly and working hard – whatever the crisis had been seemed to be over. I then found it quite difficult to remind them of the reasons they were here. I didn't want to rub it in but nor did I want them putting back on a mask they had appeared desperate to remove only a couple of weeks ago. I would remind them of why they were here, and they would shrug. A couple of weeks' sobriety, they said, was proof they weren't really alcoholics. Or the suicide attempt back home wasn't really that serious. It was as if they had looked over the abyss and were stepping away; I found myself next to them, not wanting to push, but not wanting to allow them to slope back to something they had so recently longed to leave behind.

One way in which guests avoided dealing with their own issues was to get stuck into other people's. There were always, of course, people with problems here, and we were, with their consent, fairly open about what everyone was going through. So there were plenty of others to observe, counsel and criticize rather than looking at yourself; there was often a wilful avoidance of your own shit. Bernard was a man whose wife had kicked him out of his family home for constant drug use and who had come here for a short period. He would sit down and quietly dispense advice to everyone. He wanted to be a healer and a sage, and would get quite slippery if anyone ever gently suggested that he needed to do some work on himself. His motivation was in some ways admirable: he genuinely wanted to help out and give guidance. But he was doing so because that proved he was still strong and sagacious. I gave him a book to read about addiction, written by a professor of psychiatry, and he annotated it heavily with his critiques and comments. He was always the judge, never the judged.

Gail was a warm, kind woman who was a chronic over-eater. She was extremely large and got out of breath doing the smallest tasks, even laying the table. The children loved her because she kept giving them sweets and treats. It was her way of showing affection, and we had to ask her to stop plying them with chocolate bars and cola bottles. She did the same with the animals, overfeeding the chickens and the pigs when we weren't watching so that we had to go and buy more food much earlier than we had expected. She was a person completely without boundaries and didn't know how to protect herself. She would mother the men here, wanting to meet their needs and longing for them to depend on her, to need her as much as she needed them.

They confided in her too. She was a generous listener, perhaps empowered by the idea that these men wanted to confide in her. But she was as leaky as a sieve, so secrets would spill out, her confidants would resent her and she would then do anything to be needed once more, debasing herself, doing favours, buying presents, making grandiose offers she couldn't fulfil. The place became full of gossip and Chinese whispers, awash with rumours, cliques and intrigue.

Gail did none of it with any malice; she just didn't seem able to help herself. She asked questions and listened, probed some more and kept going, constantly moving forward in her enquiry until she was peering inside someone's darkest corners. She had a wonderful gift of empathy, and a great calling to be caring, but it wasn't wholesome. Having glimpsed an individual's inner turmoil, she would walk around the place trying to get us to be more indulgent of them – something the person, of course, quickly cottoned on to. They realized that Gail could be their go-between, the intercessor between themselves and us, the perceived authoritarians. She was so completely unanchored that she could be easily manipulated, spun around and around by some old hands who wanted an ally in what they saw as a battle between themselves and our regime.

It meant, of course, that there was no longer a direct line between certain guests and us. Gail was in the middle, sidling up to them, intervening, interceding, acting as the clumsy confessor. She dropped clangers all the time, letting slip all sorts of things she shouldn't have been holding in the first place.

I discussed the issue with Tony, who was extremely fond of Gail. 'It's what I call helping someone halfway across the road,' he said. 'Gail's so keen to help out, but she doesn't quite have the competence and, rather than helping people get to the other side, she leaves them in the middle. It's worse than leaving them on the wrong pavement.'

I couldn't, clearly, ask people to stop being kind to each other. It was one of the most moving things here, to watch the ways in which those who needed care became, themselves, carers. That was part of the therapy: the realization that there were people around with troubles as bad as, or worse than, yours. An individual's self-esteem would soar as they understood they were cherished for the wisdom and insight they could offer. I didn't want to stop any of that. But sometimes the community felt like a school playground in which allegiances were being constantly forged and broken. The house suddenly seemed cliquey, with groups of two or three standing apart from the others, smoking and whispering. Fra and I watched it for a week, until it got too weird.

We called a meeting and tried to get to the heart of what was going on. We all sat round the table and talked and listened. It was pretty messy: Gail had been trying to befriend a new guest called Frank, who had told her he had been taking far more pregabalin – an anti-anxiety drug – than he was prescribed, and Gail had tried to curry favour with us by coming and telling us, so Frank felt betrayed; and Crisp had got involved because he felt Gail had an eating disorder and was ignoring it by diving into other people's problems; and Gail said, 'Look who's talking'; and dear old Marty was just looking sad and depressed, and tried to smooth things over; and on it went for an hour or two . . . But it all got put out there, with an openness that was sometimes excruciating but also strangely soothing. It was the opposite of all the secrecy and gossip that had gone on for weeks before. Halfway through the meeting, it felt as if we couldn't possibly live together any more, there was too much fury, but by the end people were nodding and listening and apologizing. We were admitting weaknesses rather than pointing them out. And afterwards it was as if we had been drawn together again, as the heat dissipated, and we sat down to the usual evening meal.

In many ways, I thought it was my fault that things had come to a head. I had been wary of too much frankness, too cautious about nudging people to put their problems out in the open. I thought Francesca and I would be picking at wounds if we asked questions, whereas we might have given people a chance to air them. If we weren't taking some sort of confession, I realized, guests would confess elsewhere, often flattering and confusing another guest who was as much in the deep end as they were. I had always imagined running a very egalitarian set-up, in which we all worked and took decisions together, but in that first year we came to understand that something different was needed. Consensual community building is hard enough, but doing it with people who had been referred by psychiatrists, social services and rehabs was almost impossible. I didn't want to admit it to myself, but most of our guests were irrational, or compulsive, or simply unwell. They weren't in the right state to be able to participate in decision-making. They wanted direction and leadership, and I hadn't provided it.

We had, by then, been here for a year. Summer was sliding into autumn again. Hairy beechnuts were hanging off the trees, slowly opening to drop their glossy three-sided nuts. Marty and I swept them up and offered them to the pigs, who scoffed them noisily. Squirrels were scampering about, racing us to gather the hazelnuts again. The chickens were still strutting around the site, scratching the ground for worms and picking woodlice off bits of rotting wood. It was getting dark earlier, and in the evenings Frank lit the stove again and the whole place felt cosy. The fruit trees were heavy with greengages, plums and pears, and Fra made dozens of jars of jam, using it to bake *crostata*, a shallow Italian cake which contrasted sweet pastry with slightly bitter fruit. Maggie Purple gathered five kilos of green tomatoes and made huge amounts of chutney. Marty picked hundreds of blackberries, and Gail turned them into fruit chews and crumbles. Fra mixed more blackberries with elderberries and sloes to make hedgerow conserve. Under the stairs now there were close to a hundred jars of produce: pickled cucumbers, peppers *sott'olio*, dried chillies, jams, chutneys and honey. Crisp and Marty had begun cross-cutting the last of the logs, so the area by the pigs had a large carpet of beige wood shavings. The log stores were full again, and it felt as if we were well stocked, prepared to survive another winter.

Year Two

'Let him who cannot be alone beware of community . . . Let him who is not in community beware of being alone'

– Dietrich Bonhoeffer

That autumn the first snow falls thick in early November. The sun glints off the deep drifts and the children go tobogganing down the slope towards the chickens. Their plastic sledges twist as they slide down, so they rotate like a sycamore seed in the wind. All the lines seem blurred, as if the cotton-wool snow has taken the edge off everything: there are no longer any hard angles, only gentle curves.

Trees seem less barren as their bare bones become adorned by fragile white flesh. Dead branches snap under the weight and others bounce up as the snow falls away, shrugged off by the disdainful tree. With every footstep you can hear the snow compressing, like teeth being ground together. I warily look upwards now as I walk in the woods, wondering which branch will break next, or which is about to dump a dozen kilos of snow.

From then on, for three months, the temperature barely rises above zero. The pristine white snow turns to ice and it doesn't thaw for months. Animal footprints from November are still visible in the glassy ice in December. The snow, once so light and fresh, now looks translucent. Paw and boot prints and tyre tracks from the wheelbarrow have become engraved on the ground. There's no secrecy any more. Long after nightfall you can walk around without a torch as the moon reflects off the snow: it's as if the day has simply been dimmed to create an ethereal, other-worldly light.

We haven't seen grass for weeks and trying to find stuff outside is almost impossible: the snow lies like a thick blanket across everything so that you have to guess, or remember, where you put the shovel or the ladder. There are long icicles hanging from the gutters and water butts, like a graph of seismic activity. The hoar frost, a hairy white fluff like an old man's eyebrows, hangs from the trees, shrubs and fences. We can't get our car out. We try pushing it up the hill that leads out of the woods, but it slips back like soap down the side of the bath, causing a splash of snow as the back end thumps into a snowdrift.

Just looking after the animals takes hours. All the water butts and hoses are frozen, so whoever's on duty has to come inside the house and fill up endless buckets and watering cans, then lug them outside towards the various troughs and drinkers. Simply opening the doors to the coops is tough, as the latches are frozen. One door has already been broken. Cleaning out the animals requires a lot of muscle, as all the shit is rock hard.

We've been walking the girls to school and going shopping with rucksacks on our backs. The wheelbarrow seems glued to the ground – its metal runners are a few inches under the ice – so I carry the logs in my arms. The snowman we made a month ago is still there, one-eyed and with a drooping nose, but nothing has melted. The honest smell of woodsmoke is constant. Crisp frees the barrow with a metal bar, and I can hear the noise of logs hitting the metal of the hod as he brings in the firewood. We shut doors as fast as possible and light candles as soon as it gets dark.

I worried that this brutal winter would affect morale, that the various people staying here would become dispirited, but it seemed to have the opposite effect. Everyone relished the challenge, enjoying the tough reality of trying to keep warm and get food on the table. They, like me, seemed okay with trudging knee deep in snow to bring in eggs or whatever. Perhaps it appealed to our survivor's instinct. In contemporary life we all find it far too easy to survive: it's such a doddle to find food, to warm and clothe ourselves. We live surrounded by incredible comfort and yet are completely removed from our primitive instincts. That, presumably, is why survivalism and post-apocalyptic fiction and films are so popular and why there's an unprecedented craze for bushcraft: they take us back to a simpler life for which many of us secretly long, a life in which we struggle for the basics and forget all the ephemera. And that, I think, is one of the things that draws people here.

One morning, I realized a predator had taken one of our chickens. There was a doughnut of feathers around a bit of blood in the snow but no footprints at all. I assumed that one of the many buzzards that circle above the trees must have seen the appetizing grey bird outlined against the snow and nosedived for its dinner. I found it interesting that my first reaction wasn't 'Poor chicken' but 'Poor us'. Losing her meant that we would have about two hundred fewer eggs over the following year, unless we replaced her, and that would have cost us a precious tenner. Sometimes, I felt as if my heart was being hardened, not softened, out here.

That December we had a dozen people with us for Christmas. A few of our guests had gone home, but a few had stayed, and some locals without family came up. Max came and ate cheese. It was an eclectic bunch: we all looked weary and weather-beaten but wore wigs and paper hats and sang songs. The fact that there was no booze made it seem more serious somehow, and made the frivolity sincere rather than forced or fuelled. It felt, with all the snow and strangers, like a proper Christmas.

Late January. Weeping icicles created slim boreholes in the dirty melting snow. You could see the dead wood all over the woodland floor, lying at odd angles like the limbs of sleeping children. The dark bark was sodden but covered with intensely red dots that made it look like the ground had measles. They were miniature bowls, a light pink on the outside but, inside, a scarlet so smooth and perfect I just stared at them for a while. It looked as if they'd been moulded on the tip of a finger. They were, I learned later, scarlet elf cups (sarcoscypha coccinea). The snowdrops were nudging their way up, their blunt green shoots giving way to an emergent white spear that opened out to offer its perfectly pointed petals. They brought so much hope: of the gentler spring to come, of a fresh start.

There were many more people wanting to come here than we could accommodate. People camped in the woods, or slept in their vans, but there was a real shortage of shelter. I mentioned the problem to Maggie Purple.

'You need to talk to Morag,' she said. 'She's got a shelter she doesn't need.'

A couple of days later Maggie sent a photo: the structure was a cross between Bag End and a yurt. It had a large, circular wooden door with curling black hinges that led into a short, wide entrance and then a circular space almost twenty foot in diameter. It looked perfect.

'The only trouble,' Maggie said, 'is that Morag hardly ever answers her phone.'

We eventually got hold of her. She told us to meet her the following Saturday night. We would need to hire a van, she said, as the wooden poles were fifteen foot long. So, the following Saturday, Marty and I ended up driving a huge van around Glastonbury, trying to find the pub where Morag was hanging out. The town is a pretty far-out place, attracting all sorts of questers and seekers who long to find their own Avalon. Its enormous abbey didn't survive the Reformation, and in recent decades the New Age has gushed into that gap. In the shadow of the iconic tor, sitting like a pencil on the breast-shaped hill, there are shops called 'The Portal for the Immortal' and 'The Psychic Piglet'. Posters advertise events offering 'free hugs' and 'hemp truffles'. On one shop counter we moved a pile of books on fairies to see a sticker that read 'God wants spiritual fruits, not religious nuts.' The town is the Somerset equivalent of Haight-Ashbury, the only place I know where you'll see a busker playing a dulcimer.

Yet whilst the 'sacred isle' is unorthodox, it's also full of idealism, and Morag of the Marsh turned out to be pretty surprising: a beautiful, dreadlocked folk singer. She said she liked the sound of what we were doing and didn't want anything up front for the shelter. She said we could put it up, live in it a while and let her have what we thought it was worth in due course. Considering a new yurt or shepherd's hut costs thousands of pounds nowadays, it was a generous deal.

So we followed her little car out of the town and on to the dark, bumpy embankments on the Somerset Levels. It was a freezing night with a full moon, and it felt like we were being led up a very long garden path. The road cut behind old warehouses with smashed windows, and became a ribbon between rhynes, the drainage channels of the Levels. Eventually, we came to a yard with dozens of caravans and makeshift homes. Some had cling film over cracked windows, others had flues puffing out white smoke. There was stuff everywhere: old tyres and anvils, strips of metal and planks and boards.

We loaded the poles, crown, door and canvas into the van and got a quick lesson on how to put it up.

'There's a hole for a flue in the canvas, so get hold of Gas-bottle Ben if you want a woodburner,' she advised.

The next day was sunny and we began putting it up. Four of us bolted the big circular door together and fitted the poles into the oblique holes in the crown, lifting it to about twelve feet. We wrestled the canvas over the whole thing and then put the transparent window over the central space. We began to peg it down and realized we were half a dozen pegs short. So Marty and I axed out the extra pegs from some ash that was kicking around the workshop and bashed them in place. We put down pallets all over the ground, to lift the floor away from the damp and cold, stuffing donated sheep fleeces into the voids and screwing interlocking boards on to the pallets as a floor. Everyone lent a hand, bringing in rugs, a bed, a desk and a few lanterns. It looked really cosy. I got hold of Ben and he sold us a fifty-quid woodburner made out of an old gas bottle.

The empty shelter reminded me of festivals and camping adventures of years gone by. It smelt of grass and woodsmoke. It exuded something of the unexpected, as if it were used to unconventional characters. As accommodation went, it was pretty basic, but that's what people were usually yearning for when they came here. They wanted, I think, to shrug off all the daft sophistication of modern life and get down to the bare bones. One of my favourite books, published in 1973, is Lloyd Kahn's *Shelter*: the barns, sheds, yurts and houseboats that appear in its pages are so simple, and their attraction lies in the fact that they're eccentric and vernacular. They're built by amateur hands to suit circumstance and climate. They are, unlike much modern housing, full of soul. Our set-up was beginning to look a bit similar. We had a three-sided court-yard now: the long house on one side; the workshop, tool shed and greenhouse on another; and, opposite the house, the new yurt, the explosives chamber and the children's 'twig-wam'. In the middle was the grassy clearing, with the kids' scooters, some swings, see-saws and bikes. Beyond – out in the woods – was the Abode. It felt like a little neighbourhood, as if each of us were providing a metaphorical awning for the other.

One of the many lessons we learned in those first couple of years was to be cautious about people who had been referred to us by well-meaning parents, partners, siblings or children. Unless someone contacted us themselves, explaining personally why they wanted to come, it would often go curly: their loved ones might want them to get help, but they didn't want it. They might go along with it to stop being nagged, or to have a break, but once they were here they would be half-hearted at best, if not actually hostile.

Tracey had been referred to us by her mother. She was, her mother said, a hardened alcoholic, someone who was unable to start the day unless she had refuelled. Her sister brought her down from Lancashire one bright morning in February, and as soon as she rolled up, it was obvious she was hammered. I could smell the spirits on her breath. She was clumsy, physically and emotionally, and her skin was so dry her face appeared strained when she tried to smile; her teeth were a bit brown. She had short blonde hair that always looked as if she had just got out of bed.

On the walk around the woods I asked when she had last had a drink.

'I haven't drunk since yesterday,' she said, trying hard to look me in the eye.

I knew she was lying, and she knew I knew, but there was no way to prove it. We didn't, back then, have a breathalyser or a drug-testing kit. It wasn't a good start.

'You'll have to be extremely tough on her,' the sister said as I walked her to the car. 'She's a lovely woman, but drink makes her devious.'

We quickly saw the truth of both parts of that portrait. Tracey was a warm, generous woman. She was run-down not just because of drinking but because she had become the carer to two elderly women: her mother and a friend of hers in the village. She had been doing their shopping, cleaning and ironing for years. We would later realize that a vast number of the people coming to us were exhausted carers, the kind of people who had been giving all their lives until they had nothing left to give.

For the first few days Tracey was shaky and nervous. She could barely eat anything and would often rush to the loo to be sick. But as she began to get her strength back, she worked hard. She wouldn't stop in the afternoons, like everyone else, but kept going, constantly trying to keep herself busy. That was another thing we quickly learned: those in recovery often had to be persuaded to down tools rather than urged to pick them up; they needed to be helped to slow down, rather than – as with some guests – crowbarred out of the armchair. Tracey would be axing up the kindling until the bell rang for our evening meal. And when she came in, she was resentful of those who hadn't worked as hard as her.

'If you ate properly,' she said to Amy, a young anorexic, 'you would be able to put in a decent shift.'

'I did all the washing-up after lunch,' Amy replied.

'But you're not pulling your weight,' Tracey said.

The accusation itself was bad enough, but the reference to Amy's weight, however metaphorical, was provocative. I could see Amy scratching her thin arm so hard she was almost piercing the skin.

Frequently, we were mediating in arguments not just between guests but between guests and the families or friends they had left at home. Tracey's phone would ring all day, and often at night: her mother complained that she needed her there; her partner ranted, drunk and jealous, about who she was spending time with. Some days we thought she was finding a bit of stability, only for the phone to ring and for her to spiral downwards again. Many rehabs ban or at least limit contact with codependents, even confiscating all means of communication. We never wanted to be so hard line but we quickly understood the reasoning behind such draconian rules. Had we banned mobile phones, our lives would have been a whole lot easier. It often felt as if our guests were only half present, as if they were still being called away, distracted, guilt-tripped and dragged back into whatever it was they had been trying to escape.

The best advice anyone ever gave me about writing is that the most important key on the keyboard is the delete key. I gradually realized that the same rule applied in woodland management. I used to think that all trees were there to be revered and admired, rather like elderly relatives, and that none of them should be felled, whereas in fact many trees are like bad sentences needing a firm red pen. A woodland needs to be thinned and managed.

Since the entirety of our little woodland came about through natural regeneration, it was a dense, dark place. Many trees grew only a few centimetres apart. The paths were narrow and you often had to duck to avoid being scratched by overhanging hawthorns or blackthorns. There was one tree that dominated and darkened much of the wood: goat willow. In its defence, goat willow provides an early source of nectar for the bees; it also provides 'witch's aspirin' since its bark contains salicylic acid (from *salix*), the source of 'real' aspirin. In the old days, girls who didn't wear a sprig of goat willow on Palm Sunday would have their hair pulled. But beyond those attributes, it's only useful as a pioneer species. It establishes itself everywhere and sends up huge, divergent stems that knock over other, smaller trees.

We decided to spend a fortnight that February thinning, felling and coppicing. An old friend and mentor of mine, Herb, came over from Hilfield Friary, and every morning Crisp, Herb and I would sharpen, clean and refuel our chainsaws. We looked like orange snowmen in our bright boots, Kevlar overalls and gloves. We began on the 'plateau', a grandiose term for a dense, overgrown area high above where we housed the chickens. We wandered around for ten minutes, chatting about what to fell and what to leave. 'Hit it hard,' was the advice of a forester friend who lived near here. Part of the difficulty of thinning in dense woods is that trees are likely to get 'hung up', meaning they don't fall to the ground but get snagged in other trees. So we cleared an area to the east, creating an open space into which we could knock over the goat willows.

Felling is never as easy as it sounds and is, obviously, a potentially lethal activity. Basically, you cut away low branches and remove the buttresses from the bottom of the trunk. You look up at the tree and decide which direction to fell it according to the lean, the weighting in the crown and the surrounding conditions. The first cut is the sink cut, a thick wedge taken out of the front of the tree; the back (or felling) cut is slightly higher so that the falling tree can't jump back at you. Those two cuts create a 'hinge' in the middle of the trunk on which the tree then, hopefully, 'folds' and falls in the intended direction, as you retreat.

It was hot work. Within a few minutes I had knocked over a couple of large trees and had stripped to a T-shirt. I always tried to lift off the ear defenders once a tree was about to go, because the sound of a falling trunk is awesome: the quiet creak giving way to a thunderous rip and a final thump as a few tonnes of timber smack on to the rocky ground. We were working far apart but constantly watching what the others were up to, just in case.

As each trunk came down we snedded it, using the chainsaw to take off the lateral branches. With such a lethal machine in our hands, it took a bit of concentration. And it was when you switched off that dangerous things happened: having brought down a big beast, I couldn't sned it because a tiny hawthorn, the size of a wrist, was trapped under the trunk and bent like a bow. So I nicked it at the base with the tip of the saw and the tension made it spring up sharply and smack me in the kisser. There was, as little Emma would have said, 'blood everywhere'.

We stopped for a break and sat on two stumps. There's no other form of land management that so quickly and radically alters a landscape. We had created a glade. Robins were already moving in, staring at us before hopping a few metres away and staring at us again. We could see, for the first time, dozens of strong saplings, rising wirily out of the leafy undergrowth. Their time had come. And the trees we had left in place suddenly looked more majestic. They now had the necessary space and light to put on girth. We could, in this one small spot, finally see the wood for the trees.

We sat there drinking tea. I still had a twinge of regret about felling. All over the glade, the brown mud and leaves were interrupted by bright beige and orange stumps. There were drifts of sawdust where we had been working. It felt like a place of destruction, but I was consoled by the fact that almost all the trees would coppice vigorously, meaning their deep roots would create dozens of new shoots from the old stumps. There were snowdrops in bunches, and one or two early bees were foraging, imitating the noise of the chainsaw as they hovered. The glade was alive now, and the winter sunlight was streaming in.

We got going again, cross-cutting the large trunks into four-foot lengths and chucking them down the slope to the path below. After an hour there was a beautiful stack of logs, ten foot wide and six foot high. They were held off the ground by two logs, placed perpendicular to the pile to stop the bottom ones rotting, and kept in place by hazel rods front and back. But all that was the easy part. It was the brash – the twiggy branches at the top of the tree – that was a bugger. And goat willow is full of it. We wove it into windrows, neat dead hedges along boundaries and ditches. We covered the stumps, or stools, with tangles of brash to protect the regrowth from browsing deer. 'Make as much mess as possible' was the advice of another forester.

A few days later we moved into the adjacent area. It was covered in dense hawthorn and blackthorn: dark, dangerous and unwelcoming. It was hard work for little or no return. There were no massive logs here, just matted thorns. After a few hours, we had bloodied forearms. We built a pile of small branches for charcoal making. It wasn't much, but the rich orange circles of hawthorn looked attractive. And it was great to see what you unearthed in the process: a previously unknown cave, a few fossils, some brave saplings forcing their way up like spears despite the shady canopy.

The second week, we were working at the far end of the wood. We brought down a huge multi-stemmed ash and another massive goat willow. It took all morning just to clear up the mess. All around them were overgrown hazel stools, thick, gnarled and intertwined. We cut them off at ground level, on a slight slope so that rainwater would run off. The hope was that, if the deer didn't get them, they would send up plenty of shoots in the spring. Again we made a huge log pile and Marty wove his fantastic dead hedges along the sides of the paths.

There was still more brash around than we knew what to do with, so we dragged it to a central spot. A new guest called Katharine made a tiny fire with dead wood and we spent a whole afternoon grabbing brash and branches, billhooking them down to size and chucking them on. It was wet green wood, so it didn't immediately catch, but once the fire got a bit of momentum, it roared and squeaked.

As the sun set, we downed tools, gathering round and just watching the flames. We were all bruised and aching, but the fire was hypnotic. We could see each other's scratched faces in the glow, and exchanged nods of satisfaction. The fire quietened people, making them content with the silence, so no one said anything for a long time as the fiery specks rose high into the clearing we had created.

'Without wood, a fire goes out,' Katharine said eventually. 'Without gossip, a quarrel dies down.'

'Where's that from?' Crisp asked.

'Old Testament somewhere,' said Katharine.

'We should carve that above the log store,' I said.

It had been a good fortnight. And we knew, as we watched the twigs glowing and snapping in the flames, that now the creative fun could start: next month we were planting three hundred trees.

* * *

Our community was beginning to feel a bit like one of those backpacker hostels where you're always meeting people from other countries, those who have been long on the road and who tell you stories of their journeys and dreams. There was the swapping of advice about where to go, and what to see, when you left here. Books changed hands; people played cards and chess and chatted about the meaning, or meaninglessness, of life. It was a cosmopolitan crowd and there was that same quiet excitement of discovery you get when you're roughing it abroad. And yet we were at home, feeling rooted. Rather than racing around to see the world, the world was coming to us. And no one turned up empty-handed or empty-headed. I enjoyed the sense of adventure that came from having a gate that was always open. A community avoids being elitist only if it has space for the uninvited, and the uninvited were at the very centre of this sanctuary. For all the hard work involved, it was incredibly enriching. Every time a stranger rolled up, there was curiosity and surprise. The children, particularly, were fascinated by the array of people who sat around the dining table. They seemed to have absorbed the old notion that strangers are important messengers, bringing news from afar. They ran up to new arrivals and quizzed them, asking blunt questions.

In late February, a man called Kev was referred here by a local charity working with rough sleepers. He wandered up the path looking tired and wary, to be greeted by Emma screaming, 'How old are you?'

Kev frowned and looked at the sky, smiling now. 'Fifty-three, I think.'

'And have you got,' asked Benny, who had been doing maths at school, 'any addition issues?'

Kev looked at me, confused.

'She means addiction,' I clarified.

He bent down to give his answer to this precocious five-year-old. 'Right. Yeah, I have. I'm an alcoholic.'

'That's okay,' said Benny, behaving like some sort of rehab counsellor. It somehow put Kev at ease though. And as with any new guest, the girls were pleased they had found a friend who would teach them, they assumed, some card trick or a song.

I was always noticing how this project seemed to be influencing the children's language acquisition. There were so many wanderers here that little Emma, trying to copy a song about a 'rock star', sang instead about a 'rucksack'. She heard so much talk about 'chopping wood' that when we were impatiently trying to chivvy her along, saying 'Chop chop!', she defended herself by saying, 'But I *am* chopping.'

The children seemed to relish always having someone to play with. Having a lot of play in a community hugely improves its feel and ambience. Whenever we went to see other communities, I kept an eye out for a chessboard, for a snooker table, or a deck of cards. If a place didn't have them, or something similar, I tended to think there was something amiss. Donald Winnicott, the English psychoanalyst, felt that play was central to our emotional wholeness, to our sense of discovery, spontaneity and creativity. The fact that there were children here, constantly wanting our guests to play with them, gave those adults a licence to play, permission just to mess around. They were flattered, too, that they were trusted with our children. So playing became one of the many informal therapies here, because play – as anyone with children knows – is serious stuff: it teaches about freedom, fairness and fantasy, boundaries and honour, rules and ruthlessness, about each other and everything else.

* * *

It slowly became apparent that this refuge was working. 'You guys,' Max said one evening, 'seem to see something in me that I can't even see myself.' 'I don't think I'd be alive if it weren't for you guys,' Mikey, a new guest, said a few days later. Even people who only stayed for a few days said how helpful it was: they mentioned the unconditional welcome, the sense of equality, the proximity to nature, the fact that someone was finally willing to listen. And yet, looking back, what we were offering in the beginning was slightly lackadaisical. We never really sat down with people and talked through why they had come. We listened to them but didn't probe. We knew they were probably hoping to find a purpose or lose a habit. But often even they didn't know why they were here. We didn't really confront issues, we just hoped the place would work for them. We had no application form, we didn't ask for references, we didn't write a care plan. Everyone was in transition, but nobody really knew where they wanted to get to. There was a lot of kindness, but not a lot of direction; a good atmosphere, but not always good practice.

We were, perhaps, so keen to create a community that we were more likely to indulge than challenge. Some people would lounge around doing nothing and, because they were down, I would let it go. 'Take it easy,' I'd say. 'Catch up on some sleep.' I wanted people to relax and recuperate and it became very hard to distinguish between those genuinely unable to work and those who were simply workshy. It was almost impossible to get people to commit to anything: we gave people a trial week, after which we invited them to stay for three months, but often they would be gone after a few days, called away by an ex, an urge, by anger or shame. It's what's called in Alcoholics Anonymous a 'geographical': the itchy feet that persuade you that a fresh start in a new place will cure all your problems. (It doesn't usually work: as they say in AA, 'Wherever you go, there you are.') We couldn't really plan anything, as people came and went so quickly.

It became very hard to balance the need to be welcoming and open and yet maintain stability and sanctuary. People would roll up at all hours. One Sunday morning we had three visitors show up before ten o'clock. We had become a bit like the Samaritans: a number to call if you were in crisis. Often I would listen for half an hour and make arrangements for people to come down, never to hear from them again.

We could manage when it was just the nine or ten of us, but quite often there were another three or four around, and suddenly one small house was squeezing in twelve, thirteen or fourteen people. Perhaps we were too hospitable, when we could have been slightly more reticent and not bent over backwards every time someone turned up unannounced. I had often spoken to guests about how, in a place like this, enchantment can quickly turn to disenchantment, but now it was happening to me. In every room there were people talking, laughing, shouting and strumming. It was noisy and there wasn't a spare chair in the house. There were dirty tea cups and plates on every surface. I felt claustrophobic and confused, squashed on all sides. You had to turn sideways just to walk through the kitchen. It often seemed like we were living in a village hall, the kind of place where everyone had a right to rock up. And I didn't want to be unfriendly, so I chatted to everyone and listened to their woes. But sometimes I just wanted to crawl upstairs, get under the duvet and pretend I wasn't here. There was never any down time. We were laying everything on for other people, but with three children and a day job, I didn't have enough time to enjoy it myself.

The effect on the family was stark. We had been here for over a year, and for most of that time the children had asked excitedly, at bedtime, 'Who's coming tomorrow?' But for the last couple of weeks Emma had gone to bed crying, saying over and over again, 'I want it to be just us.' Things were beginning to take off, we had momentum, and she was, understandably, bewildered. She was disturbed by the constant presence of other people and, more to the point, by their demands on our time. She wanted her parents, if not to herself then only shared with her siblings, not half a dozen needy visitors. Benny was sufficiently ebullient to enjoy the human traffic, but Fra had, for a few months now, gone quiet.

'It feels as if the community gets bigger and our house gets smaller,' she said.

I had been deaf to the alarm bells, but they were ringing loudly now. It wasn't just that lights were left on and doors open; that dirty plates and mugs were lying around, and tools not put away; it wasn't only that things were constantly being broken or 'borrowed' – all that, we had expected. It was the even smaller things that got to us: someone hadn't cleaned the paintbrushes, so they were rock hard. Pillowcases had been used as rags in the workshop. Tracey's mother visited with her dog, which bit the kids' football, so it was now punctured. She said she would buy a new one, but would have to wait for her next benefit cheque. All food was communal, so Mikey ate the Easter egg we had put aside for Emma.

'Didn't it look like a child's Easter egg?' I asked him, feeling miffed.

'It did, but you said all food is communal.'

'But it's not even Easter.'

'I don't know when Easter is.' He shrugged.

I stayed silent. The thing that was sure to press my buttons was the idea that Fra, or the children, were losing out, being pushed aside by the many guests we had here. It was my fault as much as Mikey's.

'My problem,' Mikey said, being conciliatory, 'is that the glass, for me, isn't half full or half empty. It just ain't big enough.'

I looked at him then and realized the issue. Most of the people who came to us always seemed to want more. They were guzzlers who struggled to know when to say when. We had expected to look after the hungry and thirsty, but not in this sense. This was something completely different. I didn't think they could be sated. It wasn't enough to give them food and water. They wanted more, and then some.

It was just a feeling, but I had the sense that people were here for what they could get, not what they could give. Every evening there would be half a dozen people sitting around the fire, talking excitedly about their spiritual journey, or creative ways to be green, or whatever. They would discuss musicians and writers and sing songs together. But it felt slightly inauthentic; I can't really explain why. There was an element of exhibitionism to it all, as if this woodland were a stage where they could become the main players, assuming identities and strutting their stuff. It felt subtly awry. It had a competitive edginess to it, rather like when you merge a flock of chickens and they go at each other to establish a pecking order.

I began to think that a lot of people, maybe myself included, were living out their fantasies here; that, despite our attempt to confront reality, this was still some sort of dream or act of wish-fulfilment. It was an illusion of community, a paper-thin facsimile. We might have been living and eating together but what we were creating wasn't really much different from what was outside: it was still full of masks and disguises and egos. The warm glow of community I had sensed only recently, when Mikey and Max had said how well it was working, now felt simulated and false. I didn't buy it. And I felt bad that I didn't, because it set me apart. It made me an outsider in my own home. Worse, Fra felt alienated. Each evening she would retreat, sadly shutting the door on the exuberance in the garden room.

I wondered whether we were the sort of ingrates who couldn't ever be contented. We had longed to set up a sanctuary, we had given up comfort and careers and savings to do so: and here we were, with a bustling community in a working woodland, and it felt wrong. I kept going back to Dietrich Bonhoeffer's *Life Together*, trying to understand what was going on. There, at the beginning of the book, it described exactly what was happening, and the advantages of it: every community, he wrote, suffers the shock of disillusionment and crisis. A true community has to shatter the illusion, has to accept the destruction of the idolized community of daydreams. As the ideal of the proud visionary is destroyed, there will, says Bonhoeffer, be many accusations and much despair. If he was right, it sounded as if there were tough times ahead.

It's dawn, late winter. On the way to chapel I see Marty wandering through the woods with the air rifle, looking for rabbits for supper. The stars are still visible as the sky changes from dark to light blue. There's something different about the birdsong this morning, as if the birds sense spring is just around the corner. It's louder now, as the sun illuminates the tops of the trees. I feed the pigs, let the chickens out and check to see if the geese have laid any eggs. They're supposed to start laying around Valentine's Day, so our eggs are overdue.

Today we're planting three hundred trees. A local forester, Pete, rolls up shortly before eight and, soon after, people start turning up for volunteer day: Tony, Kate, Maggie and a few others. We've spent the previous few weeks walking round the woodland, trying to work out what should go where, so we lay out the stakes with the point where we want the 'whips'. Whips are the small saplings – about knee or thigh high – which look, in winter, like a dead twig with roots. You plant by placing them in a slit you've made with your spade. People tend to think tree planting involves digging a huge hole, since that's what you normally see during ceremonial plantings by princes and politicians. But for these you make a quick slit, bundle up the roots, slip them in and close up the slit with your boot. Then someone else comes up behind and slips a light green tree-guard over the tiny 'trunk' to protect it from deer and rabbits. Another couple of people bash in a stake and cable-tie it to the guard.

It sounds like a breeze, but we quickly come up against all sorts of problems. It's tricky trying to place the stakes in non-geometric lines. However much I try, it's hard to be consciously random. Because I space them six foot apart, the whole first batch looks dangerously like the road plan of a Roman city: all perpendicular and perfectly parallel. Unless you're a bit of a neatness freak, it seems unnaturally ordered.

'Left a bit,' Mikey shouts at me, knowing I am trying to avoid straight lines.

'Right a bit,' Tony laughs, enjoying my sense of confusion.

There are other difficulties. Being an old quarry, there are areas where the ground is rock hard and lots of the stakes snap like uncooked spaghetti as we try to drive them in. Even getting a spade in the ground seems impossible in places.

But over the next few hours we find a good rhythm, and by the time we stop for tea, we have already planted almost a hundred. Large clearings are transformed by an army of low, slim columns. You can't even see the whips inside those circular tubes, but that's part of the attraction: the whole planting project is the opposite of instant gratification. It's an investment whose rewards you reap only in fifteen or twenty years' time at the very earliest, which means you've got to have a clear notion of what you want the place to look like a generation down the line. It's an exercise in looking to the future: inside that semicircle of invisible oaks, we hoped to dig a large pond; that clearing by the cave could be for the sauna.

For us, the primary purpose of all this planting – quite apart from the beauty of trees – is fuel: we're going to need a lot of firewood to heat the house and its water in the years, and decades, to come, and the perfect tree for that is ash, *Fraxinus excelsior*. As the poem has it, 'Ash wet or ash dry, a king shall warm his slippers by.' It's also the right tree for our secondary purpose: to have plenty of timber in the future for furniture making. The wood of the ash is strong but elastic, it cleaves beautifully (its name comes from the Latin for 'to break') and has a clean white colour. If, in years to come, we ever bore of making furniture, ash is also ideal for making snooker cues, tennis racquets, rounders bats, hockey sticks, tent pegs, oars, and so on. Historically, it was always the wood used to make spear shafts and ships, which is why the rampaging Vikings were called Aescling, 'men of ash'.

Fortunately, we know that ash thrives here because it already makes up about a third of the trees in the wood. In many areas there are tiny forests of saplings, often over a hundred in a few square feet. They look, at calf height, like vertical, crooked knitting needles. The natural regeneration is so prolific that all we'll need to do in some areas is fence off the deer, let in a bit of light by thinning out some sallow, and those saplings will shoot up.

The other advantage of ash is that it doesn't overly darken the wood. Its leaves are pinnate, allowing light to filter through to the understorey; they're the last trees to leaf and the first to shed their leaves. Their honey-coloured bark is attractive. They grow fast and coppice vigorously. So it's not surprising that the tree has always been considered the most important one in the forest. In both Greek and Norse mythology humans were made from ash. Odin was speared to an ash – the mythical Yggdrasil – for nine days to receive runic illumination; the symbols derive from the shapes of ash twigs. Nemesis carried an ash branch, and ash was used both for the symbolically important maypole and for the Yule log.

The other trees we're planting are the usual native broadleaves: pedunculate oak, field maple, hazel, rowan and cherry. A major consideration is simply aesthetics: we want to create a woodland that is hopefully both eye-catching and calming. Grey alder we'll plant where it's wet, not least because it will improve the poor soil by fixing nitrogen. Marty is in charge of the shrubs, putting in yellow and red dogwoods, spindles, and the odd Guelder rose and wayfaring tree.

The afternoon was hard work, since we had the stoniest area still to do. Energy levels were flagging. Our hands were covered with the green goo from the tanalized (impregnated with preservative) stakes and our shoulders were aching from whacking them in with the slender post-rammer. Up on the rocky plateau it was much harder to get them to go in vertically, so some of the guards ended up badly off. Each time you tried to sink the spade you would hit rock, or builder's rubble, or something else under the moss and roots that stopped you making a clean slit.

One of the people who had turned up for our volunteer day had been referred by the local social services, a chap called Roy. He told me within minutes of us meeting that he was a schizophrenic with addiction issues. I explained our golden rules about no boozing, no using and no violence, and he gave me an eager, brown-toothed smile. He was trying to stop all three, he said.

'Have you got a history of violence then?' I asked, more concerned about that than the other two.

'Yeah, I've been violent, but not in a bad way though.'

I tried to think what a good way might be.

'It was with my stepdad. Don't want to say it was his fault, know what I mean, but he pushed me. Really pushed me.' He nodded and held my gaze, letting me know he wasn't a man who could be pushed.

Another guy up for the day, this time referred by a local charity, was called Andy. He had done a lot of amphetamines and seemed punch-drunk now that the world had slowed down again. There could hardly be a more eloquent illustration of the psychiatric damage of drug abuse. I asked him to give me a hand, so we could work and talk together.

'What music are you into, Andy?' I said, trying to draw him out.

'Death Metal.'

'Okay. Don't know it. What's that like?'

He looked at me with disdain. 'Loud.'

He spat on the ground through the gap in his teeth, making a sound like a water pistol.

It was one of the hardest things about our volunteer days: you would have a dozen people to organize, all doing different jobs that required supervision, and all the while there would be one or two who were telling you such intimate or tragic details about their life that you couldn't rush off and fetch the sledgehammer or drawknife. I was happy to listen, but I also loved getting things done, and the two things rarely went together. There was always a delicate balance between being patient and being driven. If you listened too much, things would never get done; but then, getting things done wasn't the purpose of this place. The jobs were far less important than the people. As one of our wise volunteers once said, 'It's not about the work we do in the woodland; it's about the work the woodland does in us.'

We moved on to the clearing at the far end, where we planted another sixty or so hazels, field maples and ashes. We now had a good system: slit, plant, close, move on. Someone came up behind and banged in the stake. Someone else slipped the guard over the top and tied it to the square stake. By half past four we had planted all of the three hundred trees and it looked great. For the first time since we had moved here eighteen months ago, the place finally resembled a working woodland: large logs were neatly stacked in piles all around. Hundreds of new trees had been planted. Benny and Emma brought out a ribbon each and wrote 'Happy Birthday' on them. They tied one around a rowan for their grandmother and, since it was also the birthday of another friend, Pam, they tied another round a maple for her. I went to feed the pigs, and to shut in the geese and chickens.

It was dark and cold by the time we all came in. Tony, as always, had brought doughnuts, and we scoffed them with tea. A guy called Terry was with us for a week, and had started cooking a risotto in the kitchen whilst Marty slumped in the armchair, playing Arlo Guthrie's 'City of New Orleans', and 'Will the Circle be Unbroken?' Mikey was listening and trying to sing the harmonies as he picked it up. He couldn't sing, but we didn't care. Crisp was making the girls laugh by pretending to stretch his thumb to double its length. Leo was crawling down the corridor towards the kitchen, and I could hear the sound of a metal bowl chiming against the flagstones.

'Francesca!' Terry shouted from the kitchen. 'Leo's eating the cat food again.'

Fra got up, and we all laughed as we heard her admonish Leo in Italian. He started crying, not knowing why he couldn't eat the rabbit stew in juicy jelly.

Everyone was exhausted but, apparently, happy. Crisp lit the candles on the table and played Scrabble with the girls. Fra lit the woodburner. Marty forgot the words to the song he was singing and got upset that his memory was going. Terry's risotto was pretty rough – undercooked by a good five minutes, so the rice stuck to your teeth and the onions were crunchy – but it didn't seem to matter. We were all so hungry it went down okay.

'Maybe give it a bit longer next time,' I suggested, as I picked raw rice from between my molars. 'Take it slow.'

Terry frowned, not liking the suggestion. 'I like it like this.'

'Okay,' I shrugged, thinking it better to have a bad meal than a bad vibe.

There was only one other house near ours. One or two of the windows were broken, and behind the cracks were strange objects: a live parrot with no feathers, old vases so dusty they looked grey, brass jars that had been knocked over. We had gone round to say hello soon after we moved in: there was an old woman with wiry white hair and her son, a thickset man whose face at rest was a scowl. They showed us their pet fox.

We rarely saw them after that, but they made their presence felt. Dense black smoke would blow over from their house, spreading around the whole area like grey fog. They were burning anthracite. Their dogs howled like wolves all day and night. Guineafowl shrieked, sounding like metal being filed. None of this bothered us too much: everyone has the right to keep warm and keep animals. But then one day someone ran into the kitchen to say they had almost been hit by a stone. I went outside and saw our neighbour Barry throwing rocks on to our log shed up by the boundary, smashing them on to the roof and creating quite a hole. I went upstairs to get a better view, to make sure, and there he was, happily chucking rocks over the boundary. Quite apart from the damage he was doing to the shed, it meant we would have wet logs. I went round to remonstrate, but instead of denying it or apologizing, he explained what he had been up to.

'Lot of people round here don't like what you're doing,' he said. He was wearing army fatigues and his eyes were so close together it looked like he had a squint.

'So you throw rocks around?'

'You don't belong here,' he said, smiling nastily as he declared war.

'Do you decide who belongs here?'

'Lot of people don't want you round here, you and your funny farm.' He exuded menace as he stepped towards me. 'Don't want your paedos and addicts round here, we don't.'

I decided to listen to his fears, thinking naively that it was better to do so than to deny them. We had spent many months strategically engaging with the local community, talking to them about what we were doing and listening to their advice. They had all, until now, been incredibly supportive and generous. The more I listened to Barry, however, the more aggressive he became, telling me how he wanted to strangle the neighbour on the other side of him and enjoying my unease at his violent language.

We tried to ignore him from then on, but it wasn't easy. We would see him walking his cowering dogs along the road and, when he saw us, he would feign hitting them with the shovel he was carrying, with the sole purpose, it seemed, of showing us he meant business. He would shout obscenities through the car window.

'Daddy, what does "wanker" mean?' Emma asked one time, after Barry had leant into the car and spat out his spite.

He began taking photographs of the children on their way to school and even took snaps of Francesca through our bathroom window. Dog shit and pig's trotters began to appear in our drive. It sometimes felt as if we were besieged: whenever we were laying the hedge by the boundary or doing fencing there he would repeatedly fire off his shotgun. He would swear abuse at us as we put out our recycling at the end of our drive, opposite his house. He called the council every time we moved livestock or manure. It seems absurd, but I began to think that we really were in the wrong, that we were ridiculous to be offering shelter to ex-offenders and recovering addicts against the will of our neighbour.

Looking back, I can kind of understand why I wanted to listen to his concerns. I had concluded *Utopian Dreams* by drawing a circle around our Bristol house and making that our given community. I had been influenced by those lines from G. K. Chesterton about neighbours, about how 'we have to love our neighbour because he is there . . . He is the sample of humanity which is actually given us. Precisely because he may be anybody he is everybody. He is a symbol because he is an accident.' It's easy to live and love amongst a clique, amidst the likeminded and the lovable. The real challenge of following the famous command about loving thy neighbour is to love those we don't choose to live alongside. That was the challenge Barry presented, and I was determined to try to listen to him despite the shit he, literally, threw our way. I made such an effort to empathize with him and to understand his anxieties and grievances that I came to the conclusion that he was probably right. I got a brief glimpse into what it might be like to be in an abusive relationship, because all the humiliations and intimidations were not only scary but strangely persuasive. You think you truly are in the wrong, that you deserve what you're getting. I kept trying to listen and to understand, and didn't see the absurd and bullying behaviour as anything other than an indictment of our folly. If the man felt so aggrieved, it was because of us. What he was doing was our fault, and we deserved it. We bent over backwards and, of course, he kicked us to the ground.

For months now we had been without the right equipment. We had been carrying cordwood in barrows or on shoulders and chucking pigs in the boot of a small car. One afternoon that spring, I went to get a load of pallets from a local builder's yard. I overloaded the roof rack of our old Citroën and when I braked too suddenly the whole pile fell forward, fanning across the road like floats in a swimming pool. The windscreen was smashed into a spider's web.

'We have to get a pick-up,' said Crisp when I got back.

We had spoken about getting one for a while, but we couldn't afford it. We could barely afford to fix the windscreen.

Marty was quite a petrolhead and went on eBay to see what there was. We bid on cheap things like Indian Tatas, until eventually we got a battered red Mitsubishi from the early nineties. Marty loved the idea of a road trip and got the train to Oxfordshire to bring the thing back. By the time he got it here, the lever for the windscreen wipers had snapped.

That pick-up – scratched, dented and rusty – would be the cause of many more adventures over the next few years: it often wouldn't start, so you always had to have jump leads behind the two seats and to park it, where possible, facing down a hill. Occasionally, the indicators would stop working, and you would have to put your hand out of the window, or ask the person in the passenger seat to indicate we were turning left. Grass grew in the muddied gullies of its windscreen. The key would break off in the petrol cap. Somebody who was staying here tried to fit it up with a stereo but got the wiring wrong, so you never knew what you were going to hear when you turned the key. The defender relay broke, so to start the engine you had to lift the bonnet and fiddle with the temporary wiring we'd sorted out. But the pick-up made logging easier, and it certainly made us look like a shoestring operation any time we went to pick something up. Marty started playing Neil Young's 'Out on the Weekend' to make us laugh. He would sit in the armchair, the harmonica held by the metal arms on the guitar, doing the introduction perfectly: 'Think I'll pack it in, and buy a pick-up . . .'

The trouble was we were spending money we didn't have to make this place work. As the community expanded, I was constantly having to buy the simplest basics for people: towels, pillows, torches, candles, lamps, and so on. Then there was the expense of all the other stuff needed for a smallholding: watering cans, drills, axes, coops, beehives, fencing, wheelbarrows, buckets, insulation, tiles, and all the rest. 'Where's our card?' guests would ask me, as if my debit card was communal and our resources infinite. The basics of infrastructure and tools were costly and the quicksand of personal debt made me anxious. Not just for obvious reasons, but also because we were constantly accumulating new clobber when the hope had been to escape incessant consumerism. We were still shopping for stuff: spending money online and racing round shops. Fra and I did feel genuinely enriched, but we were also – if not impoverished

– always within sight of poverty. And when people came round here and commented on our 'voluntary simplicity', on our pared-down lifestyle, I rather tartly told them there was nothing 'voluntary' about it.

The problem had sneaked up on us. To begin with, we had just had a spare room which we allowed people to use. Since then, we had been the victims of our own success, in a way, because we now had six or seven people living with us, all having hot baths and boiling kettles and using the computer. We were adamant that we didn't want to charge rent, because we wanted this place to be available to the very poorest and because rent makes people understandably reluctant to work for their keep. But now we had the opposite problem. Because people were working for their keep, they were reluctant to pay for anything.

We put up with it for another month because, looking back, I think I was still in thrall to that oldest of utopian aspirations, the abolition of money. And I liked the liberating creativity of frugality. We had to be resourceful, and that required imagination – an inventiveness and a determination to waste nothing. That's why, I think, quite a few homeless men and wayfarers felt at home here, because they were habitually resourceful themselves, living, like us, a fairly hand-to-mouth existence in which you had to grab any gift going. We were frugal to the point of absurdity: not just making candles out of beeswax, baking bread and knitting but making tent pegs out of old logs, using offcuts of narrow piping to protect the edge of an axe, using tuna tins to safeguard the top of fencing stakes that might otherwise rot. We constantly raided skips: we took a magnet from an old speaker in order to sweep outside the workshop for nails and screws; we used a white plastic curtain rail to make a bow for the kids. Someone tried to use the inside of a washing machine to make a wind turbine. The price of sheep fleeces was so low that local farmers would just give us theirs, and we'd use them to insulate various shelters and sheds. A rusty old wheel rim was used to wind the hose around. We turned old oil-drums into kilns, leaking welly boots into waterproof tiles. Tony loved pallets and helped us make floors, compost bays, kindling, benches and gates with them. We made a 'pallet chalet' and planned a 'pallet palais'. Friends of ours from Bristol had moved abroad for work, and they offered us the chance to clear out their old house, so Marty and I went up there in the pick-up, arriving after dark. The electricity had long been cut off, so we ransacked the house with torches like burglars, loading up mirrors, pillows, bookcases and blankets in the dark. Once we had got all the pickings back to Windsor Hill Wood, they gave the place an appearance of eccentric simplicity.

There were few things we couldn't use and as local people began to realize that, they started bringing us their junk. It was fine at first: the odd toolbox or old duvet was quite useful. But we came to understand that for some of them we were just nearer, and friend-lier, than the local tip. They would bring us things they had foraged in a skip, stuff from their late grandmother's garage, anything they couldn't use themselves. It was almost as if they were setting us a challenge, to see how we would upcycle it, and when we began to say no, one or two got miffed and expressed surprise that we didn't want their broken plastic chairs or a rusty exhaust.

But despite that resourcefulness, money was truly becoming a profound problem. James Baldwin once said that money is like sex: you think of nothing else if you don't have it, and of other things if you do. I was now worrying about money much of the time. I was having to spend more and more time writing, trying to earn the money to pay the mortgage on the adventure play-ground where everyone else was having great fun. From my office

I could see people sawing up trees, turning things on the lathe, carving spoons, making rounders bats, and all the rest. I was longing to do more carpentry with them, but more and more I had to sit down and pick up my pen to pay the bills.

That March, at the weekly house meeting, we tentatively suggested that people were going to have to contribute towards the cost of things other than food.

'Like what?' asked Mikey, frowning.

'Seeds,' I said. 'If we're going to grow as much veg as last year, it's about thirty or forty quid up front.'

'I don't see why we should pay for it,' said Mikey, 'if we might not be around to eat the produce come the summer.'

I felt my internal cogs speeding up but tried to maintain my self-control. 'Mikey, you're eating all the honey and chutney we made last year. They're free to you because someone else invested time and money before you rolled up. Whether you're here or not in the summer is irrelevant.'

'I just don't see why we should cough up for something we might not eat.'

'Because someone did that for you before you arrived – so you could do it for someone else before you leave.'

Mikey was shaking his head, as was Crisp. Not for the first time, I saw the stark ideological difference between us. I had always thought a community was the meeting point of generations; it was a place where predecessors prepared the ground for the future, and where new arrivals were taught to do the same for their successors. Most of the people around the table now didn't agree.

'Growing your own is so inefficient anyway,' Crisp said. 'It takes up so much time. It's not even cheaper. Might as well just buy it all in Tesco.'

Suddenly, people were talking about what they weren't prepared to pay for. Amy was a vegetarian and said she wasn't happy paying for air-rifle pellets that gave us rabbit, wood pigeon and squirrel. Tracey said she didn't like kale and so wanted a rebate on her weekly food contribution. The floodgates were open. Those with allergies and intolerances were chipping in too, saying they shouldn't pay for this or that. I silently wondered when our craved-for simplicity had become so complicated.

'I'm sorry,' Fra said, her face pale and her flat palm laying down the law. 'If we start making exceptions for every taste, things will be so confusing we won't know where we stand. What are we going to do next? Weigh the food people eat and have them pay accordingly? We all pay thirty quid a week towards food, and that's that. I'm sorry,' she said again, 'we share food costs evenly, and we need to start sharing bills too.'

The week before, we had looked over past bills and realized that the electricity consumption in the house had trebled, which meant – with rising prices – that the cost had almost quadrupled. Our Internet usage was way beyond our maximum, not least because Crisp would have dozens of pages open as he downloaded every song and film he could.

'You've obviously got the wrong suppliers,' Crisp said, shaking his head. 'You're being ripped off.'

'And if it turns out,' I said, 'that they are the best, cheapest suppliers, what then? How do we share the costs fairly?'

'I don't think we should,' he said. 'We're working here as unpaid labourers. The least you can do is supply hot water, cups of tea and a bit of broadband.'

I could see his point. From the guests' point of view, they were toiling for free. But out of tact I couldn't mention the flip side of that. They weren't competent workers but people in pretty profound crises who struggled to concentrate on or complete any task. That same week someone had put the entire cladding on a shed upside down. I had asked him to take it down and do it again. He tore the feather-edged boards off, ripping quite a few in the process. He then went and sat down and had a cuppa before putting the whole thing on upside down again. More things were getting broken or stolen than fixed up. Someone had bust the tap on one of the water butts. I had spent two days laying a hedge with Mikey and then came back one afternoon to find that a volunteer had sawn up all the long horizontal branches that were woven in and chucked them into a wheelbarrow for firewood. My much-loved ash tool-rest, a perfect shape, which I had sanded and oiled for years and which was an integral part of my pole lathe, had been axed up and turned into kindling. Most of the people here were genuinely trying to help out and I always kept my cool. I knew many of our guests were on heavy sedation, and many had been drug users for years, if not decades. Some had such low self-esteem that I sometimes thought they deliberately did things badly to prove that they weren't up to the job: they would be clumsy to reinforce their notion that they were incompetent. All that was fine. Things were bound to go awry. But I really didn't want to be told that I had to sink deeply into debt because there was a team of able labourers around. That was bollocks.

Marty had been watching the exchanges. He was the calm, wise head amongst us, and was pained by the tangible tension in the room.

'Couldn't those of us who can afford it just make an *ex gratia* contribution?' He had recently committed to being here long term and, as he had a pension and was renting his flat, he had a higher income than any of us.

I nodded, acknowledging his kindness. 'That would certainly make a big difference.'

'No, I'm absolutely opposed to that. It's all wrong,' Crisp said. 'That means there's no equality any more. It'll skew the way things work if some of us are making donations and others aren't.'

With Crisp there, we wouldn't be able to agree on anything. Fra was shaking her head and we got up from the table knowing nothing had been resolved.

I think we had ignored the financial issue until now because we liked the idea that this refuge was a place of contingency and uncertainty. It felt right that it was a breadline operation, receiving alms as much as giving them. I don't want to make out we were living in poverty – we lacked nothing and always scraped through to the end of the month – but frugality was acute and habitual. It made us realize that whilst many were reliant on us, we were just as reliant on others. It meant, I hope, that we weren't smug or conceited or patrician; we were takers as well as givers, completely dependent on the kindness of strangers. And that kindness continued to be extraordinary. A lot of professionals – foresters, carpenters, consultants – gave their time for free. Locals would bring round blankets, watering cans and old mugs. Cardboard boxes of books arrived. A local woman who had overheard Francesca lament that there was never enough money in the kitty to buy orange juice brought round a few cartons. And every time we were scratching our heads, wondering how we were going to find the money for fencing or compost or straw, a cheque appeared in the post, always for exactly the amount we needed. Once someone brought us, unprompted, a garden fork, just a few days after ours had broken in the rocky quarry. Each time it happened it restored our faith not just in people but in the project: it seemed as if what we were doing was important to outsiders, many of whom had never been here. Whether it was providence or coincidence, we were being supported and sustained.

It was noticeable too that whilst we were looking after the animals, they were also, in a way, part of the therapy of the place. We had recently replenished our flock of chickens by taking half a dozen ex-battery hens from the British Hen Welfare Trust. The birds were no longer laying at the rate demanded by industrial farming and were due for slaughter unless rescued by the Trust. Tracey and I went to pick them up from a nearby farm and the birds were a sorry sight: since they hadn't been scratching around like normal hens, their claws were an inch long and their beaks had been cut off at an unnatural, blunt angle. They had hardly any plumage and their skin looked grey and saggy. Tracey was shaking her head, indignant at the look of them. We put them in cardboard boxes and, once we got home, let them out on to the grass. They didn't know what to do. They crouched there, head held low beneath their wings in apprehension.

Over the next few weeks Tracey looked after them. They couldn't eat normal corn so we ground up stale bread. Tracey sat with them, encouraging them to scratch around under the beech tree. She would lie down and let them crawl over her, raising her arms to form a perch as they flapped nervously. I was interested not only in the change in the birds – their claws slowly eroded back to normal, their tan feathers returned – but also in Tracey. She identified with these exhausted, mistreated birds and seemed to gain huge amounts of self-esteem through caring for them. Turning this place into an animal sanctuary was benefiting the humans too.

There were plenty of other ailing animals. We found a wounded wagtail in the woods one day and Tracey gamely tried to nurse it back to life, offering it worms on the tip of her finger. When it died, she buried it at the edge of the chapel. One of the geese got ill too, so my old man, a retired GP, went and bought a course of antibiotics.

'What's the name of the patient?' they asked him at the chemist.

I watched him look at the ceiling. 'Jemima,' he said.

He and Marty battled to get the yellow gunge down the goose's long neck, its strong serrated beak biting hard as they did so. Again it was Tracey who became the carer, holding the goose on her lap and stroking its tough white feathers.

Marty too found the animals good company. He would spend his afternoons sitting outside the pig paddock in an old camping chair, carving a spoon or a spatula to pass the time. Occasionally, he would look up and chat to them, laughing at how deaf both he and the pigs seemed to be. He got in with them, too, stroking and scratching them. They were, for months, his confessors, the silent recipients of his secrets.

'I would never have had so many women problems,' he chuckled to me once, 'if I had met a pig forty years ago.'

Marty was a constant for us through the many arrivals and departures of guests. He was so generous he was almost leaky. Rarely did a guest leave without a bit of a financial side wind from him. He would give them lifts to the station or airport, his tariff only a Toblerone. He was always making us laugh. One morning he came in saying he had made a mistake in the night. He was so impressed with our purchasing a pick-up online that he had bid for a Land Rover on his phone. He hadn't really meant to, it was the other side of the country, but he had won the auction. He now had to go up to Newcastle to pick up a motor that was so ancient it was ventilated by rudimentary metal rectangles that were opened with a rusty lever.

In April, Marty had moved into a different shelter, deeper in the straggly woodland. He organized a housewarming one Sunday afternoon. He wore an almost-matching linen suit, the trousers tucked into his wellies, as he passed around cherries. There was something both bohemian and elegant about him; he was intellectually sharp but also quite a space cadet. One Wednesday he smiled at Maggie Purple and asked her, 'Isn't Maggie Purple coming today?'

Marty was a great combination of idealist and realist. He enjoyed communal living but was often gently cutting to the credit-card hippies who rolled up here.

'I heard that meditation causes cancer,' he said to a guy who was so often sitting cross-legged it might have seemed like laziness.

'You're kidding?'

'Nope. That's what this article said.'

'Meditation?'

'Yep, if you smoke whilst meditating it can cause cancer.'

His love of the pigs did occasionally land him in trouble. One time, he and I went to see Dave to get something on the pick-up fine-tuned. Dave was every driver's dream mechanic: quick with service and slow with bills. He had often done stuff for us for free or, rather, for a bit of veg or firewood. After he had fixed the pick-up, we stood around nattering.

'What I love about Harriet –' Marty was enthusing about our sow – 'is the way she comes up and nuzzles me when I scratch her back.'

'What do you mean?' Dave said, frowning.

'She's just so friendly, so loyal. Every time I go and see her, she'll come towards me and rub my thighs with her shoulders.'

'Are you being funny?' Dave said. I'd never seen him looking so ill at ease.

'No, she really does.' Marty was nodding. 'She's a beauty.'

'What are you talking about?'

'Harriet. Our sow. She's a lovely animal.'

Dave had closed his eyes and was smiling now, shaking his head. 'I thought you was talking about my Harriet,' he said.

'How do you mean?'

'My wife, Harriet. I couldn't work out what you was on about.'

'Oh, no!' Marty giggled, amused at the confusion. His high-pitched laugh was contagious, and Dave rolled his eyes, both relieved and amused.

From then on, every time we saw Dave we would ask after his Harriet and he would ask after ours.

Mid-April. Tracey had started going for walks in the early-morning sunshine. It was good to see her strolling out, getting exercise and fresh air. She was writing lots of letters, and often walked through the morning mist to catch the post. She was trying to get her finances sorted out, so she would wander off again in the afternoon, across the fields, to the bank in town. It all seemed positive, as if she were making an effort to turn things around: getting in touch with people she had hurt, getting her finances back on track. She would return more bubbly, a little more effusive. Her breath would smell of mint, and – more tellingly – she would usually return with a little present for one of our children.

Her constant industry was surreptitiously replaced by sleepiness. She was spending more time shut away in her yurt. She was getting clumsy again. It all came to a head one lunchtime when I was looking after Leo. I had to go and drain the pasta and asked Tracey to hold him for a minute. As soon as I got my hands on the saucepan, I heard a crash and little Leo's scream. Then there was a long silence, by which time I had run back into the garden room and picked him up from the floor. Tracey was holding one of his ankles. He was silent, his face growing redder, and then he really screamed.

'He didn't fall on his head,' she shouted over the noise, looking almost as pained as Leo.

He rolled his eyes and then either fainted or fell asleep for a few minutes. In that time, I told Tracey she had quite clearly been drinking. She started crying and apologized. Leo came round and sobbed quietly. The other guests looked on, unsure what was going to happen next. We had a one-strike policy; everyone knew that's how it was, and they knew I would have to ask Tracey to pack her bags.

Once we had eaten lunch, I took Tracey into my shed. She knew she had broken the rules and that she couldn't stay, but we sat and talked more than we had in all the previous months. It made me realize the ways we had failed her: we hadn't really made time to sit and listen to her, we hadn't insisted she go to AA, we hadn't breathalysed her randomly, as we often would with future guests. We hadn't been either sufficiently caring or sufficiently tough. We had lived and worked together, given her a break from the rut she was in, but it hadn't been enough. It was the first time I had to ask someone to leave, and there was much guilt and grief. You always wonder what else you could have done. You take an individual's failure as your failure. I knew we had to hold the boundaries, that this place would fall apart very quickly otherwise, ending up being not a sanctuary but more of the same. I understood that it was vital that people didn't mistake our easy-going vibe for anything goes. And yet asking someone to leave was still hard. It turns you into the opposite of what you want to be: I thought I was managing in this community because I was understanding and empathetic, but here I was being not the good cop but the bad one.

It finally feels as if spring is here. Today the sky is an infinite blue and although it's still bitterly cold before sunrise, the temperature has been rising ever since. The place looks completely yellow: the daffodils and dandelions are out, there are the shallow domes of pale primroses, vibrant sprays of forsythia, carnation-like *Kerria japonica*, star-shaped celandines. Jemima the goose has recovered, and she and the other geese are laying their majestic white eggs again. Suddenly everything looks different: what appeared dead only a few weeks ago is now performing a slow-motion explosion. The paths through the woods smell of wild garlic and the green points of the arum lilies are beginning to poke through the undergrowth. Although we've had a couple of hardy people camping here in January and February, it's now a more mainstream option. So we put down the black sheep fleeces under a rug in the bell tent and move a sofa bed in there.

We've met a local man called Mark who works in recycling and scrap. A burly ex-army man, he's amazingly resourceful: he walks through the woods picking up bits and bobs, putting them in his pocket or rucksack. Sometimes he drives his Land Rover around the site to load up random things. In return, he bring us almost anything we need. Whenever we give him a list of obscure objects, he can usually source them within a day or two. When we want a huge campfire kettle, an odd-sized auger bit and an oil drum, he has, by the end of the weekend, found the lot. As long as we give him a slice of cake and cup of tea, he always offers them to us for free. Like most of our exchanges with the local community, it's non-monetary.

We needed the oil drum in order to make charcoal. We cut

five golf-ball-sized holes in the bottom of the drum: one right in the centre and the others at the four points of the compass near the edge. We slice off the top completely but cut it from above, leaving four metal arms – horizontal semicircular indentations – on which that 'lid' can be rested and rotated to control the airflow.

It's a sunny morning, and Mikey, Marty and I spend a contented few hours cutting up brash and thin sticks at lengths of between four and eight inches. We're in the clearing by the Abode, and it feels as if the outside world doesn't exist. We have a saw horse and a bow saw each, and it's blissfully quiet work: just the sound of the saws rattling through the wood and Marty singing snatches of old folk songs. The whole woodland feels alive with noise and movement: the drilling of a woodpecker, the irregular jig of a butterfly, the lazy bounce of a rabbit so used to us he barely moves away. Mikey is stripped to the waist, showing off his muscles and tattoos.

I'm beginning to understand why living in a woodland is so healing. The trees are so resilient: even after coppicing and pollard-ing, when they've been knocked down hard and cut off at ankle or head height, they keep coming back. Each winter you inspect the bare beige stools and stumps, convinced that this time you've overdone it, that you have been too harsh on the tree. But then they make their comeback, a vigorous, defiant return, like a boxer who's been floored but refuses to stay down. The indomitable sycamores, oaks, ashes, hazels and willows burst back, creating a fountain of new shoots to replace the one strong trunk. This is where we were coppicing the winter before last, and now the stumps have sent up dozens of new shoots. This endless sylvan resurgence must surely be encouraging for people fighting misfor-tune and tragedy. The untouched trees in a coppice cant are called 'standards'. They're the noble, mature trees which you leave as they are. There's something about those standards that dwarfs you. They give you something to look up to. They put things in perspective. I look over at Mikey and Marty, both struggling with their own grief, and they seem serene, almost blissed out by this work. It really is as if they're coming back to life, like the coppiced stump on which everyone had given up.

After a couple of hours we've got large piles of slender sticks at the ends of our saw horses. The hazel ends form white circles; the willow and hawthorn ones are more sunset orange. Mikey wanders over the ridge to stoke up the fire and make a cuppa. I can see him bending down now, getting his head under the kettle to blow on the embers, still glowing from breakfast. The wood hisses and cracks as the flames increase, and he fills up the kettle from the water butt on the Abode.

We drink tea and discuss the best way to load the kiln. As usual here, it's the blind leading the blind. We've read a few articles and watched some videos online, but it's mostly common sense. On a large kiln you're supposed to place long, relatively thick pieces of wood to channel the oxygen from the air inlets to the centre of the kiln. But our oil drum is fairly small, so we decide just to put lots of kindling around the holes and place small twigs radially around that.

We lift the kiln up on four bricks so that the air can get in underneath and start loading it. It takes a while, as we stretch down to the bottom of the drum to place the sticks as neatly as possible. It's like log stacking: the more tessellated they are, the more, obviously, you can fit in. Half an hour later the thing is full and we're ready to go.

'I've read that it's tradition for a woman to light the kiln,' Marty says.

'I'll go and get Katharine.' Mikey wanders off and comes back with Katharine, who's covered in flour from her baking.

'What do you reckon? Just a match under the holes?'

'Better have a cloth soaked in paraffin,' Mikey suggests. 'Let it burn for a minute or two.'

'I've got paraffin for my lamp back at mine,' says Marty.

'And I've got the perfect thing to light it with,' says Katharine, smiling. She wanders off and comes back with one of her socks. 'All my socks are odd. This one is half of the only pair I have. A pair seems all wrong. So, here.' She passes it to Mikey, who wraps it around a hazel pole and soaks it in paraffin.

He passes it back to her, and she lights it and then bends down and holds it under the drum. We all crouch down, cheeks on the dry undergrowth, checking to see that the flames have found the holes. Slowly, smoke begins to rise from the open top of the kiln. Katharine moves round to the other holes and the smoke gets thicker. Within minutes it's gushing out smoke like a steam engine. We watch it, hypnotized by the silent speed of the smoke and the ferocity of the flames, which are now flashing above the metal rim. Marty deftly puts the lid on to the metal arms of the drum, and the holes act as chimneys, channelling the smoke into beautiful columns that rise vertically for a couple of metres. The sunlight is angling down through the trees now, and it's a beautiful sight: the power of the burn contrasting with the peace of the woods.

I walk off for a while. The periwinkles have turned the banks green and purple. The hawthorn blossom is white, making the trees look as if they're covered in confetti. The goat willows have fluffed up, producing sprigs that look like dusted rabbit's tails. The beech leaves, just sharp spears a week ago, are now unfolding, the concertina being pulled flat by the promise of sunlight.

The inky dots on the fringes of the ash trees are opening too. Purple waterfalls of aubretia cascade from the rock face.

After lunch we come back to the kiln to inspect the smoke. Charcoal is created by shutting off the oxygen supply at the precise point at which all the moisture, resins and tar have been burnt off so that what remains is 'pure' wood: the brittle, instantly ignitable charcoal. Charcoal burners traditionally had a one-legged stool, which would stop them falling asleep in the night and missing the key moment. One of the advantages of using a small oil drum is that it takes only a few hours and you don't need to stay up all night watching it.

The colour of the smoke is the only indicator you have of the right moment to shut down the burn, so Mikey and I keep going over to look at it. We grab the smoke, feeling the humidity as we let it waft between our fingers. You get a feel for it, a sense of the moisture and heat that's coming off. The smoke is still just white, so we go off to chop some wood for a while and when we return, it's time. The white smoke has disappeared and all you can see now is a translucent haze. We kick away the bricks, and the drum falls flush to the ground. We shovel squares of turf around the base and smack it tight with the back of the shovel. We twist the lid so the chimneys are closed and put turf all over the top, patting it down so that no oxygen can get in. It's like a pressure cooker now, and tiny gaps in the turf piles whistle. We plug the gaps, pushing in clumps of soil and grass.

The kiln is still hot three or four hours later. You can touch it now, but we don't want to lift the lid too soon in case the whole thing reignites and we lose our eyebrows. So we leave it until later that evening, shortly before sunset. It's exciting to scrape away the turf and start lifting off the lid, unsure of what we're going to find. Inside, the wood, previously packed to the brim, is barely above halfway. But it looks like perfect charcoal: a shiny blue-black colour, it snaps easily with a faint metallic sound. It's also incredibly light: without all the impurities and moisture, it feels less than half its original weight. The sides of the kiln are coated with a black tar that cracks off easily. We tip the kiln on to the ground and start putting the charcoal in large paper bags and mail sacks, ready for our next barbecue or market stall.

Two weeks later, a couple of old-fashioned men of the road rolled up. They looked weather-beaten, with ruddy cheeks that might have been the result of fresh air, or booze, or both. They had heard about us from other wayfarers and wanted somewhere warm to stay for a few nights. We gave them a meal and gently suggested they should feel free to have a shower. That evening, after doing the washing-up, I went to look for our girls. They weren't anywhere obvious, so I asked one or two of the other guests.

'They're playing hide-and-seek with Gary and Bob.'

'Where?'

'In the woods. I saw them go out twenty minutes ago.'

I walked among the trees at a brisk pace, trying not to look alarmed. This was the stuff of sinister fairy tales and nightmares: unknown adults luring kids into the woods away from their parents. Eventually I saw Emma with her hands over her eyes, counting to one hundred as her forehead rested on the bark of a large ash tree. I watched the scene for long enough to understand that it was all innocent. Benny looked at me from behind a log store, her eyes screaming at me to keep quiet. I glimpsed Gary and Bob fifty feet away, not even looking for the girls but rolling up cigarettes as they sat on a horizontal trunk.

The children didn't see the dangers, and perhaps it was good that they were sufficiently innocent to trust all the adults at Windsor Hill Wood; we certainly didn't want to overburden them with fears. But their safety and innocence was the most precious thing here. On one occasion, one of our 'outpatients', a guy called Chris, was bouncing on the trampoline with Emma. There was something about it that Fra thought looked wrong. He was lying down and encouraging her to bounce on him. It was probably harmless, but Fra walked over and – to Emma's dismay – explained that she wanted her to come inside. We must appear to the children like party poopers, the ones who always stop the fun for no reason.

We had always taken seriously the objection that in running this refuge we were putting our children at risk, and both my and Francesca's antennae were highly tuned to any danger. It was very rare that the children were out of our sight. My writing shed gave me a good view of the central clearing and all the paths into the woods from there. Fra, from the other side of the house, could see the same.

We had a notion, though, that, paradoxically, the way to keep this place safe was not to make it more defensive but more open, because we had noticed over the first eighteen months that the best gatekeepers were the current residents and the diaspora of Windsor Hill Wood 'graduates': former residents, guests, volunteers and friends – all those who had spent time here and knew its inherent vulnerabilities; those who, without exaggeration, counted our children as their own. They were often far shrewder than we were about certain behaviour patterns, and even more protective of this place – their 'only home', as many call it – than we were. I remember a new chap who turned up and, as they often do, told us his life story. Amy, a guest who was with us at the time and who was OCD, could spot inconsistency at a hundred yards. She came to me later and outlined all the reasons we should be on our guard. I hadn't picked up on any of it.

It sometimes felt like we were a magnet for the West Country's blaggers and chancers. We kept hoping we would get more street-wise, but we must have seemed like a soft touch to the hardened survivors out there: a well-publicized open-door policy, rent-free rooms in the Somerset countryside. No matter how explicit we were about our expectations, about rules and boundaries, we were frequently left dealing with sizable amounts of debt and discord. And although we grew more canny, that was probably the way it always would be. It was the nature of somewhere like this to be vulnerable. The only way, we felt, to keep it safely vulnerable – if that makes sense – was to keep it open, literally and metaphorically: to keep the gate open but also to make it a place of honesty and transparency.

There was a warning at the back of my mind in case that open-ness ever became too much. It came from a passage in Abigail Alcott's diary. She was the mother of Louisa May Alcott of *Little Women* fame, and the wife of Amos Bronson Alcott, a transcen-dentalist who set up the Fruitlands community in Harvard in the 1840s. Abigail complained that 'we have always been too crowded up. We have no room to enjoy that celestial privacy which gives a charm to connubial and domestic intimacy.' Of the idealistic, vegan men, she lamented that 'they spare the cattle but they forget the women and children.' Her husband's principles meant that her home was constantly invaded, and he looked after guests more than his family. I was always aware that I was in danger of doing something similar. I felt guilty that I wasn't spending enough time with the children. There were so many demands on my time that I seemed to race past them sometimes. The danger of their feeling ignored or forgotten was far more likely than the more alarming dangers that came to mind. A few days after Fra had hauled Emma off the trampoline, Mikey wanted to make space in the shed for his bike and so he chucked the children's paddling pool on to a pile of rusting metal, ripping it. They couldn't, understandably, comprehend why their pool was less important than his bike.

'Mikey,' I said, calling him over, 'can you see what's happened here?'

'I put my bike in the shed.'

'In place of what?'

He looked around and saw the brightly coloured paddling pool chucked on the corrugated iron. 'I took out that old tarp.'

I explained what it was, showed him the rips and asked how he thought the children would feel about it. He had an underdeveloped empathy gland.

'Mate, they're too big for a paddling pool at their age.'

'That's their decision, not yours.' I was struggling to keep my cool. 'It would be good if you could replace it with a new one by the end of the week.'

He stared at me in disbelief and then wandered away, shaking his head. My anger was as much aimed at myself as it was at Mikey. I was ultimately responsible for the fact that he was here. It wound me up that he was sidelining the children because that was what I feared I was doing.

Every windowsill in the house and surface in the greenhouse had seed trays on it: little rectangles of compost with the timid shoots of tomatoes, chard, peppers, chillies, spinach, aubergines, courgettes, squash, leeks, and all the rest. The shallots were in and the seed potatoes had been chitted (placed in egg boxes in the light and encouraged to sprout) and planted. Wrinkled rhubarb leaves were unfurling on the end of their fat red stalks. Rows of garlic stood perfectly vertical, like eager cadets. The raspberry canes were coming to life, the crooked twigs suddenly producing their serrated leaves. The mint was becoming bushy, creating a green rug amongst the gooseberries and redcurrants.

We had found a dozen scaffolding boards and were making more raised beds with them. Mikey and Max were weaving a knee-high hazel fence. They wandered off into the woods and came back with armfuls of twenty-foot hazel, which they then bent left and right between the uprights. After a few days, it looked rustic but tidy. Katharine was planting out. Marty was bringing over barrows of compost from the pile in what we called Walnut Tree Bay.

Work here is rewarding because, in the old permaculture adage, it's all about integration rather than segregation. Everything seems to have a purpose and nothing goes to waste: the manure comes from the chickens and nearby horses; eggshells are mixed with wood ash to act as a slug repellent; the slim timber from the woodland is used for weaving a fence; pigs plough over land where we'll plant next season. Nothing is unwanted: all the peelings and slugs and snails feed the chickens. We pick up pallets for free and turn them into bird boxes and laundry baskets and chests for blankets. What some people consider weeds – dandelions and nettles – feed the bees and us. We make pesto from the wild garlic and last autumn's hazelnuts, selling a few jars to locals, which is more about making friends than making money.

Integration is what happens with people too. Most come to us feeling useless, but it doesn't take long for them to see how they can become integral and indispensable. Whenever visitors start to go weak at the knees eating Francesca's sophisticated *tortelli di erbette* or *di zucca* – pillowcases of handmade pasta filled with chard or pumpkin – we always make a point of saying we should really thank Bill, who had weeded and manured the veg for so long, or Mikey, who had looked after the chooks so that we had eggs in the first place. Misfits just seem to fit in, to tessellate well. One person's lumpy bits sit well with another person's gaps; or someone's weakness allows another to discover their own strength. Someone drinks too much; another doesn't eat enough. One's obsessed with order; another thinks anything will do.

The majority of people who come here don't want to be helped; they want to help out. They yearn for a position and a role. They want to be a part of something. Well-being is connected to integration, and the real ailment of people here is their 'placelessness', their lack of belonging. We're always hearing people say they feel that they 'don't fit in'; and the real problem is that there's nothing left into which they can fit. The metaphorical 'public square' where people used to gather is diminished or non-existent. The social glue has dissolved. Most of our guests are suffering, primarily, from loneliness. It's never expressed so explicitly, partly because loneliness seems embarrassing, a sign of being without friends or family. Globally, the number of people living alone rose eighty per cent between 1996 and 2011. Only a few years ago, the planet reached the point at which more people live in cities than in the countryside. We're used to isolating and insulating ourselves, aspiring to the values of rugged individualism. We're solo survivalists, relishing our autonomy and freedoms and trusting in technology and transport to keep us connected. And so community, as it's currently understood, is delivered through a screen. It's strangely compatible with rootlessness. We discover we have less and less in common.

Everything here is a balancing act. Guests relish being integrated, but then we have to teach them, too, about distance and boundaries. The trouble is that people who are uncomfortable with their own solitude will be equally ill at ease in company. They yearn for recognition, conversation and endorsement, and are so eager to avoid being alone that they waylay whoever they can. It means that over time I've become slightly aloof. And as a community we are often devising ways in which we can protect our own and other people's privacy. Francesca and I are lucky inasmuch as we have a private language. We resort to Italian when we want to chat without being overheard and understood. We try not to do it too much because it would be excluding, but it makes a huge difference just to have that subtle verbal intimacy in a crowd, even for a few minutes.

One of the diehard stereotypes about communal living is that communities tend to be full of outgoing extroverts and gregarious, eager-to-hug types. But we all need a door we can shut, a place to which we can retreat. I hope this small sanctuary suits shy introverts and the socially timid too, because solitude is still so easy to find. All it takes is a stroll into the woods. I think part of the education of living communally is that being alone becomes a cherished, rather than a dreaded, experience. It's only in community that you can distinguish between solitude and loneliness.

In M. Scott Peck's iconic, slightly slick book about community, *The Different Drum*, he discusses the processes through which a group has to travel before becoming a true community. The stages he identifies aren't dissimilar to the rhyming quartet of 'forming, storming, norming, performing'. The first stage, Scott Peck calls 'pseudocommunity', in which everyone tries to create instant cohesion through being wonderfully pleasant and snuffing out any disagreement. It's hugs or handshakes all round, in a polite,

but false, setting. People veer away from confrontation and difference. 'Pseudocommunity,' Scott Peck wrote, 'is conflict-avoiding;
true community is conflict-resolving.'

Years later, it's clear that what we had in that early period was a
pretence of community built on the avoidance of dispute. The
excitement of having created a woodland gathering was such that
I didn't want to endanger it by pointing out the differences, even
incompatibilities, between us. The people who were sheltering
with us seemed so fragile that I was reluctant to place on them
more expectations or orders, and so I allowed drift and indulgence. I relished the idea that I was laid-back and easy-going, and
didn't want to reveal that, actually, I thought people should be
punctual and hard-working. It was only later that I understood
that people who have led chaotic lives yearn for rhythm and rules
and expectations. They don't want indulgence but responsibility.
I thought it was a kindness to allow people to get out of bed when
they wanted, to work when they felt like it, to come and go as they
pleased. I thought we were offering them rest, whereas, given
such lack of direction, they were – I realized later – simply restless. Responsibility can come only in response to a call, and I
wasn't giving them anything to which they could respond. The
place was too flabby, too easy come, easy go.

And yet I remember why I resisted over-organization. I had
read in *The Different Drum* that 'organization and community
are . . . incompatible.' I didn't want to shoehorn people into an
inflexible system; I didn't want to establish a set of rules or rotas
until we had lived and worked together and talked about what
was best for us as a group. We wanted to allow something to
emerge rather than impose a structure from the outset. Only if it
evolved organically, from our own experience of this place and
these people, from doing these tasks, would our eventual

community truly be suited to its purpose. But there was more to it than that. The vast majority of people coming here had been dependent most of their lives: dependent on drugs, on relatives, on a prison regime or on military order. I was reluctant to be the new crutch, the person they looked to or relied on to manage their behaviour or conduct. The American psychiatrist Irvin Yalom once wrote that his task as a therapist, even as a parent, was to make himself 'obsolete' in order 'to help a patient become his or her own mother and father'. I was keen for the success of this place to be the result of everyone, not just me; for it to be a group of leaders, not a group of people who were led. That was the aspiration of all the therapeutic communities I admired – Toc H, Fairweather Lodges, Soteria, the Philadelphia Association community homes and Lothlorien: all spoke about democratization and empowerment as an essential part of recovery and reconciliation. They all, to varying degrees, believed in getting alongside, rather than above, people; in 'doing with' rather than 'doing for'.

My style of leadership, such as it was, was to step back and allow others to come forward, to find their own sense of responsibility and inner drive. But as soon as I stepped back it allowed the most assertive, controlling or manipulative people to assume command: to dish out their opinions, to keep and leak secrets, to say what should happen, and when and why. Whenever I saw that domineering behaviour, I would gently try to face it down, but it was often going on when I wasn't around and so I didn't see it. I had no problem with peer support, with people offering loving advice to one another, but there was sometimes something darker going on. Manipulators were exploiting the compliant. The self-righteous or self-confident were bossing the fragile.

One day I overheard a couple of people murmuring about how

it would all work far better if Fra and I weren't around. We had it all wrong, they said; we were impeding the efficient operation of the community. I hadn't ever expected gratitude, but nor had I anticipated being scapegoated. I knew that St Benedict had insisted that the greatest obstacle to true community living was moaning and grumbling, and this seemed to encapsulate it. I used to warn people when they arrived not to idealize us; I now realized I should have warned them not to demonize us either. Ironically, I was getting it in the neck not for being too authoritarian but for being insufficiently so.

Nothing could have prepared me for the vitriol. Crisp was increasingly infuriated by what he saw as a lack of clarity or leadership. For various reasons, he was acutely uncomfortable outside a regimented structure. If it was missing, he would take it upon himself to rotarize every hour of the day. He began sitting at the head of the table during house meetings, telling us what we should all be doing, giving out jobs while throwing his large palms towards us. To begin with, I was content for him to take the lead and watch what happened. Over the next month or two he assumed more than just a leadership role: he was dogmatic and fiercely forthright – any time there was dissent he would shake with rage. Francesca, he said, would have to pave over her rose bushes because we would need somewhere to park the tractor he demanded I buy. The spare room had to become a bunk room for half a dozen people. Everybody had to work identical hours outside, whatever the weather, even if that meant Fra left the children – all still under six – on their own with adults we sometimes barely knew. There had to be equality at all times. When gentle voices were raised against these proposals he would become irate, commencing on a monologue that would veer between global politics and microbiology. One guest came to me in tears, saying she was scared of him. We tried to resolve various issues but each time we came to an agreement, Crisp would renege on it the next day. As someone said to me in exasperation, 'Crisp has a problem for every solution.'

Alarm bells were ringing pretty loudly, but what really convinced me that things were unsustainable was the attempt to eradicate the founding vision of the community. We had been short of many things here – money, time and sleep especially – but the one thing that had never been in question was the vision. We were here to offer refuge to those in need. That was our purpose for being here. But it became clear that various residents were – consciously or otherwise – trying to nudge that purpose into something else. One or two people started saying that now there were a dozen of us here, we should pull up the drawbridge and not accept any new arrivals. Another guest said they were far too busy to make a newcomer feel welcome. It became habitual not to make a pot of tea for everyone but make your own and get on with things by yourself.

The tragedy of it, and the reason I hadn't acted sooner, was that we all loved Crisp. He was so fun and lively that everyone wanted him to stay. He could, when he was in the mood, be a welcoming host to new, troubled guests. He was strong and could plough through hard work. He could be gracious, inspiring and amusing. I realized how much I had missed him since Christmas: for almost four months he and I hadn't sat down together and talked. We hadn't done anything together for the common good. For the last few weeks we had walked past each other with barely a nod. I yearned to be close to him, because he was such an openly vulnerable man, fretting about his health and his weight. I think the reason he really found it hard here was that communal living strips away disguises, and his carefully crafted character – that of the medieval mendicant and street-performing carpenter – was falling apart. He was, we discovered, called Crispin, and his father was a boarding-school headmaster. I wondered how much transference there was going on when he battered me for being a cold, distant figure who didn't lead in the way he wanted. I could easily identify with the longing to escape privilege by becoming a commoner, but Crisp was conflicted – wanting monkish poverty whilst being angrily envious of wealth.

I finally sat down and chatted with him in front of two other people. It felt as if a major rupture in our little community was about to happen, and I wanted others to hear what went on. I said I didn't think this was the right place for him. He agreed and said it needed to be run completely differently. Perhaps we were both right. I got the impression that we were both in the wrong place: Crisp was desperate to be in charge of something – if only his own destiny – but he wasn't; whereas I really didn't want to be in charge, but I was. He eventually got up to leave, deciding his stay here was over. We shook hands, and he left.

The relief and sorrow were profound. The relief was because, for many months, he had held the whole place hostage. His sudden mood swings and bullish opinions had made things extremely tense. Many of us only realized once he had gone that we had been cowering, beaten into submission by a man who insisted on being the only alpha male. He was the sort of person – and I've met many like this – who longed for community, as long as the set-up was entirely on his terms. But there was great sadness too. This was a man who had been an extremely close friend and ally. More than anyone else, he had turned this home into an 'extended household' and helped transform this scrawny quarry into a working woodland. Fra and Marty both cried when he went, mourning the departure of a good and troubled man. It felt like the end of the beginning: the illusion had now been truly shattered, and there was much melancholy and disappointment.

Once he was gone, we almost immediately sat down and spoke about all the issues we had avoided discussing for months: things that weren't going right, things that needed addressing, things that were good. Now, finally, we were relaxed. We agreed that the contribution to the common purse would increase to £45 a week to take account of bills. We agreed to have a weekly house meeting, for no longer than an hour, every Tuesday after lunch, with Marty chairing and taking notes.

A friend from Bristol came down one Sunday afternoon in late spring. A self-confessed introvert, he had always said he could never live communally. But he had often been down to help out, chopping wood or painting sheds. He was a bit older and wiser, and had always looked out for us.

'How're you doing?' he said when he got here.

'Honest answer?' I stared into the distance. 'We're frazzled. Absolutely burnt out.' I told him everything that had been going on, and he looked alarmed.

'I don't know how you do it,' he kept saying.

'Nor do we any more. Or why, more to the point.'

He listened for a long time and was sufficiently worried to suggest a solution. He wanted us to have a management committee: essentially, a bunch of *consiglieri* who could steer things a bit from a distance and make sure we were being sensible and realistic. Over the next few weeks we put together a team of people we already knew a bit from previous places: a psychiatrist, a GP, a chaplain, Herb from Hilfield Friary, a fundraiser, an environmentalist and a wise woman from the local church. They all understood that the project was run from our family home and were happy for Fra and me to veto any suggestion they made. They were advisory rather than directorial.

We met for the first time in Bristol. The meeting lasted almost three hours. Francesca and I poured out all the grief and stress associated with the project and as we did so, it felt as if we were finally allowed to be honest. The *consiglieri* came up with a few immediate suggestions: we should, they said, limit the number of people staying at any one time. There shouldn't, they thought, be more than ten living on site, which meant us as a family of five plus five guests. Where possible, the contribution to the common purse would be paid a month in advance to avoid the difficulty of people coming and going at the drop of a hat. If anyone missed a meal, there wouldn't be a rebate or refund. We would set up a bank account so cash wasn't sloshing around in biscuit tins. All guests would sign a 'licence to reside' so that we could escort anyone off the premises if they were using or boozing or being aggressive. The committee wanted us to have weekends away, even a holiday.

From then on, our *consiglieri* would meet with us every two months. There would, over the following years, be plenty more crises and strange surprises, but never again did it feel as if we were losing control of the project. We had, behind us, a bunch of wise, well-connected comrades. They would frequently come and visit, getting to know our guests, the livestock and the woodland. We were also sending out a newsletter every six months or so and as our mailing list had grown to quite a few hundred, we had a large pool of people who responded quickly to our calls for help or advice. We bought a breathalyser and a drug-testing kit so that there were never grey areas.

The other thing that made a huge difference was the arrival of an unexpected, unusual man.

'Someone came to the door whilst you were out,' Francesca said one afternoon in May. 'A guy called Eve.'

'Eve? A bloke? You sure?'

'Yeah, a bloke.'

'What did he want?'

'I dunno. He said he would come back another time.'

'What did he look like?'

'Big black afro and a long black beard.'

'Certainly sounds like a bloke.'

A few days went by, and we started teasing Francesca, telling her that she must have misunderstood the guy's name. 'He must have been Steve,' we said, 'or Ian.' But then I saw a guy coming into the woods one day from the footpath: a guy in sandals with a bushy beard and tight, curly black hair. He raised his arm silently in greeting as he walked briskly towards me.

'You Toby?' he said softly as he got closer.

'Yeah. You Eve?'

'Short for Evelyn.' He rolled his pale-blue eyes, like he'd been explaining it all his life. 'The choice was either Eve or Lyn. I chose Eve.'

'Do you need somewhere to stay?' I asked. He looked like one of our wayfarers with his long beard and charity-shop clothes.

'No, I'm fine. I've got a place. I just thought I'd come up and see if you needed anything.'

'Sleep,' I smiled. 'Money.'

'Can't help you with either. But I'm good at working stone. And wood.'

'Got a lot of them round here.'

We chatted for a while. He said he'd been watching us for a few months from the footpath on the field above the woods. He said it had looked busy and he thought he'd wait until it had calmed down a bit. He seemed pretty calm himself, a cool kind of idealist who wanted to lend a hand where it was needed. With those sandals and that blue-eyed serenity, there was something that made me think we had been sent what, in the old days, would have been called a paraclete, someone who acted as a comforter or advocate.

It's now high summer, and the woodland feels dense, almost cushioned. The foliage offers cover, the canopy a ceiling. The woodland weeds – the cow parsley and nettles – are defiant, chest high, as if they're squaring up, rising for a fight. The dull, dead brown of winter has been replaced by red and yellow dots. Coltsfoot stands like a skinny dandelion. Wood anemones rise on slender stalks. Cowslips emerge from their hourglass sepals. The off-white spheres of Dutch clover huddle in the grass. Field poppies emerge bright red on their hairy stems. The hirsute, purple heads of self-heal dominate the clearings. I'm learning all the wonderful names of the wild flowers around us: germander speedwell, ribwort, meadow vetchling, meadow cranesbill, hare-bell, and all the rest. I've been reading H. E. Bates's rhapsodic tribute to trees, *Through the Woods*:

'the wood has no single minute of eclipse throughout the year. It never fades, never cheats. It has mystery but no falsity. It is staunch and even majestic but never overpowering. It is a place of quiet and conflict, of absolute peace and tigerish bloodiness, of passion and death. It is a contrast of power and delicacy, space and little-ness. Yet all the time, throughout the year, it has its own special atmosphere.'

Eve started coming up every day. He always walked up from town, through the fields and woods, emerging from between the

trees like a wild man with his long beard and rustic hat. He had
real panache, wearing cool gear from charity shops and looking
lean and muscular in the sun. He would make himself a coffee
and chat with guests for hours, listening and smiling as they told
him their stories. He had no money, he said; he lived on nothing.
He slept on a friend's sofa and did odd jobs around town in return
for food. That's all he seemed to want: work, company, food, shelter. It would have been easy to label him a dropout, but he was
hard-working. He was simply at odds with everything about
contemporary society, be it greed, or mechanization, or whatever. He wanted to work with his hands, to make beautiful things
through his own imagination and not inconsiderable strength.
And not for money or fame, but merely for the pleasure it gave
him and other people. He walked, or hitched, everywhere. If
someone lent him a bike, he cycled.

Eve and I talked about making a cob oven to bake bread, pizzas
and casseroles. We needed a large base for it, I told him, and Eve
said that the woodland would provide what we needed. He started
walking around with a couple of dogs he was looking after, studying the land from different angles. Often I would see him between
a group of tree trunks, as I was on my way to feed the pigs or the
chickens, standing there with his head on one side as he sized up
a mound or a gulley.

'There's a long wall under here,' he said to me on one occasion.

I looked at the moss and ivy, struggling to know whether to
believe him. 'How do you know?'

'Look at the earth.' He prodded it with a long metal bar. 'The
embankment here's too regular, too straight for nature. Listen.'
He dropped the bar into the ground and instead of sinking, it
gave a metallic complaint. 'And over there –' he pointed at what
looked to me like a stand of overgrown hazels – 'there's more.'

For the next week Eve looked for buried stone like a pig snuffling for truffles. I would see him on his hands and knees, dusting away at the ground as if he were an archaeologist. After a few days we had a huge pile of beautiful stones. Many were perfectly rectangular, dressed stones that looked like huge versions of a Jenga block; others had one flat face and an irregular bulge behind. Eve spent hours looking at them, turning them over and getting to know them. As he put them down, he said, he would listen to the sound they made, as if memorizing the shapes. He would heave blocks the size of a suitcase to another side of the clearing where we planned to build the oven, organizing them according to some scheme the rest of us hadn't yet understood. Eventually the whole clearing was covered with stone. We started going a different way through the woods because it was impassable there.

One Sunday morning at just before seven we were woken up by the sound of loud banging. It was a constant, irregular bashing, as if someone were knocking thin sticks together. I put on some clothes and went to see what was going on. There, in the workshop, was Eve, standing next to a pile of kindling and an axe block.

'Morning,' he said cheerfully.

'Hi,' I said, wandering on to let out the chickens. Not for the first time I wondered what it was that brought people to this place. He must have been here for at least an hour to have made that pile, which meant he had arrived before six. And that on a Sunday morning. He was an altruistic man, but I was curious as to what else drove him to work that hard, that early, for other people. He was certainly giving, but I wanted to know what he was getting back. Normally I would have asked, but with Eve there was an elusiveness that made that kind of enquiry completely inconclusive. He would deflect the question or duck it. It was as if he had a protective barrier around his inner life, and part of that barrier was his hyperactivity; he would rush around doing things for people so that he never had to stop. Instead of saying goodbye, he would always say, 'Got to keep moving.'

'I figured you'd need lots of kindling for the winter,' he said, when he saw me coming back from the chickens. He didn't stop as he spoke but kept bringing the small axe down on a short length of pallet planking that he was holding vertically on the block. He sliced it like a chef cuts carrots: deft and fast. Little strips of wood flew off the axe block and somersaulted until they landed somewhere on, or near, the pile of pale wood to his right.

'It's not even autumn yet.' I smiled.

'Will be soon. How many woodburners and fireplaces have you got here?'

I tried to count them in my head: the Abode, the bell tent, the yurt, the garden room, the sitting room and, most of all, the main boiler. And by then, the explosives chamber had been converted into accommodation, so that, too, had a stove. (Our chapel was now simply a tarpaulin strung between some trees.) There were probably one or two other stoves I couldn't think of. 'Seven or eight,' I said.

'That's a lot of kindling you'll need.' His tanned cheeks rose as he smiled back at me.

'What are *you* going to need this winter?' I asked, curious as to what we could do for him.

'Me? I'll be fine.' That's all he said. I thought there was an edge to the way he said it, like nobody cared for him; the way a child says it doesn't matter when it really does. He was still chopping fast, the axe making a metallic *ching* each time it split the wood.

'Will you let us know what we can do for you?'

'You're already doing it,' he said, with that same enigmatic smile.

I left it at that. He very rarely spoke about himself, or his past. He told us snippets about his previous life, but it was hard to know what made him tick. He hinted occasionally that he felt people had taken advantage of him and his generosity and that he had fallen out with them as a result. Behind that calm, almost seraphic exterior, it was clear that there was something unsettled, some unresolved resentment or sadness.

The structures and strictures of our community continued to evolve. We agreed to have a cleaning hour once a week on a Thursday morning. We cleaned all the communal areas – the bathroom, kitchen, garden room, laundry room and boiler room – and, if there were enough people around, the workshop and tool shed too. It became quite a fun ritual, with loud music and fights over who got the mop first. It also became a time of bonding, because everyone was at it, doing the most humble jobs. No one was allowed to slink off and do something more interesting instead. We found that some OCD guests couldn't stop when the hour was up and we teased them gently as they kept scrubbing through the tea break. We each had other duties too. There was a bread rota, whereby one person was responsible for making bread all week. The quality of the loaves varied greatly: one week we would have focaccia and milky rolls and the next it would be dark bricks.

We had an A4 sheet of 'ground rules' on the noticeboard and website, and every few weeks I found I had to rewrite it and reduce the size of the font to get new dos or don'ts on it. We were reluctant to add new restrictions and regulations, but we kept coming up against issues we hadn't thought of. One new rule was that there should be no romantic entanglements between residents. I had read about a similar rule at Pilsdon years ago and hadn't really understood the need for it. It seemed quite an invasion of people's privacy and intimacy. But then, here, it made a lot of sense: the last thing people in recovery need is to cling on to another vulnerable person like a lifeboat. Communal living is complicated enough without love and sex being thrown into the mix. AA recommends not getting together with anyone for the first year, or more, of sobriety.

We did have people, however, who arrived as a couple. Mikey had moved on at the end of June, finding a flat and a job in Bristol, and Stew and Alice had arrived from Yorkshire a week later. She was a thin, tattooed woman, with a caring manner. She had become agoraphobic, though, especially since her ex had been granted custody of her daughter. She was grieving the loss of her child and the insult to her maternal skills, and had closed herself away. Alice was so anxious she had pulled large clumps of her hair out, and what was left had been cut short. Her man, Stew, was muscular and had half a dozen earrings in his right ear. He had shut himself away with Alice for the last year, smoking weed and drinking. They were a great couple to have around: Stew was strong and exceptionally calm. He never lost his cool, he just listened and quietly made jokes. He loved the woods and the manly jobs that needed doing. And Alice was a warm woman who was happy baking bread. I was particularly pleased that she, a self-declared sociophobe, felt at ease in our little household; it suggested there was sufficient space to which she could retreat, sufficient privacy and silence that even an introvert could be comfortable.

One of the joys of working with Eve was the fact that he gave curt orders without frills. There was no bashfulness about being in charge.

'Go and make a former,' he said to me. 'It'll need to be sturdy.'

'What size?'

'Whatever you want. Depends how much wood you want stacked under the arch.'

Stew and I went to the workshop and cut two large half-ovals of ply. Using pallet planks, we joined the two together, reinforcing it, as it would need to take a lot of the weight from the stone. In the end it was about a metre high and a metre deep.

For the next week, we built the stone base for the oven, constructing an arch over the former and slowly working our way up to the large, flat rocks on which the oven would be sculpted. It was back-breaking work, putting rocks in place and pulling them off if they weren't right. But by Friday we had a stunning stone base and the fun – actually making the oven – could start.

We had got some clay from a friend in a nearby woodland, and a local farmer gave us a few bales of straw. The weather was wonderful: the sort of July day when it was warm before breakfast, and about a dozen people rolled up to learn how to make the oven. Once everyone had had a cup of tea, we rolled out a large tarp and placed the clay in the middle. We sprinkled water on, added a few bags of sharp sand and then invited everyone to dance barefoot in the mix. There were half a dozen kids, and they loved being allowed to get muddy, jumping up and down as they tried to mix the dense clay with the sand. Marty sat on his campfire chair with his guitar, playing lively folk songs to keep us all moving. The best technique was to grab a partner, hold hands and twist your feet deep into the sludge, allowing the mud and sand to ooze up through your toes. Gradually the mix began to look like cob, a decent, supple mix of speckled brown mud.

We laid out twenty-one fire bricks on sand levelled out on Eve's magnificent stone base. They formed the rectangle on which the oven would sit. We then got damp sand and created a conical, beehive-shaped former, which would give the oven its shape. The children found a short plank and, holding it by each end, they 'walked' it over the sand to make it firm and smooth. We kept stepping away to check the shape. The kids were better at it than we were, so we let them get on with it.

We laid wet newspaper over the sand and then dolloped the cob mix on top. This was the thermal insulation that would keep the oven hot, so we laid it four knuckles deep, squeezing each new brick of cob down on the previous bit. Slowly the sand disappeared beneath the dense, rich mud. The children then took their plank again and thwacked the big beehive shape with the end to pack it all together. They each jostled for their go, desperate to hit something as hard as they could. Then we mixed up more cob with some chopped straw and added that to the previous layer. It now looked like one half of a giant egg, a perfectly symmetrical dome.

The next day we cut out an opening. The door, I had read, is supposed to be 63 per cent of the height of the oven; that's the ideal proportion so that the heat circulates properly inside and yet allows the smoke to escape. We put our hands in through the opening and scooped out the damp sand inside the dome, scratching away with our fingers until we felt the newspaper. We gave the opening a lip, made from the leftover cob, and then carved a huge plug for the door from a lump of ash. We lit a nightlight candle and placed it inside, and the kids shouldered each other out of the way so they could see inside the dome they had created. After that we lit a fire and watched as the smoke snaked out of the top half of the opening.

'Who wants some pizza?' Fra asked the next day, once the oven had completely dried off. As Fra made the dough, I carved a pizza paddle out of half a scaffolding board. Marty made a 'rooker' to scrape out the ash, and Stew made a 'scuffle' to clean the oven between batches of loaves and pizzas.

The dough we baked in that oven came out subtly different from how it would from a mechanical oven: the crusts were tougher, the bread or pizza bases stronger. Things tasted properly baked rather than just heated up. It felt so simple: the kids scavenged for dry twigs in the undergrowth; we made a fire; we broke bread together. It was satisfyingly primitive, so much so that Stew and I decided we would light the fire only by old-fashioned friction. This idea didn't last long, but for a week or two it was fun. Someone had come here and taught us how a short while ago, and so we kept doing it: rotating a spindle in a plug using a long bow, moving the bow backwards and forwards as fast as possible so that the twig started to smoke and, eventually, produced a glowing ember. Stew had collected a bowl of 'King Alfred's cakes' – the black growths you find on the bark of ash trees. We cut them open, and when we got an ember we placed it in the spongy, dry centre of the 'cake'. If you breathed on it gently the orange dot would slowly expand; we used the white wisps of a thistle as tinder, which would suddenly catch and create a flame. The first time you do it, you can't believe you'll ever create fire through muscle and breath, but the feeling of elation when that tiny flame appears is profound. There's something deeply spiritual about making a fire purely through ingenuity. We felt, not for the first time, like cave men.

'Oh, come on,' Marty said once, as we faffed around with our bows and spindles, racing each other to make fire. 'I've got a lighter here.'

But that wasn't the point. We didn't want to flick a switch or strike a match. Speed had been replaced by slowness; satisfaction took time, and concentration. It required equilibrium and control: you were watching the smoke, treasuring that orange dot, learning how hard or how soft to breathe on it. I've since taught fire by friction to really troubled guests as well as schoolchildren who've come to visit here, and the effect is always the same: they gain an extraordinary confidence, a sense that if they can do something so subtle and essential, they can do almost anything. After one session, an excluded local schoolchild who had mastered fire by friction said to me softly: 'I'm not afraid any more.'

We made a shelter for the cob oven using ash poles. The roof we built out of hazel rods and turf. Bridget, a young volunteer from Glasgow who was here for a few weeks, started carving a sign for the whole area, taking a line from Ecclesiastes: 'Eat thy bread with joy.' (We thought it wise to leave out the other half: 'and drink thy wine with a merry heart.') But she got side-tracked, and only got as far as the 'j' of joy, so for months people looked at the sign and joked about what it was going to say: 'Eat thy bread with jam?' asked Stew.

Finding peace and quiet to write in this public, open place was like trying not to get splashed in a crowded swimming pool. There was always noise: so many shrieks, so much laughter and happiness and tantrums and tears. I would retreat to my writer's shed only to be interrupted by problems that needed to be dealt with both urgently and slowly, both immediately and passively, through listening and understanding rather than through action. Hours would slip by as someone sank into the armchair and told me their woes. Often it would begin with them letting off steam about something seemingly petty: how furious they were with

Bridget because she had asked them to hang out their laundry, or with Alice for not feeding the pigs when she said she would. Sometimes, that's all it was, and the more I listened to the complaint, the more it petered out. Sometimes, however, something much more serious would emerge.

The only way I could find time to write was by getting up extremely early. I began to head out to the shed at four o'clock most mornings, writing for a good three hours before chapel. Even at that time it wasn't infrequent that I would see one of our guests having a fag outside, unable to sleep for whatever reason. They didn't usually disturb me at that time, but we would wave to each other across the clearing, aware at least of the other's workload or lack of sleep.

But it wasn't just the need to write that got me out of bed in the night. At the time I didn't realize how much it affected me, but each day I was listening to a colossal quantity of trauma, pain and sadness. I would go to sleep wondering how we could help someone, or wondering why they were acting strangely, or struggling to get my head around repeated weirdness. Often I would wake up suddenly, not with the problem solved, but with a possible answer. Or I would have a vivid dream and would then lie in bed, motionless, trying to understand where it had come from and whether it applied to what was going on here. Sometimes, too, people would phone in the middle of the night.

There were other reasons I got woken up. A guy called Rongo had got in touch, saying he needed somewhere to get clean. He had a drug habit he wanted to beat, and the sort of friends he needed to escape. His voice was dreamy, as if he were high right then, but when we met him a few days later we realized that was what he was like. He was peaceful and chilled, as if nothing much could trouble him. He did everything in slow motion, as if he were still zonked. His parents, he said, had been seventies hippies, and 'Rongo' was Maori for 'peace'. The name suited him somehow.

I showed him the yurt, and he liked it, but there was a problem.

'I scream at night when I'm coming off it,' he said. 'This canvas isn't going to keep the noise in.'

'That's okay,' I said, 'as long as we know. I'll tell the others.'

So for the first week or two of his stay, I would hear him groaning and yelling in the middle of the night. I would try to get back to sleep, but the noise of someone in agony wasn't exactly soporific.

That July we had a stall at a fair in the local town to sell some of our produce: bags of kindling, charcoal, plants, coasters, candle holders, jigsaws, and so on. A sceptical-looking farmer with mutton chops came up to us, screwing up his face as he looked us over.

'You from that commune?'

I smiled wearily. 'We're a little community, yeah.'

'You them ravers, having those dance parties all night?'

'I wish we were.'

He almost shut his eyes as he glanced from Stew, with his piercings, to Marty, with his grey beard. He wandered off, unconvinced.

We spent most of the day trying to persuade locals that we weren't layabouts, or ravers, or nudists, or drug fiends. But I could see where the rumours came from. It was partly the fact that there was a nearby wood with a circular clearing where there were often late-night parties. But there were also little incidents that must have fuelled the gossip. There was one morning when

Benny and Emma thought it would be fun to do some face-painting on the adults, so they covered Alice and Rongo's cheeks with blue butterflies and smudged tiger stripes. Later that morning a gruff farmer arrived to pick up his boar, who had been serving our sow. I wasn't around, so he was greeted by those two softly spoken adults with brightly coloured cheeks.

'You lot look like Smurfs,' he said.

The most embarrassing incident was at a music festival near here. I had bumped into Morag, the woman who had given us the yurt. We had said months ago we would give her some money for it, and there she was, in the corner of a field: tattoos, piercings, dreads, dancing on the spot to the rhythm of some distant music from a marquee. We hugged, and I gave her a few notes just as Benny's primary-school teacher passed by, looking away quickly as though she didn't want to witness what appeared to be a drug deal. What should I do – run up and tell her I wasn't scoring gear? If I did that, didn't it only sound more likely that I really was doing something dodgy?

We often laughed about what the local community must think of us. But we were building a decent reputation in the town and surrounding villages. We had made raised beds for a local school and a couple of benches for a housing estate. We gave away our surplus eggs, vegetables and logs. Many of the misfits and loners from the town came up here, and people saw that we were doing, hopefully, a good thing. Our kids went to the school and nursery in town, so we weren't aloof or frighteningly alternative. We found that if we called ourselves a small farm, instead of any of the other communal labels, people were immediately at ease and could understand what we were up to.

But what really made a difference to our integration was the wife of Scrap-metal Mark. Kath was a special needs teacher at one of the local schools and had come up to a volunteer day one Wednesday.

'I've got this vision,' she said enthusiastically. 'I want to run a forest school. To have a place in the woods to teach children who aren't suited to sedentary learning. All those kids who are excluded or a bit behind.' She looked at me, waiting for an invitation.

'And you think you might want to do it here?'

'Well, I'd like to talk about it maybe, see what you think.'

So I gave her a tour and she was, in her words, blown away.

'This is unbelievable,' she said, looking around. 'It feels completely safe but the kind of place children could have an incredible adventure.'

She spoke about what she dreamed of doing with the children she looked after. It was that time of year when the forest floor was dusty dry and felt almost like a velvet rug. The whole place had a buzz: the noise of flies and bees frantically darting to and fro. Butterflies were flitting silently, bouncing unevenly through the air. We looked at the tree house and pigs and cob oven, at the fire pit and all the rest, and Kath wanted to make a start right away. She kept telling me how effective forest school was for children, how kids nowadays were excluded from nature and woodland play, and that once they were back in that primeval environment they were again in a world of wonder. They were awed by the height of the trees, spooked by the eerie shade, alarmed and excited by sharing a habitat with all sorts of animals. It was a place where knives became not weapons but tools; where kids could build their own houses from anything they could find.

Kath came up again a week later to decide the best site for her school. We walked around the woodland again, looking for somewhere that was flat, safe and accessible but not too close to the rest of the operation. We stopped in various clearings, in old quarry ruins, on high ledges and low cuttings. In each place I told her what the plans were for future projects: 'Here, we'll build a sauna one day,' I said optimistically; 'This is where we'll dig a large pond'; 'This is where we're going to have a compost loo.'

We went back to a clearing at the edge of the woodland. Behind it was the steep quarry face, now covered with the thick trunks of ash and oak. There was a beautiful view over the spear-like shafts of marshy grass where we wanted to dig our pond. It was yellow with the dusty pollen of *Alchemilla mollis*, or lady's mantle. The place had a natural canopy of branches, leaning away from the rocks behind towards the light, so it felt somehow like a shelter already.

'Let's do it here,' Kath said. 'This is perfect.'

Over the next few months she began to transform the space. She and Scrap-metal Mark put up a parachute as a cover, so there was a beautiful green circle above her campfire. They had found roughly rectangular boulders to put around the fire and four scaffolding planks to make a square of seating. They built a rustic log store and a wash-up and storage area using all the spare hazel poles and planks that were lying around the place. Quite soon it looked like a stunning base camp: rustic but well ordered, with huge campfire kettles resting on welded horseshoes. There was a mud kitchen, huge wooden cotton reels, gnarls of old rope, dustbin lids as drums: it was a kid's dream.

Kath's forest school hugely enriched our community. Once or twice a week she would deliver a minibus of schoolchildren up here and the woods would echo to the sound of their shrieks and screams. Mark kept bringing up things he had found in various skips and house clearances, placing them amongst the trees: he propped the inside of an old piano vertically against one huge trunk so that it looked like a sylvan harp. The kids would drag their fingers across the taut wire as they ran past. Mark and Kath seemed to know almost everyone locally and through them word was getting around that we weren't weirdos but normal people trying to get by. The schoolchildren, their parents and grandparents started to understand what was going on and began making friends with those who were living here. Having been, always, a completely shoestring operation, we now had a trickle of income, as Kath paid a small land rent into our common purse. Mark would always stop and talk to the rough diamonds who'd ended up here: the former soldiers, the ex-offenders, the tattooed tough nuts whose shaved heads revealed plenty of scars. This woodland, I often worried, might have been a bit effete for them, full of gentle folk baking bread and weaving willow. But Mark's presence transformed the vibe, made it a place where muscular men could talk about warfare and prison, about engines and the price of scrap metal.

Quite often when a wayfarer wandered in off the road we would joke that underneath their straggly beard and ill-fitting clothes they were really a secret millionaire here to check us out before offering us hundreds of thousands of pounds. People laughed at the joke, liking the idea that they were only pretending to be rough sleepers and that we saw through the impoverished exterior and glimpsed a possible saviour.

And then something a bit like that really happened. In early August, almost two years after we had moved in, we got an email through our website from someone who said he represented a maverick philanthropist. This representative, called Jim, wondered if he could come and visit us.

He came a week later and sat at the garden-room table having tea with us all. I asked him about the philanthropist, but it was all fairly secretive, so he told me about his family instead.

'My daughter won the Miss Birmingham competition last year,' he said proudly.

'You must have a very beautiful wife,' I replied.

There was a moment's silence and then everyone started laughing. 'Thanks a lot,' said Jim.

'What are you saying, that he's ugly?' guffawed Marty.

'No, I meant . . .'

'Yeah, whatever,' said Stew, chuckling.

It was the first time anyone with a chequebook had come round to check us out, the first time we had ever had the possibility of someone giving us some funds, and I had put my foot in it. But Jim was laughing too, and there was an upside to my gaffe. Jim was looking round the table and had picked up on the atmosphere: he could see the troubled faces but heard the laughter and the teasing as well.

'Listen, just to get this out the way,' he said when things quietened down, 'we'd like to give you five grand.'

We were so shocked we didn't know what to say.

'There's no need to fill in any forms or anything,' he went on. 'Just give us the bank details and jot down a paragraph or two about how you'll use it.'

'Pig arks,' said Marty, quick as a flash.

'You'd give them pigs four-poster beds if you could,' smiled Alice.

'Does this mean I can get another blanket?' asked Rongo.

'Man, five grand,' I said. I couldn't believe it.

'The person I work for,' Jim said, 'really likes what you're up to. He believes in it.'

'How did he hear about us?' I asked.

Jim shrugged. 'I don't know. He's quite well connected. Someone's obviously told him what you're doing.'

'And you just travel the country,' Stew said in awe, 'giving away his money?'

'Yep,' Jim said, smiling – 'and getting insulted for my troubles.'

It meant we could start seriously to improve our accommodation, buying a shepherd's hut to replace the saggy bell tent.

A pig's gestation period is three months, three weeks and three days. We weren't exactly sure when Wally, the horny but hapless boar, had served Harriet, but we knew she was due to farrow any day. Marty spent most of his time up there with her, scratching her back and checking for milk from her many teats. He often sat in a chair, picking away at his guitar, or drawing portraits of her.

Marty couldn't help himself: when he went to the bakery, he would buy a treat for her. Or he would walk miles out of his way to some orchard he knew where he could get some windfall apples, which he would then offer her one by one on his open palm. When we had checked that she was 'in-pig', we were supposed to rub oil on the sensor to pick up the heartbeat of the piglets in her womb, but Marty wasn't happy with smearing cheap vegetable oil on her undercarriage; he wanted extra-virgin olive oil.

'Isn't that a bit of a waste?' Alice asked, smiling.

'Not for my Harriet, it's not. Has to be olive oil. She's a sensitive soul.'

We let him get on with it and watched him rub the sensor across her belly, waving his fist in the air in triumph when the slow bips of her heart were replaced by the rapid trilling of several others.

Once we got milk from her teats, we knew the farrowing was

imminent. We chucked some straw outside her ark and she took it inside almost immediately, picking it up in her mouth and then shoving it around with her snout. She was nesting as surely as any human mother.

That evening Marty had his tea out there, sitting with his plate on his knees. An hour later he came in and told me it had started: one piglet had already been born, he said as he rushed back up there.

I joined him, and we both squatted inside the ark, separated from Harriet by some sturdy four-by-twos, in case she objected to our presence. Every ten minutes another piglet would pop out, falling on to the straw. They were covered in a film, but once that was removed their coats were as soft and velvety as a foal's. Their ears were pinned back on their tiny shoulders (they normally cover pigs' eyes like blinkers). As more piglets came out, they started clambering over each other to get at their mother's milk. Harriet kept growling and grunting, until all seven had been born. When they were all lined up, suckling away, their black and white stripes made them look like a bag of humbugs.

Marty and I just watched them, occasionally jumping over the timber to help one find a teat. It was amusing to see how quickly these newborns became boisterous and argy-bargy. They would all collapse and fall asleep and then suddenly wake each other up and start charging around, looking for more milk. At almost midnight I headed off to bed, leaving Marty there patting Harriet, telling her how proud he was.

The next day, the kids wanted to see the new piglets, so I walked them up there in the early morning sunshine. The dew was glistening on the long grass, and the usual robin was sitting on the corrugated metal dome of the ark. I lifted the children one by one over the electric fence and quietly opened the back door to the ark. We could just see, in amongst all the straw, some grey hairs poking out. The kids were excited and crammed in closer to see the piglets.

'Hey, that's not a piglet,' Benny said. 'That's Marty.'

The grey hair rose slightly from the straw, and Marty's face followed. He screwed up his eyes, adjusting to the light. 'Morning,' he said.

'Have you slept in here all night?' Benny asked, astonished.

'Yep. Needed to make sure the old girl was okay.'

He sat up and tucked himself into a corner of the ark so the children could see the piglets. They were all asleep, piled high on top of each other against the ample pillow of Harriet's belly.

'This one here –' Marty pointed out a piglet with the narrowest strip of white – 'is called Pinstripe.'

By now Marty had been living with us for almost nine months. His grey hair was down to his shoulders and his beard was hiding his ears and his neck. He had become the unofficial elder of the community, teaching songs to the children and cracking jokes with everyone. He was wise and well-read, but in between those moments of lucidity he would be completely absent-minded. I was constantly having to devise new, polite ways to check that he had done things. 'What are you cooking tonight, Marty?' I asked cheerily one time, half an hour before teatime.

'Me? Tonight?' He sat up in the armchair. 'What day is it? Oh, crikey!' He chuckled at his forgetfulness. 'Right, yes. Tonight. Tea. Well, I've planned –' he had a boyish face when he was being cheeky – 'beans on toast.'

Another time, I would ask how the pigs were doing as a way to check if they had been fed.

'Oh no,' he would say, slapping his forehead. 'The pigs. I knew there was something I had to do this afternoon, and then I got chatting to Alice.' He jumped up, chuckling again.

Marty's foggy mind became a bit of a joke amongst us. One day he asked who was coming to volunteer day and Alice suggested he look at the wall chart.

'Wall chart?' He looked amazed. 'We've got a wall chart?'

'In the corridor, where we write up all the visitors. We talk about it every Tuesday.'

'We do?'

For more than a year we had written up the names of those we were expecting. We always spoke about it in the weekly house meeting.

'Quite remarkable,' Marty said. 'I never knew we had a wall chart.'

Another time he came into the garden room doing a little jig. 'I've found it, I've found it,' he said.

'What?'

'The kitchen light. The light for above that table. I've been looking for that switch for almost a year, and I've found it. It was hidden behind the aprons.'

Everyone looked up at him, smiling at his excitement. 'Why didn't you just ask?' Stew wondered.

'I kept thinking I'd find it one day . . . and today's the day.'

I didn't know whether it was his age, or his medication, or his self-medication back in the day, but he was almost childlike in the way he would get so absorbed in one thing and forget everything else. He was very worldly and well travelled, but there was an innocence about him to which people warmed. He had an easy-going empathy. He listened to everyone and went the extra mile, and far beyond, to help them out if he could.

* * *

We realized quite quickly that there was one group of people we struggled with perhaps more than any other: those with eating disorders. One of the key points about our life together was sharing our meals, sitting around the table in the egalitarian act of breaking bread or serving soup. When there was someone with us who shunned that offering, who was slyly disguising what they were eating or secretly throwing up, it really seemed to affect the harmony, not just of mealtimes but of the whole place. It was much easier to make sure an alcoholic didn't drink, or a drug addict didn't use, than to ensure an anorexic ate. With addiction, the battle lines were at least clear: you were trying to encourage abstinence, to stop someone using something. But with eating disorders you were trying to encourage the consumption of something absolutely necessary for survival, to normalize – rather than eradicate – a relationship. An eating disorder is, we came to understand, just as much an addiction as all the others. As Marya Hornbacher wrote in her anorexia memoir, *Wasted*, 'You become addicted to a number of . . . effects. The two most basic and important: the pure adrenaline that kicks in when you're starving – you're high as a kite, sleepless, full of a frenetic, unstable energy – and the heightened intensity of experience that eating disorders initially induce.'

We only learned about anorexia and bulimia as we went along. Diana was a young woman in her early twenties. I remember looking at her when her father first brought her down. She was sitting on one of the tree trunks, staring at the ground. Her face seemed so doleful. She was red-haired, and the corners of her mouth were pulled down at the sides. She barely spoke, but when she did she couldn't pronounce her 'r's. Her father had a cup of tea and then cleared off: no hugs or kisses; he just gave her a plastic bag and drove away.

'Treats,' Diana said to me, not making eye contact.

I peered in the bag and saw chocolate bars and boxes of Mr Kipling cakes.

She didn't say much for the rest of the day.

About a week later I heard someone shout that the pigs were out, words that always made me despair. I knew it would mean hours of coaxing them back to where they had come from, trying to persuade huge beasts about twice my weight and strength that they should return to the muddy field rather than stay on the velvety woodland floor with its acorns and hazelnuts. When we finally got them back in the meadow, Marty and I spotted that someone had disconnected the electric fence.

'Who unplugged the electric fence?' I asked at tea that night.

'It kept hurting them,' Diana said. 'Every time their snouts touched the wire they would yelp in agony.'

'So you switched it off?' Marty asked.

'I think it's cruel to keep hurting them every day.'

No one knew what to say. Diana had a self-righteous streak and seemed to relish being set against the rest of us, as if other people's opposition was a sign that she was right all along.

'They don't get hurt if they learn it's electric,' Marty said. 'They learn that wire hurts and so they don't touch it.'

'I switched off the chicken fence too,' she said proudly.

'Because you didn't want them to get hurt?' Stew asked. 'Let a fox get them instead?'

Diana couldn't keep to our simple system and kept taking autonomous decisions. At the end of every week we would tot up the receipts in the kitty tin and work out how much we had spent on food. Sometimes there was a surplus, sometimes a shortfall, but the main thing was that the receipts tallied with the amount of cash we had all put in. One week we had about eight quid less in the tin than we should have had. I added up all the receipts again and the shortfall was eight pounds.

At the next meal I asked if anyone had forgotten to put a receipt in the tin. Everyone shook their head.

'No one's bought anything for eight quid? That's what we're missing.'

'Eight quid?' Diana asked.

We could all see it coming. 'Go on,' I said, looking at her wearily.

'Well, I missed Friday lunch because I was at the doctor, and then I didn't like the casserole. Or Marty's omelette.'

She had single-handedly decided to award herself a rebate. She had given herself a pecuniary reason not to eat, which was the opposite of what was required. She needed incentives to eat, not to avoid doing so. I carefully explained to her that we didn't refund money if an individual was fussy, or for being absent from meals. Money was put in the common purse, and that was that. The whole thing would become unworkable if people fished out coins because they didn't drink coffee or eat cake or had tea without milk. It would simply become absurd.

She was silent, staring at the table with her mouth turned down.

It was relentlessly attritional. It often felt as if there was a constant erosion of myself by a sort of Chinese water torture, a non-stop dripping of water on the same spot. It was as if I was pinned down and constantly under pressure but couldn't draw attention to it because each individual incident was merely a tiny droplet. The yurt is leaking. Someone's seen a fox outside the chicken coop. Diana is self-harming. Alex has been drinking and needs to be breathalysed. Leo's crapped his nappy. No one has watered the tomatoes. Someone new has just rolled up and wants to stay the night. Benny needs help with her homework. Stew has found a used needle in the explosives chamber. There's a GP on the phone to talk about a patient she wants to refer. A broadsheet wants an op-ed piece by 4 p.m. The idiot neighbour is taking photographs of the gate. Someone has let the geese out and they've eaten all the blueberries. No one's laid the table.

I was having to get up earlier and earlier to get things done. I was often up well before four just because my head was so full. I had no spare bandwidth, no spare disk space. Friends and family had started saying I was looking haggard, and I was aware that my patience – which had held up fine thus far – was now badly stretched. I was becoming a bit tired of everyone's negativity and their monosyllabic replies. No one had any oomph, any get up and go. I was having to charge up everyone, quietly coax them into gear. One night I was baking a cake for someone's birthday and I suddenly felt dizzy. I got tunnel vision and thought the walls looked watery; it was as if they were moving towards me. I grabbed the worktop and stumbled outside for some fresh air. No one noticed, and after five minutes I headed back in and finished baking the cake. I knew I had to slow down, to try to take things easy. But I didn't know what could be cut. I was a father of three kids; I had to write to make ends meet. Something had to give but unless I was careful, it was likely to be me.

There was simply far too much to do: all the children, animals, people, shelters, plants; all the little and big emergencies. The children were lightning rods of everything here and I could usually read their behaviour as symptomatic of what was going on around them. Even in the afternoons, when there was no school to rush for, they were, I think, aware of how busy we were. They could see us frantically trying to hold the place together and they had begun to reflect my behaviour back to me, like an unwanted mirror that revealed my faults. Each time I asked Benny to do something she would say, 'Two minutes'; and Emma had begun copying her, saying in her toddlerish voice, 'Chew minutes.'

I sat them down one evening and explained that when they said, 'Two minutes,' it felt to me as if they were saying, 'I'm ignoring you.' That was the real message they were giving me, and I said I found it frustrating. So the next day, when I asked them to do something, Benny stopped what she was doing, and looked at me.

'Daddy,' she said, 'I'm ignoring you.'

That, I thought, must be the message they had received from me: that I was ignoring them. I was too busy with yet another guest, with building or fencing or whatever. I kept saying to them, 'Two minutes,' as I listened to another stranger in the house.

I didn't think they were hard done by: they had two parents permanently around the house and we very often sat together, just us, and had a laugh. They were growing up in an enchanted space that offered them adventure and excitement. But they were vying for attention with five other adults who were, in many ways, like demanding children themselves. Some of those guests were extraordinarily adept at somehow ousting our children.

'Can we have a chat?' Diana asked, standing at the bottom of the stairs as I was trying to put the kids to bed one night. She always seemed to need a chat when my attention was on the children.

I could barely hear her because the girls were on a beyond-bed-time high, screaming excitedly, and Leo was wailing because he couldn't find his beloved pot-bellied 'Kaloo'.

'Later, Diana. I've got to put the kids to bed right now.'

'I've done something really serious,' she said.

It sounded like an emergency, or close. 'What?'

'I'd rather not say in front of the children. Can I just talk to you for a minute?'

'Kaloo!' Leo wailed. 'Kaloo!'

The more I resisted her interrupting my time with the children, the higher she raised the stakes. This time, she had got out all the kitchen knives. She said she wanted to do something drastic. I didn't know whether it was a bluff to get my attention, and she probably didn't know either.

Something similar happened every other day; she would manoeuvre herself next to me at the expense of the children. When I was sitting on the sofa with them reading a book, she would come in crying, standing by the door and asking if she could have a word. When I took them to the park, Diana would turn up ten minutes later on her bike.

I knew that human organizations invariably found a scapegoat, that there's usually someone who takes the blame for everyone else's troubles. I really didn't want Diana to become the person at whom we always pointed a finger. But by now, every time money or livestock went missing, we wondered what she'd been up to. It had got to the stage where people rolled their eyes or shook their heads when her name was mentioned. She was absorbing all our energy, which wouldn't have been a problem if we had felt we were getting somewhere. But her pleas for help were never accompanied by explanations of why she actually needed help. She didn't talk about her bulimia, or abuse, or anything else. 'You wouldn't understand,' she always said, and you got the impression she perhaps didn't want to be understood.

By then, we no longer avoided issues. If someone was

struggling, and being scapegoated, it needed to be talked through. Francesca and I, exhausted by Diana's antics, discussed it in private and then called a house meeting. Everyone came in and sat round the table. Francesca, always calm and patient, explained why we were there. Rather than make any accusations, she laid out her own regrets: she felt we were struggling to help Diana; that Diana was asking for a lot of attention but was perhaps receiving the wrong sort – rebuffs, and criticisms, and so on. We always spoke about how difficult situations made us feel, in the hope that a guest would connect with their own feelings, and that the discussion wouldn't become an argument but a meeting of emotions. Diana got extremely emotional: her breathing was juddering, and then she started crying for a long time. Alice passed her the tissues. Marty put a hand on her back. When she was able to talk, she shared a lot about her past, and quite suddenly the atmosphere was completely different. People who had, for weeks, been telling me how tricky they found Diana, now warmed to her and said kind words. It was as if she were now at the centre, rather than on the fringes. That was the way it often worked here: if someone was closed and we only saw irrational behaviour, it was very hard for this place to work. But once someone had been completely open about what they were going through and had, like Diana, made a public confession to the group, that person and their behaviour began to be understood and irritation was replaced by affection.

There were so many people who came and went. Sometimes we made progress, often not. But I always found it fascinating, and was absorbed by the sleuthing, trying to understand what lay behind the irrational, odd behaviour we saw. We used to get frustrated when things didn't work out. Some guests, so used to rejection, tried to pre-empt it by rejecting us and storming off, never to be seen again. Others got paranoid, thinking we were a cult that was trying to trap them. Plenty blamed us for not curing them, or for not caring for them as they demanded. People would test you to see if they could trust you, deliberately doing wrong things to see how you reacted. Disappointment and chaos were always with us. We realized we couldn't necessarily straighten people out. We could just live with them, let them be, allow them to act up and examine, with them, their performance. In many ways, all we were doing was teaching guests to watch their dramas as well as act in them.

It was obvious that many guests who came to live with us came from broken homes and that, in living here, for perhaps the first time they experienced what it was like to live in a comparably stable family. It was also the first time, for many, in which the virtual world of the screen had been replaced by the solidity and serenity of manual labour. We were amazed to discover how many people simply longed to split wood, carve spoons, clean out the pigs, make chairs and plant trees. And many people loved coming and doing jobs here, even though they had pressing ones to do at home.

'In a group,' a counsellor friend once said to me, 'people become slightly psychotic. They re-create their own social worlds within it and cast you as characters in their own psychodramas.' I was beginning to see what she had meant. There was no audition or discussion; you were just allocated a part in their fantasies. It took a lot of stability to withstand an individual's desire for you to play a certain assigned role. But we felt we had to stay with them, to keep accompanying them. I began to think that the greatest thing we could do for people was to allow them to become who they truly were, to give them space and confidence to find their voice. I often thought of the Trappist monk Thomas Merton's suggestion that 'many poets are not poets for the same reason that many religious men are not saints: they never succeed in being themselves.'

Probably the majority of our guests had experienced professionalized care. They had, they said, been mentored by paperwork and policies, not people. Here, the care is purely personal. There's no bureaucracy. It is, in the old mantra, 'the relationship that heals'. But often, of course, it doesn't. Often it was too painful, and people would leg it as soon as the initial enchantment was replaced by disillusion and disappointment, or before they were forced to study their own behaviour patterns and the reasons for them.

There were always strange moral dilemmas. What to do about the man who walked through the garden room completely naked? I was always on high alert for sexual perversion, and couldn't work out whether he was a complete innocent or a dodgy flasher. I knew by now that people communicated through often bizarre or erratic behaviour. There was one guest who asked us to look after a brick-shaped wodge of notes – about ten grand. Where had that money come from and why should we be responsible for it? More to the point, what was he trying to say to me in giving me so much cash to care for? One guest told me not only that he was feeling suicidal, but that he also had fantasies of taking his children with him. What should I do? Alert the police, tell his ex, or respect the confidentiality of the confessional and hope he didn't do anything?

Alice had planned for her daughter, Molly, to come and spend a week with us towards the end of August. It would be her birthday and she wanted it to be special for her.

'How old will she be?' Marty asked.

'Six,' Alice replied.

'We've only got three weeks to decide what to do,' Stew said.

'Twenty-one days,' Marty said idly, stopping strumming for a second, 'is the gestation period of chickens.'

We looked at each other and knew what Marty was thinking.

'Yeah,' said Alice happily. 'Let's do it. Can we hatch out some chicks for her birthday?'

'It would be wonderful,' I said. 'But we haven't got an incubator, and none of the hens seems particularly broody.'

'And Floppy's not exactly strutting his stuff.' Stew laughed.

Floppy was our cockerel. He had been given to us by a farmer in the next-door village who said he was called Floppy because of his droopy comb. But the name suited him in other ways. He was, literally, hen-pecked. He had bald patches on his hackles and hocks where the ex-battery chickens had jabbed at him with their sharp beaks. He didn't have that leggy, sprightly step of a rooster keeping his harem in check. He looked kind of forlorn and his wobbling wattles gave him the appearance of a jowly drunkard.

'I saw him doing his thing the other day,' said Marty, picking away at the strings of his guitar again.

'It's worth giving it a go,' Alice said. 'Can we call Scrap-metal Mark, see if he can source an incubator?'

We called Mark the next day, and of course he knew someone who had a small seven-egg incubator they didn't want any more.

'What do they want for it?' I asked him.

'Nothing.'

Alice made Mark a large carrot cake. Once we had swapped the cake for the incubator, we gathered seven eggs and placed them carefully in the tiny machine. It was the shape of a halved football. We filled the central bowl with water to maintain the humidity and set the temperature at 37.5°C. Every forty-five minutes it would turn the eggs, whirring methodically as the disk moved. If they were on schedule, they would hatch out on little Molly's birthday.

But watching those eggs, it seemed inconceivable that anything would happen. They just looked like smooth pebbles. And then, the day after Molly arrived, and bang on her birthday, the first cracks appeared. Benny, Emma and Molly raced to the incubator, giving us all a running commentary as the tiny beaks began to break through.

'Happy birthday, Molly,' Benny said, hugging her.

'Are they all mine?'

'Yep,' Alice said, her hand on her daughter's shoulder.

We spent the next hour going in and out of the laundry room, watching the damp yellow birds emerge. I made the mistake of trying to work out their gender by googling 'how to sex chicks'. I didn't get the sort of advice I was expecting.

It was one of those moments when, for all the difficulties, I realized how magical this place was for children. Our girls had a new best friend and were making up absurd names for her new pets. As they sat on the grass outside, each with a couple of chicks on their lap, I thought they weren't having too hard a time of it.

Some people, when they arrived, were so shy or timid they couldn't talk. Kelly was the opposite: she was so jittery she couldn't stop talking or doing things. That summer, she had been released from Eastwood Park prison. She had a weathered face: very attractive, but lined and weary. She looked as if she had been through tough times, and she brought an edgy honesty to the place. Blunt and straight-talking, she was also slightly brittle, as if her tough-nut exterior was a tense shell that hid vulnerability.

One evening, we were all sitting out in the sunshine by the cob oven. Stew was sharpening a stick so that Benny and Emma could toast some marshmallows on the embers of the campfire. Marty had his guitar out. There was another guy who was down for the week, Olly, who was a phenomenal guitarist, so he and Marty played together, occasionally smiling at each other across the flames as they sang. They were playing some protest song from the sixties and Marty was singing it as if he was on the barricades with the riot police in front of him. The rest of us were just listening.

'Come on, sing, you buggers!' Marty shouted happily. 'How are you going to change the world if you don't sing along?'

Once the girls had scorched their marshmallows, I put the kettle on the embers to make tea and we sat around chatting. Leonardo was asleep on Fra's lap. Stew was sitting on the ground with his legs apart, Alice sitting between them. Olly kept asking questions about things here, how long people had been here and where they came from.

'Us five are all inmates,' Marty said, jutting his chin towards the others. It was the jokey word he used instead of 'guests'.

I looked across to Kelly and saw her strained face. A couple of minutes later she got up and walked off. She was heading for the far end of the woods, up to the mound we called Heartbreak Ridge. It was where many people went in their most melancholy moments. I followed her at a distance, letting her sit by herself for a few minutes before I scrambled up the muddy slope, grabbing on to roots and trunks to pull myself up. She heard me and looked over.

'You okay?' I asked.

She shrugged. She was staring down into the trees below, where two wood pigeons were boxing with their wings, causing a sudden rattle and flurry as they jumped up and flapped at each other.

'Marty would never have said that if he knew,' I said. She had only just been released, and I knew she had been horrified by the use of the word 'inmate'. She didn't want everyone knowing she had done a long stretch inside, and she certainly didn't want them using it to needle her.

She looked across at me. 'I thought you must have told him,' she said; 'that he was having a go at me.'

'Nope.' I shook my head, sitting down next to her on the grass.

She was staring out at the sunset, a stony look on her face. I put a hand on her shoulder.

'I didn't think anyone had noticed I'd gone,' she said.

'Well, the singing was more in tune, so I figured you'd headed off.'

She smiled, putting her elbow on my right knee. It was one of those intimate moments, far from anyone, that required complete trust about boundaries. It had to be explicit that it was innocent. Not for the first time, I realized how important it was, doing this, to have a solid marriage, and for everyone to know it. Kelly must have been so used to people hitting on her, and needed to know that my physicality was paternal, or fraternal, and nothing else.

'Even if people did know,' I said, 'I don't think they would think any differently about you.'

'Yeah, right,' she said dismissively.

'Maybe you should tell them. You might feel easier about it. And they would share with you what they've done, where they've got in trouble. Otherwise, you'll assume you're the baddie and everyone else is a saint.'

We chatted some more. She was uncomfortable being comforted and soon put her tough-nut mask back on. But by then we had shared a few secrets, and the bond between us had deepened. We walked back to the cob oven arm in arm, watching the badgers shuffling like hairy armadillos, their bodies rocking from side to side as they scuttled about, scratching out a living in the undergrowth.

'Where have you two been, eh?' shouted Stew as we emerged into the clearing.

'Just chatting,' Kelly said.

Marty and Olly were playing again, more quietly now. Leo was still asleep on Fra, and the girls looked as if they were on a marshmallow high, running around the place playing air guitars.

I'm constantly trying to analyse our motives, to work out why we're doing this. I read years ago about a nun who said to Dorothy Day, the co-founder of the Catholic Worker Movement, that 'it's a grave temptation to want to help people.' I thought it sounded like a strange thing to say, but I can understand it now. I fell into that temptation with both feet. I'm sure that my motivation in doing this wasn't all bad, but there was probably a fair bit of vanity and pride mixed in with the altruism and obedience. Perhaps I wanted to be a hero. Looking back, I can see that there were subtler motivations too. Three of my grandparents, both parents, two uncles, an aunt and both brothers all work in medicine in one way or another. I've always felt like that character from *Goodness Gracious Me* who says to his Asian parents that he wants to be an actor. 'In our family,' the parents say, 'we pronounce it "doctor".' Looking back, I wonder whether, not content with being a creative, I too wanted to be a healer, wanted to join the family firm through the back door.

I'm still trying to work out whether it's really a calling, or maybe some deep psychological need I'm too daft to understand. I had the privilege and horror of going to an English boarding school. For all its advantages, that education has always been a cause of sadness for me. I lived apart from my parents and friends for much of my childhood. I sometimes wonder whether part of the appeal of this strange lifestyle is that I'm back on the wrong side of the tracks. In *Iron John*, his intriguing book about masculinity, Robert Bly talks about the need for all young men to undergo a period of katabasis, a descent into the ashes or the underground: 'For young men who have graduated from privileged colleges, or who have been lifted upward by the expensive entitlement culture, their soul life often begins with this basement work in the kitchen.' The more elitist their upbringing, he suggests, the more soaring their careers, the more necessary the solidity and stability of menial labour. I found I felt not humiliated but strangely liberated when I was doing the most humbling jobs here: mucking out the pig troughs, cleaning the communal loo, doing the washing-up. I felt grounded again. I was back in my home county and connected to the soil.

Perhaps that's what I had wanted all along: to create a space where life was classless, a place where people didn't label you according to class, rank, criminal conviction or whatever. It wasn't always easy to encourage people to stop using lazy labels. Many people would come and try to get a handle on others by constantly referring to geographical, racial, class or career labels, and often I would try to intervene and persuade people to let all that crap go. It wasn't as if we didn't describe people, but we wanted to avoid using descriptions in a pejorative way, to allow people to escape their backgrounds and pasts, whatever they were. And when I tried to analyse why we needed to be so vigilant about the language we employed, I wondered if it was because I too wanted to escape a bit of my background.

Year Three

'People may come to our communities because they want to serve the poor; they will only stay once they have discovered that they themselves are the poor'
— Jean Vanier

Compared to the cosy enclosure of summer, autumn feels exposed, as if you no longer have curtains in any of the rooms. We have a bit of a view at last, but it feels like everyone can see in too. The wind rips russet and copper leaves from the trees. They're all different: the oval, brown beech leaves have oblique veins that look perfectly parallel and ordered. The sycamore leaves go blotchy and curl like a fortune-teller fish. The hawthorn ones seem crispy and fried. The oak's round lobes make the brittle, brown leaf look like a cartoon hand with stubby fingers. All that's left are the black skeletons of the trees against the grey sky.

The air is still warmish, but it's been raining for days and the ground is sodden. It squelches with each step, and people start trudging head down, trying to avoid the puddles that accumulate around the site. Mud and damp have made their autumnal return, and everything looks brown or grey. The water butts are overflowing again. The mood is sombre, and we're all feeling solitary and subdued.

* * *

Alice and Stew, and Kelly, had moved on, and a lad called Ben came to stay. He was short, with small feet and quite a belly on him. His mother and stepfather didn't tell me the name of any specific condition he might be suffering from, but they said he had severe learning difficulties and there was something in his chubby face that confirmed the fact. He didn't quite look normal: he had bulbous eyes and unusually shaped features. He pursed his lips any time he was concentrating or confused, bringing them to a wrinkled point as he tried to work out what was going on. There was also something in his expression that made him look extremely angry, as if he might explode at any moment. But when he smiled he seemed so happy it was contagious, like the sky had suddenly cleared after a storm. The contrast was so marked I could already feel myself, in the first few minutes with him, trying too hard to get the smile, not the scowl, to emerge.

It didn't take long to understand one possible source of his rage. I was giving his mother and stepfather a cup of tea and a slice of cake that first afternoon. Ben had already hoofed his cake and was standing by the window, staring at his phone and mumbling about the lack of reception.

'He can wash up,' his mother said. 'He'll wash up all day if you ask him to.'

It sounded like she was offering us her skivvy.

'And he's got an NVQ in food preparation, so he can cook okay. Cooks curries sometimes, isn't that right, Ben?'

The stepfather was rolling his eyes at the thought of Ben's cooking. He looked desperate to get away.

'I've got a full-time job,' she was saying, 'and Andy's work often takes him away. We can't have Ben mooning around the house all day drinking.' She lowered her voice, but it was clear that Ben could still hear what she was saying. 'We just need to get rid of him for a while.'

I wasn't sure I had heard correctly but didn't want to ask her to repeat it.

'No reception,' Ben said, as if actively blocking out what he'd heard.

'We just need, you know –' the mother leant close to me – 'to be shot of him for a bit. Get a bit of normality back.'

She didn't show any trace of embarrassment. Ben was still staring at his phone. It appeared, not for the first time, that we were hippie babysitters for parents who didn't know what to do with their troubled children. She kept going on, saying how Ben could do little tasks like 'ironing under supervision', which kind of defeated the point.

They said goodbye to Ben – no hugs or handshakes – and took their dog outside. It promptly crapped by the workshop. I watched, waiting for one of them to pull out a plastic bag, but they left it there for us to clear up. They jumped in their Jag and sped away. They must have been in third gear by the first bend in the drive.

I looked at Ben now, sitting in one of the armchairs. He was shy and sad. He was in his mid-twenties but looked like a little lost boy who had been abandoned by his mother. I sat down next to him and tried to chat, but the barriers were up. He looked at me with suspicion, frowning all the time. It would prove an uphill task trying to get that smile to appear.

There were other arrivals. Gerald was a tall, thin man in his fifties. He had grey hair, and skin that had the lard-like pallor of a boozer. He had come to us saying, like they often did, that he wasn't an alcoholic, just someone who drank too much. He was so eager to please that he would interrupt to give his assent before he had really heard what you were saying. He repeated your name too often as he was talking, like someone who was constantly caressing you to get their own way. I knew pretty soon that he was slippery, a perception that made Francesca and me put up our invisible defences and retreat a bit from his rushed intimacy. He was excessively grateful, but it wasn't the sort of gratitude that implied serenity or true thankfulness, rather the kind that seeps from someone who is full of resentment at their previous treatment. At least you're not like all the others, he seemed to be saying; and with that came the subtle warning that he could withdraw his gratitude as quickly as he had turned it on. It was almost a warning shot across the bows. He was a bitter, cynical sort of man: eloquent, well educated and deeply disgruntled.

Only later did I see that there was more to it than that. There was plenty of resentment, but that uncomfortable gratitude was, I realized, a way of expressing that he felt unworthy of any attention or kindness. He resented himself far more than anyone else, that was the real poison; and all that conversational caressing was a way of expressing, rather explicitly and childishly, his sense of worthlessness.

He was incredibly clumsy. I had seen him plant out a row of tiny lettuces only to walk backwards and trample the lot. When he cooked, all the kitchen surfaces, and much of the floor, were stained and splashed; it looked like some kind of abstract painting. He would drop things all the time. His way of washing up was to spread the dirt around with a clean drying-up towel.

Like most cynics, he had a good sense of humour and could make us all laugh. But that cynicism meant that he struggled with the everyday miracles and emotional candour of AA. I took him along to meetings, but he sat there with his arms crossed, saying nothing. All that guff about the 'higher power', he said, was mumbo-jumbo. You got the impression that if the solution was spiritual surrender, he wanted to stick with his problem. It wasn't even a problem, he said. The real problem was . . . and he went on to list all the reasons why he occasionally had a glass or two of vodka before lunch.

There was an area of the woods that was almost completely inaccessible. It was thick with curving brambles, young hawthorns, chest-high nettles and a stand of Japanese knotweed well over twelve feet high. You couldn't walk there at all. The whole area was only about the size of a couple of five-a-side football pitches, but we reckoned it would be a perfect place to put the pigs. By now, the top field, where they had been for over a year, was sopping. It was just deep, wet mud and even in summer you would sink up to your calves and often lose a welly as Harriet came up to nudge you over in search of food. Marty loved the idea of moving the pigs to the far end of the woods. It would be called 'Pig World' he said, laughing at the theme-park sound of it.

The nettles were easy: one swipe with the billhook and they fell like skinny straws. Even the brambles were fairly simple: we had a slasher a bit like a machete and Ben let out some of his anger on them. But the knotweed was tough: Gerald tried going at it with an old scythe, but the shaft broke above the blade. We tried with a brush cutter but although that dealt with it, huge clumps of knotweed would then fall on you from double your height – and within seconds you were crouching under the heavy, dark stalks like a fly caught in a pile of spaghetti.

It was horrible work: the knotweed was so dense you could be at it for half an hour and see no difference. The cream-coloured pollen would dust you, so you were sneezing non-stop. We worked up there for a whole week, with the inevitable effect on morale: Ben kept showing me his scratched forearms, pouting as if to say it was my fault. Gerald was silent, thinking – I guessed – that this grunt work was beneath him. Even cheerful Anna was quieter than normal. She was a warm, sassy character. Half Spanish, half English, she could speak four languages. Although she was a recovering heroin user, she was as far from the TV stereotype as it was possible to be. She had short black hair and smooth dark skin. She was very beautiful without seeming to be aware of it. You didn't get the impression she spent long looking in the mirror, which kind of made her more appealing. She would laugh and joke with everyone but knew when to be quiet and listen. We liked her, and so did Gerald. She told him she was a physiotherapist and masseuse and his back suddenly got worse. When she first came, I had sat her down for a long chat. She told me she had had a pacemaker fitted. From then on, we were all terrified of her going near the livestock because of the electric fences that surrounded them. We had images of elegant Anna lying in chicken shit, her ticker tripped by the fence's pulse. One assumes a modern pacemaker would have been up to coping with an electric shock, but it became a joke that she couldn't check for eggs or feed the pigs so had to do extra washing-up.

Once the ground was cleared, we started dealing with the trees. We used various bow saws to take the lower branches off the tall ash, thinned some hawthorn and cleared away a lot of dead, spongy elder. We left the elder to rot but barrowed the other, useful logs to the various sheds. It was the end of a hard week, and the sun was out. We had transformed a dark, weed-ridden bowl into a suntrap. We lit a bonfire and piled on all the brittle brambles, knotweed, nettles and brash. As it hissed and smoked, we leaned on our pitchforks and relaxed. It was as if we had

Our eccentric chapel with straw bale pews © Donna McDowell

Working on the raised beds © Donna McDowell

One of our sows, Marble, feeding her piglets in the sunshine

A toddler inspects the finished pond © Donna McDowell

Many hands making the cob oven

Francesca by the solstice bonfire

One of our guests and his dog © Donna McDowell

The four-poster bed in the so-called Explosives Chamber

One of the entrances to the woodland

The Jones family
© Donna McDowell

"THE SOIL IS THE GREAT CONNECTOR OF LIVES...WITHOUT PROPER CARE FOR IT WE CAN HAVE NO COMMUNITY..."

WENDELL BERRY

The polytunnel

Emma on top of the cob oven roof © Donna McDowell

Benny and Emma with the pygmy goats

discovered a whole new area, had conquered a barren land. The fire squeaked and whistled now, as the flames grew higher, and we all backed off a bit. Marty was watching from his camping stool a little way away. He was painting a pig weathervane that he planned to put on the eventual gate of 'Pig World'.

The following weeks were just as hard. We had to ram about two hundred fence posts into the ground. It's bad enough doing it in normal soil, but fencing in a quarry is like trying to force a pencil through a pavement. We had designed four pens for the pigs and knew where all the strainers for the gates and corners needed to go. We started off digging deep holes for them, but it was almost impossible. The spade would hit rock and rubble almost immediately and even if you stood on it, it wouldn't sink. So you had to go at it with pickaxe and mattock, which meant that the eventual hole you made was far too wide for the post. It took an hour to dig one, and we needed to do nearly twenty. It was the kind of task that required no skill, so I had hoped everyone would muck in. But Gerald wasn't used to physical work and couldn't swing the pick properly: he would nibble away at the rocks, as if trying to comb the hole. And Ben was so slow he would pause between each hit, leaning on the shaft and frowning at the mud. Anna went for it, but her aim wasn't great, so instead of a nice vertical hole we got a shallow puddle in which the post could have sat horizontally. I sometimes felt as if I were trying to coach a team of one-legged footballers; players, moreover, who didn't really want to play in the first place. The mood was glum again when we came in for tea.

It took another two weeks to get all the posts in place. Once we had dug the holes for all the straining posts, we placed them in position and back-filled with all the grit and rubble we had dug out, smacking it down hard with a tamper so that the posts were rock solid. Gerald smiled as he watched Ben going at it unusually vigorously with the tamper.

'You're having a tamper tantrum,' he joked.

'Eh?'

Gerald tried to explain the joke, but Ben didn't get it. He thought he had been accused of something and scowled again as he went back to breaking rocks. Gerald looked awkward at the thought that he was doing menial work with numpties like us. That, I always thought, was part of the cure. I never deliberately gave people demeaning jobs. I didn't want to force humble pie on anyone. But nobody was excused the mucky jobs. There were no white-collar workers here.

All the same, people often resented the muddy, rocky work. A lot of guests came here with an image of rural languor in their heads. When they arrived, they saw the peace of this place but invariably they made the mistake of thinking we had a charmed life where there wasn't much to do other than chase butterflies and gaze at the stars. And once people have an idea in their heads, you can be as explicit as you like, but it won't sink in. Despite being very blunt about the workload on our website and in all the publications we ever put out, we still got emails from people saying things like 'I love the idea of a place where I won't be bothered, and where I won't need to bother.' I replied pretty tartly to that one. Many thought this was a place to down tools rather than pick them up.

For Gerald, fencing the pig pen was, I think, a reminder of how far he had fallen. For Ben, it was a sign that he would never succeed like his siblings. Only Anna seemed to enjoy it, seemed to relish this reinvention of herself from Mediterranean beauty to Somerset labourer. She would laugh happily as we stood ankle deep in mud, trying to jam in rocks around the base of the straining post. It took many more days to make the bracing posts for them: diagonal struts that went from the post to the ground and made sure that it wouldn't move when the stock fence was strained tight. And all that work was simply for the corners of the pen. There were still about 180 intermediate posts to smack in for the actual run of the fence. We strung binding twine between the corner posts for our line and started ramming in the smaller posts. I showed them how, lifting up the post-rammer by its metal ears and dropping it hard. The ground was so rocky that nothing seemed to go in vertically, if it went in at all. Plenty of the posts lost their point as we rammed in vain against bedrock. But we enjoyed it, smacking the heavy metal rammer into the wooden posts. We felt better afterwards, with shoulders vibrating and minds cleared. Eventually, after days of doing little else, all the posts were in. It looked like a scene from the trenches, with mud everywhere and rows of posts at odd angles.

Simon from Pilsdon came over to help us with the actual fence. We stapled one end to a straining post and unfurled it all the way to the end of that run. We had the pick-up parked just round the corner, and ran a chain from the tow bar to the end of the strainer which was attached to the fence. We then walked the fangs of the strainer up the chain links to pull the fence taut. It was the first time, after weeks, that the job became truly satisfying. In a few short moments, you could create fifty metres of tight fencing. For once, it looked professional. Ben and Gerald hammered staples along the line. We did the same with a run of barb on the bottom. The hardest thing was trying to manoeuvre the pick-up to the right position each time, so that the taut fence would be pulled against the appropriate straining post. Once we had done the corners, the vehicle had ploughed all the mud, so that even before the pigs came in it looked churned. It took a few days, but we had finally fenced four beautiful pens. It looked secure and smart, the metal squares of the stock fence glinting in the weak autumn sunlight.

Unfortunately, though, we had done things in the wrong order. We were always doing things in the wrong order. It would be because something hadn't turned up (the corrugated iron) or someone had (Simon). It would be because of the weather, or someone's well-being, or whatever. I probably wasn't sufficiently bossy to say what should happen when, with the result that jobs ended up being far trickier than they should have been. The problem this time was that we hadn't finished making the three pig arks we wanted to place in Pig World, so we were now going to have to lift them over our beautiful new fence. And since Marty wanted to assemble the arks in the workshop, where we had all the tools, we were going to have to transport them in one piece, manhandling the heavy, cumbersome arks across the mud and over the barbed wire of Pig World.

They were almost done now. Marty and Tony had been working on them for a few days: a huge semicircle of marine ply at each end with four overlapping curves of corrugated iron over the top. The structure was held together with lengths of four-by-two and offcuts from a nearby sawmill. Marty had cleverly cut out hand holes to lift the things: two of us could just about get them off the ground, but the farrowing ark (the so-called 'maternity unit') had scaffolding poles down the sides to prevent newborn piglets getting squashed, as well as hefty timber to keep those poles in place, so it was much heavier. The arks had doors front and back, with bolts top and bottom. They were beautiful but, man, were they heavy.

We put the arks upside down on the pick-up and took them over to Pig World. They were far larger than the flatbed, though, and wobbled precariously as we drove along the winding path through the woods. We lashed pairs of pallets together and ran two tracks of four-by-two over them to act as a wooden railway. It all felt pretty rustic, but the arks moved smoothly across them and the fence didn't get damaged. Marty put up his beautiful sign – 'You Are Now Entering Pig World' – with the pig weathervane on top.

Jenny was one of those people who had contacted us only then to disappear off the radar for six months. But that winter she resurfaced, and said she was ready to come. She had been bereaved and was battling a bad habit.

A tall, thin woman, she looked frail, even though she was only in her forties. She had blue eyes and high cheekbones. She got so nervous she would shake as she spoke to you, frequently apologizing mid-sentence for whatever she was struggling to say. If you walked into a room where she was sitting, she would look up and explain herself, desperate to excuse the fact that she was doing something completely innocent like reading a book or lighting the fire. She seemed as fragile as a dry twig, always giving you the sense that she could break under any pressure. When she was particularly tense, her top lip would tighten painfully over her uneven teeth. She came with a small fat dog called Baxter, which she carried around in a blanket as if he were a newborn baby. If she put him down, he would whimper and whine until he was picked up. We teased her because she took him, not for a walk but for a cuddle.

Everyone was immediately fond of Jenny. She was so vulnerable, so openly wobbly, that it was hard not to put an arm around her, to hug her and comfort her. She made us laugh by constantly laughing at herself. She was quite a hypochondriac, convinced every time she coughed that she had cancer. She struggled to pronounce a lot of words, talking about Windsor Hill Wood being a wonderfully 'peratheutic place', or asking us to pick her up from the 'centograph' (the cenotaph in town). The only way she could say 'apocalypse' was by saying 'a puck of lips' as fast as she could.

I once asked her if she was busy, as I needed a hand in the kitchen. 'No, I'm not,' she said. 'I'm at your disposable.'

Another time she said 'erm' quietly, which was her version of clearing her throat and getting your attention.

'Hi, Jenny,' we said.

'Jinjin,' Leo said, waddling over to her to hug her thigh.

'Erm,' she said again, composing herself. 'Could I have a saliva of kitsch?'

'Eh?' We laughed openly because it had become a bit of a joke that she got her words confused, and she liked the intimacy of being ribbed.

'What do you want?' Fra asked, smiling.

'Erm, well, it was so good yesterday, that kitsch, and I was a little bit hungry, so I wondered if I could have a saliva?'

'A sliver of quiche?' Marty said, roaring with laughter.

Fra went to the fridge to get out the quiche, knowing it would never be called that again.

Funny, sad things were always happening with Jenny. She was once trying to retrieve a football from Baxter, who was biting hard on the leather hexagons. So she picked up the ball and swung the dog round like you would a child, only Baxter suddenly went flying through the air, a couple of his old teeth breaking off as he did so.

She would pack her bags once a week, convinced that she was unloved and that she had better get out quick.

'Am I overreacting?' she asked one day, as she met me by the door with her suitcase packed and Baxter in her arms.

'I don't even know what you're overreacting to. Where on earth are you going?' I said.

'You called me Tintin,' she said, her top lip so tight it was barely visible.

I frowned, trying to remember what I might have said. 'I think,' I said gently, 'I called you Jinjin, which is what Leo calls you. I just like it. I won't do it again if it upsets you.'

She looked at the ground and realized her mistake. 'I thought you were trying to humiliate me, talking about how silly my hair looks. I've got this curl –' she brushed a twitching palm over her quiff – 'just like Tintin.'

I just smiled and put a hand on her shaking shoulders.

'Am I overreacting?' she asked again, waving her fingers under her eyes, as if to waft away her tears. And then she unpacked, laughing at her own fragility. It became another of our catch-phrases, repeated each time one of us was feeling exposed or misunderstood.

Jenny was flighty because of her low self-esteem. I sat down and spoke to her about it, but she fretted that at some point I would become fed up with her.

'You'll get annoyed with me,' she said plaintively, clearly expecting me to contradict her and reassure her I would never get annoyed with her.

'Probably,' I said. 'I get annoyed with myself, with my children, even with Francesca. I can't imagine I won't get annoyed with you.'

'But you'll hate me.'

'No I won't. I'll just get annoyed with you. And I'm sure you'll get annoyed with me.'

She frowned, surprised both by this frankness about annoyance, and by the notion that being annoyed or annoying could be without consequences. For Jenny, and many other guests like her, it was important to know that there would always be hiccups and irritations, arguments and crises, but that none of that meant they were hated, or had to leg it suddenly. She was fickle, but was beginning to understand commitment too; beginning to glimpse what happened if you hung around.

The reason some people wanted to leave was simply because they still felt unworthy. For whatever reason, they didn't think they deserved to be here. That's why Jenny's presence was so precious: she was openly vulnerable, and that vulnerability only added to her humanity. She was an example to us of the need to embrace imperfection; such a good example that she sometimes, perhaps, exaggerated her sensitivity and instability to secure more hugs. In a place where tough nuts would roll up and boast of their survivor status, of their invulnerability, it was important to have someone who was visibly in pieces – and who somehow demonstrated that it was okay to fall apart like a jigsaw in its box. Many resisted it, myself included, holding things together even though it would have been better to let go. And because she admitted to, and chuckled about, having ballsed things up, she was a lesson in the importance not of denying pain but of acknowledging it.

Friends, family and our *consiglieri* were often worried by how much pressure there was on us and frequently counselled that we should try to get away or switch off. But it just wasn't possible a lot of the time. Every day something strange happened, something that needed to be dealt with tactfully, firmly and, usually, immediately. It would take an hour or two and, more to the point, large reserves of energy: someone has cut themselves, another is crying and wants to talk, a pig has escaped, the roof is leaking, someone is punching a wall so hard they've made a hole in the plaster and damaged their fist. Often it was just dealing with the consequences of clumsiness. Gerald forgot to switch the hob off, so we smelt acrid smoke billowing from the kitchen and found the plastic colander in a smooth, horizontal sludge. When he was asked to clean up the mess, he scratched the hob so much it became unrecognizable. For the next month, it stank of burnt plastic every time we cooked. Jenny was the opposite, so careful about switching things off that she accidentally flicked off the freezer, which contained an entire winter's supply of our own pork. The next morning, I stared in disbelief at the defrosted meat: all the effort to breed, raise and butcher those pigs, for this. We had to eat six months' worth of meat in a week: ribs, sausages, rolled belly joints, bacon, hocks, the lot. We ate pork until we couldn't face it any more. And, through it all, you had to remain jolly and make sure that no one felt too low; you had to be strict, but maintain a sense of easy-going camaraderie.

We were wrecked. Sometimes, I caught myself deliberately avoiding sitting down because I knew that when I did, I wouldn't be able to get up. So I would keep going until, when I did eventually stop, it was worse than I feared. I would stare into space, focusing on nothing. I couldn't hear anything, or if I could, I couldn't respond. I knew things were crooked when I went to a friend's party. I love parties, and this one was a lively, glitzy affair in London. But I spent the evening standing in a corner, just watching the scene as if I weren't there, hoping people wouldn't come up and talk to me. All I wanted was to lie down in a dark room by myself for a month. I felt like a computer on the blink, no longer responding properly and ignoring prompts until suddenly it goes berserk, randomly opening and closing files. Fra felt the same. We were absolutely frazzled and the worst of it was that we could see that our kids were getting a raw deal. They must have felt sometimes that they were at the back of the queue to talk to us. And when they did get us to themselves, at their bedtime, we were so shattered we didn't have any patience. We had spent the day bottling up anger at strange adult behaviour only to lose patience when faced with completely normal children's antics.

It was as if we'd created a beast we couldn't tame, an animal that kept on getting bigger and bigger and taking ever more energy, money and space. It was good that it was growing: what we'd done here seemed successful and popular, and was admired. These woods were attracting people from near and far. In the two and a half years since we had opened the place over fifty people had stayed here, some just for a respite week, but most for much longer. Many of them said that it had saved their life; dozens of others said that it had saved their marriage, or their sanity. But it felt like our house was getting smaller every week. It was so busy, so chaotic. No attempt to manage the influx of people seemed to make any difference. In those two and a half years almost two hundred people had come as volunteers or day visitors. We asked people to give us notice they were coming and deliberately didn't put a map or phone number online, but there were still unexpected arrivals every day: bikes and cars coming and going, walkers wandering in, expecting a warm welcome. I should, perhaps, have told them they needed to make an appointment and to come back another time, but that went counter to the ethos of the place. And it's not as if any of those arrivals were malicious. They were good-natured on the whole. But most were in some sort of pickle and brought behaviour that was invariably erratic and impetuous. One person snapped off most of the branches of the young fruit trees whilst chatting on his phone. Another guest, out of spite or thoughtlessness, hacked down Fra's much-loved roses. People lost control of their dogs, which then killed the chickens or knocked over children. Money was stolen, axes were broken. It was as if we'd lost control of the place, as if it now had a life of its own. And that was a problem as much for our long-terms guests as it was for us: they often found themselves not in a peaceful space but in one that was disturbed and shaken by day-trippers and itinerants.

I had often noticed, when we were on our travels, that experienced communitarians seemed to have developed an invisible moat around themselves and were able to be both warm and reserved at the same time. 'Why have you come here?' they asked us when we were on our travels, the question appearing both blunt and kind, both defensive and generous. They knew when and how to retreat, either physically or mentally, how to avoid being buffeted by every new arrival. You had to be centred and ever so slightly distant if you weren't going to be knocked around by the jostling and jockeying.

Some of our residents, though, beginning to resent the constant intrusions and queries, were slightly more brutal in their responses to visitors.

Maggie Purple was weeding inside the raspberry cage one morning when some earnest local councillors came round.

'What are you doing in there?' one of them asked, with dripping condescension.

'They keep me here because I bite,' she said, straight-faced. They edged away, not sure whether to sympathize or run.

Anna was the champion at the wind-up, though. She could look pretty fierce when she wanted to and was young enough to unnerve those who thought she must be really screwed-up if she couldn't just live with her parents.

'Why are you here?' a German visitor once asked, her head tilted on one side to disguise curiosity with kindness.

'Because –' Anna smiled nicely – 'I killed my parents.'

Comments like that usually guaranteed her a bit of distance.

There was a generosity of spirit in Jenny that made her want to look after people. She loved cooking for everyone, baking the bread or making the tea. Every time a new guest arrived she would listen to them and try to help out, albeit in slightly haphazard ways. She would serve them, seeking approval so much that she would sometimes do unwise things to obtain it. Our woodland was so full of hardened wanderers that many took advantage of her, asking her to iron their clothes, or do their laundry, or just make their tea. She was thrown by anger and, more subtly, by undercurrents of aggression. People who were aggressive were very good at disguising it as teasing, or bluntness, or 'advice'. She had it in her head that by allowing herself to be walked over, people would eventually appreciate her. I would sit down sometimes and talk to her about it. Rationally, she knew it didn't make sense, but it didn't make any difference. She would do anything to placate people, over-stretching herself and being exploited.

For weeks she had been making tea for Ben. He would be sitting in the armchair and she would generously fuss around him whilst he stared at his phone.

'Did you put the honey in it?' he would check, not looking at her as she set the cup down.

'I did,' she said.

'What honey?' I asked.

'Ben has three spoonfuls in his tea,' she said, as if she were the mother of a mute boy.

I'm not a very accomplished beekeeper, but that summer we had taken off about fifty jars of honey from the hives. It was rare and precious stuff. I once read that for one teaspoon of honey, a bee has to fly the equivalent of three times around the globe. I had spent much of the summer with seriously stung and swollen forearms. And here was moody Ben being waited on by Jenny, going through the honey for a fecking cup of builder's tea. I opened the cupboard where I kept the jars and there were a lot of empties, left there unwashed and with the dirty lids just tossed in.

I went off by myself before I said anything I might regret. I tried to work out why it wound me up so much. It wasn't only that Jenny was, as usual, being subserviently kind. And it wasn't just the fact that much of our annual stores of honey had disappeared into cups of tea. What really irked me was that Ben was taking the mickey, not just using Jenny as his waitress but being a glutton. He was trying to stop drinking and, like many of our guests, had replaced the booze with a very high intake of sugars. One morning I had to go and wake him up and found him fast asleep on his bed with a halo of Quality Street wrappers around his head. They had been a present to the community from someone, and now there was just an empty tin. The difficulty was that he had such severe learning difficulties you could barely reason with him.

Because we were living with so many recovering addicts, I found myself frequently thinking about addiction. It's become a bit of a truism about modern life that all of us, in some way or other, display addictive behaviour. The manipulation of our wants, the sophisticated stoking of our desires, the speed of delivery and the speed of the ensuing dissatisfaction – all contribute to make us, if not addicts, then compulsive bingers. The once-rare pleasures and excitements of life have become completely commonplace, and we return to them with such somnambulant regularity that they no longer give us either pleasure or excitement. The undeserved rewards are suddenly deservedly unrewarding.

People started coming to us not just with the obvious addictions but also the subtler ones, involving for example shopping or gambling. And in a dry house, you start to notice the unhealthy consumption of coffee or sugar and, especially, the twitchy dependence on technological gadgetry.

I wondered why recovery invariably takes place in a communal setting. Most recovering addicts say that being alone is like being behind enemy lines. It's obvious, but recovery's bound to be easier when you're surrounded by people trying to help you beat an addiction. If people use because of the wrong crowd, getting clean is easier if you can find the right crowd. One possible reason why AA has been so successful over the decades is to do with mutuality, support and the 'group conscience'. For those who struggle with religion, the numinous 'power greater than ourselves' to which addicts turn in step two is often conceived of as simply the 'fellowship' of the group, rather than God.

In communal living there is, sadly, less spontaneity – 'Let's plan,' Benny once said, 'what spontaneous things we're going to do tomorrow' – but there's also less scope for individual indulgence. That's why we try to give a very clear timetable to guests. We meet for work at the same time every morning. Each adult cooks one night a week. The kind of work people do offers, hopefully, an antidote to the habit of seeking instant, solipsistic gratification: wrestling a boar into the sow's pen yields a reward only when she farrows in about four months' time. Our guests are constantly doing work not for themselves but for those who'll come after them. They are, as the saying goes, planting trees under whose shade they cannot expect to sit.

There's a theory that addiction is a 'spiritual malady', that it isn't merely a physical craving for a substance but a reflection of the fact that family, tribal, cultural and spiritual ties have been severed. We are dislocated, isolated and atomized beings who have become, thanks to super-speed capitalism and acute consumer competitiveness, incredibly individualistic. We're obsessed with ourselves and what we've got. It's a point Wendell Berry, the American writer and farmer, makes eloquently in his essay 'Racism and the Economy'. 'It should tell us something that in healthy societies drug use is celebrative, convivial and occasional, whereas among us it is lonely, shameful and addictive. We need drugs, apparently, because we have lost each other.' In becoming connected to a wider group, some of that isolation and dislocation is adjusted and that need is reduced.

But there are deeper reasons why recovery coincides with community. Given the almost limitless expanse of freedom we enjoy, it's inevitable that many people will make the wrong choices; that they will be unable, in the words of Edmund Burke, the 18th century political philosopher, to 'put moral chains on their own appetites'. A community does that for them. Communal living reduces choice; it limits – let's be honest – freedom. That's one of the first complaints people have about communal living: that it imposes limits on personal freedoms and autonomy. To which communitarians reply that the reverse is also true: that the obsessive pursuit of personal freedoms and autonomy slowly dissolves community, eventually making it inconceivable.

Freedom and community are only incompatible if freedom is understood as licentiousness, a place where there are no ethical limitations; if freedom is simply, as Wendell Berry says, 'a sort of refuge for escapees from the moral law'. Whereas there's an old paradox suggesting that freedom actually consists in restraint, in choosing obedience to the central command to love one another. Most of us are understandably wary about any mention of constraining freedom because it can appear the thin end of the wedge that leads to tyranny. But in an intimate community it's extremely clear that solicitude, rather than dictatorship, is the reason for constraint. When you know each other so well, and yearn for what's best for each other, it's far simpler to distinguish between the two.

Plenty of people are aghast at the idea of their autonomy, spontaneity and choice being reduced. It goes counter to the received wisdom of the age that we become ourselves only when we follow our own desires and longings. We always want to keep all our options open and are therefore transfixed by choice: we must always have a choice, and struggle to decide; 'decision' means, etymologically, to kill off the other options. But many of those who have written about communal living in the past suggest that it's only in the reduction and conscious neglect of desire that you truly become yourself. Freedom is forfeited when we act only for ourselves: we become enslaved by our own urges and narrow ambitions.

The trouble for us was that abstinence didn't always usher people into the sunny uplands of serenity and gratitude. Quite often it had almost the opposite effect: when someone stopped using, a whole host of issues that had been buried came to the fore. We had plenty of people who were sober but still full of fury, regret, self-pity, anxiety and resentment. It's a common phenomenon, as anyone who goes to Al-Anon – the support group for relatives and friends of alcoholics – will attest: 'It was easier when he [or she] was drinking' is the cliché there. The hard work often comes long after someone has stopped, when they're grieving for the loss of their old friend – the bottle, the needle, or whatever – and are having to deal with problems they've ignored for years. That's why there's so much emotional shrapnel here, so much crossfire between irate guests, so many moments in which one has to calm down tensions and misunderstandings.

What also frequently happened was that we got people who were clean but who still had very little power over other cravings (what's called, in the jargon, 'impulse control disorders'). Living in a place where we tried to exclude the obvious addictions, subtler ones came to the fore. Many of our guests could proudly tell you exactly how many weeks or months they had been clean. But whilst some had started giving up everything – tobacco, sugar, cake, and so on – others seemed to have simply transferred their never-enough behaviour to other things. There were plenty of pretty heated debates about how much chocolate or coffee our common purse could afford to buy for particular people who would happily gulp and munch every minute of every day. There was still a repetitive dependence, a habitual return to the same small buzz. But being a communal setting, those things were seen and discussed, and we gradually made small inroads into this type of hunger and the reasons for it.

A few days after we had discovered the empty honey jars, Jenny had performed a small act of kindness: she had put aside the last of Tony's doughnuts for Fra, since she hadn't had one. At the end of a long, hard stint, Fra was sitting in an armchair asking if there were any left.

'I put one in the larder for you,' Jenny said proudly.

'I'll get it,' I said, as I was on my feet.

'Erm –' Jenny tried to stall me – 'maybe I should.'

'You're okay,' I said, stopping her. I wandered into the kitchen, found the doughnut paper and passed it to Fra. As she pulled it out of the bag we saw that there, in the side of the doughnut, a bite had been taken out, a perfect, obvious bite, like the munched apple on a Mac. Dear Jenny had had the kindness to put aside a treat but had lacked the resolve to resist having a piece herself. The way we dealt with it was, as always, open discussion: everyone was sitting round the fire, and we teased her, and laughed about it, and talked about it. We all mentioned our own foibles to make her feel better. We had done the same with Ben a few days earlier, talking with him about appetite and restraint, and persuading him that sugar, rather than honey, was fine for tea. The bitten doughnut was funny, but there were plenty of occasions in which a person's inability to resist any temptation was frustrating and, bluntly, thoughtless: someone would hoof three slices of cake before others had had one; they would glug a pint of coffee and not pour for anyone else. We got used to talking about the science of dopamine, and – even more complicated – the art of sharing. Fair division, of course, is always an issue in a community, but especially in a community made up, largely, of those struggling to control their appetites.

The girls were now old enough to jump on their bikes and disappear along one of the rocky paths into the woods. They had miles of tracks all to themselves, and you would hear them, shrieking and giggling, as they dared each other to freewheel down some new, steep descent. They abandoned their bikes wherever they wanted once they were sidetracked by something else. Benny would pick wild flowers, filling her little fist with an eccentric combination of weeds and grasses. Emma always tried to climb the quarry face, tobogganing down the rocks on her bum as she squealed. She adored animals, and used to play with spiders and ladybirds, creating habitats for them and giving them names. They would both ride the breeding sow, Harriet, clinging on as she ambled around the field, barely aware they were there.

I marvelled at how even the most communally raised kids were still, instinctively, commercial and entrepreneurial; at how the muddy Somerset countryside combined, in them, with the urbane elegance of their Italian heritage. Quite often they would establish a stall and invite us to come and peruse their wares: woodland perfume, mud slops, a few eggs, green tomatoes, some picturesque moss. They wouldn't just set up shop; they had to get dressed up, putting on wigs from their dressing-up chest, introducing themselves with absurd names.

'What's this?' Gerald said, holding up a jar full of watery green liquid.

'That, sir,' said Benny, doing her posh pose, turning sideways and pursing her lips, 'is Eau de Somerset. Would sir like to try it?' And she dipped her fingertips in the jar and flicked them at him before creasing up in cackles.

Weary Gerald smiled, and fingertipped the liquid behind his earlobes. 'Smells very sophisticated,' he said. 'What's in it?'

'Sage,' Emma shouted, 'crushed grass and pine cones.'

'Lovely. I'll take it. How much?'

'Ten pence,' said Benny. 'And there's a five-pence deposit on the jar.'

'Ten pence!' Gerald shook his head. 'I can get Eau de Somerset for half that on the King's Road.'

'Just give me the money,' screamed Benny, becoming bullish.

And so it went on: Gerald and Benny haggling and laughing and pretending to get angry with each other. Emma offered a mud soup to Anna in return for a few coppers.

The girls were growing up to be, if not feral woodlanders, then

certainly free-range foragers. But they were also wannabe sophis-
ticates. Benny once came in from the garden with a squidgy
cucumber that had hung on through the autumn.

'I wouldn't eat that,' I said.

'Not going to. I'm organizing a spa.'

And she proceeded to slice up the cucumber, placing two discs
on her eyes as she lay on the bench outside the house. Within a
minute, she was shouting for her assistant.

'Emma! Where's the mud? I need that facial.'

Emma ran past me with a bucket of her speciality slop. They
called it an 'unhealth spa', pleading to be allowed flapjacks, fudge
and crisps.

Although I often fretted about the effect of this place on the
children, there were many moments when it was, for them, an
idyllic upbringing. They had the run of an adventure playground.
They felt safe, despite being made aware of the dangers. They
were so immersed in nature they didn't even realize it was
unusual. And for all my guilt – presumably shared by most
parents – that I wasn't spending sufficient time with them, I realized that they were blessed with dozens of parents, each charmed
and tested by their innocent world. Our kids were being raised by
many more people than just their mother and father. I remember
Benny once listing all the 'uncles and aunts' she had lived with,
going through the fingers of both hands twice.

The presence of the children was also vital to the guests. The
livestock and vegetables demanded attention, but the kids, especially, took people far away from their own woes: the immediacy
of the children's needs, the noisy sunshine and showers of their
emotional lives, made the rest of us appear unexpectedly stable
and mature. It gave guests the sense of being in a serious position
of responsibility but at the same time in a place of happy

regression, where they relished role-playing and dressing up. They enjoyed the fact that whatever their backstory, we trusted them with the most precious and vulnerable part of our community (albeit watching carefully from afar).

The other thing about the children was their straight-talking. I would agonize for days about raising an issue with one of the guests, but Benny would put her head to the side, frown, and say it right out: 'Why do we have to wash our hands before meals if Gerald doesn't?' Or, when we were talking about Peter Pan round the fire, explaining to Emma the concept of a boy who doesn't grow up, she looked at me and asked, 'Do you mean like Ben?' Even when they were trying to be tactful, the children were inadvertently blunt. One mealtime Benny took a mouthful of pretty ropey food and, politely, decided to pass judgement in Italian, thinking it would be incomprehensible: 'Crudi e disgustosi,' she said.

That winter, we decided to look for a long-term residential volunteer, someone to share the load with us. We advertised, and a young woman in her late twenties called Lucy came forward. She seemed okay: enthusiastic about sustainability, which was great. But she didn't seem enthusiastic about much else. She had a downcast kind of face and the sort of backstory that suggested she had drifted for a few years, either choosing to move on or being asked to. She worked hard but always wanted to work alone. It was a risky appointment, but we were almost on our knees by then and foolishly assumed that a bit of help would be better than none at all.

Within days there were some pretty alarming warning signs. I asked her to look after the children for half an hour whilst I cleaned out the chicken coops and came back to find her playing cards with them whilst listening to her iPod.

'I don't think she really wanted to play with us,' said an unusually subdued Benny later.

Over the next few weeks Lucy's behaviour remained difficult. We had given her a very clear notion of the job requirements: it was almost exclusively about caring for our guests. But you would see her in the common room with orange earplugs on, shouting at vulnerable people to keep quiet. She would scowl behind her computer, tutting at something someone had said. She was especially perturbed by Ben, by his moody, unpredictable character. 'He freaks me out,' she said, soon after meeting him. The way she spoke to him was the verbal equivalent of a slap.

One evening, I had spent an hour listening to Anna. It hadn't been a private chat – we were just sitting in the garden room around the fire – but it was clear that she needed to talk. It was a sort of public counselling session, something that happened a lot, albeit informally. When Anna finally decided to go to bed, Lucy stormed up to me and put her hands on her hips.

'Why does she get all the attention?' she asked.

'How do you mean?'

'You've been talking to her for hours, and you've barely asked me how I'm doing all day.'

It was something we would witness dozens of times over the next few years: people would get in touch, offering themselves as volunteers, only for their strength to disintegrate as soon as they arrived. They would quickly start to demand, rather than give, attention. Lucy was the first person who had demonstrated the trend. We had been desperate for help, but she had only added to the burden. It went on for a few weeks, getting worse as time went on. By then I was sufficiently experienced not to get irritable or even angry: better to give people the chance to say why they were troubled rather than accuse them of causing trouble. It was the same conversation in the end, but invited whoever it was forward instead of putting them on the back foot.

'You're obviously finding it very tough here . . .' I said.

She nodded, looking at me with watery eyes. She told me all the things she was struggling with, not just here but with her own family. We sat and chatted for a long time, and her behaviour became understandable. However, over the next few weeks, things went downhill. Lucy and Marty had become very close, each energized by the excitement of the other's attention. They were like a loved-up couple, playfully teasing each other and giving themselves nicknames. Lucy would spend time in Marty's shelter, and the pairing-off rang alarm bells, not just because this wasn't a place for romantic relationships but because theirs was a friendship that seemed forged in defiance.

By now Marty had been with us for well over a year. He wanted to pootle around with his pigs, but I suggested that feeding the animals was a very small part of the working day. He felt I didn't appreciate all the work he did.

'How hard do we have to work to get your approval?' he asked.

He was fed up with me. He was a pensioner and was tired of taking orders from someone thirty years younger than him. He was weary, I suspect, of our constant stream of tricky customers. He wanted this to be his home but, at the same time, he didn't want to be here any more. He was roaring off in his Land Rover increasingly often. Yet throughout those simmering disagreements, Marty was never nasty or unpleasant. He put his point across, but with more sadness than pique. One day we were walking over to see the pigs when he told me he was moving on.

'I suppose,' he said, 'a place like this has to keep evolving. It can't be built around me, and what I want to do. I understand that. So I'm going to look for somewhere else to live.'

I sat on a fallen trunk and tried to absorb it. It felt like this was the end of the whole project. With his guitar and harmonica, Marty had always provided the soundtrack to the place. He provided the humour, and most of the wisdom. It was as if all the tension of the previous two and a half years had backed up and I couldn't hold it together any more. Months of sleep deprivation had caught up with me. I worried how hard it would hit Leo, who adored Marty. We didn't say much for a while, but then started laughing about all that had happened in his time here. Marty had seen it all, had always been generous, witty and eloquent. He had plenty of issues he was dealing with, but he had never been manipulative or dishonest. And probably, because he seemed so well adjusted and independent, I hadn't given him the attention I should have. He had become jealous, perhaps, as others took up more of my time. Maybe we had taken him for granted, I don't know.

Fra wept when he told her. I told him to stay as long as he needed, that he could stay for months more if he wanted. But he was gone within a week, moving to a static caravan on the top of the Mendips.

Two days after he left Lucy came up to me, looking slightly sheepish.

'I'm leaving,' she said quickly.

I nodded, taking it in. I expressed sadness that she hadn't found it easy here.

'When are you off?' I asked.

'Tomorrow.'

'Tomorrow? Where are you going?'

'I'm moving in with Marty.'

I nodded again, trying to understand what that meant.

So within a week two of our supports had disappeared. The

amusing mentor of the community had gone. The volunteer we had desperately needed was leaving too. They were, of course, free to go, but it felt like desertion, leaving us high and dry at very short notice.

A few days later I lost it. I came apart, pulled like gum until I was thin, a combination of translucence and holes. I had no robustness left, no strength.

By coincidence, Tom came again from Bristol. He shook his head. 'I couldn't do what you do,' he said.

'Neither can I.' I stared at the leafless trees as I moved my head left and right. 'I can't do what I do. Not any more.'

It wasn't the sort of fatigue that a good night's sleep could cure. I'd tried that, but I was like an old phone that you have to keep charging more often, for longer and longer, but which runs down more quickly each time. My batteries had gone. For years people had marvelled at my energy, at the way I could tear around and get things done day and night. Now I couldn't get out of the chair to answer the phone. I couldn't be bothered. I couldn't see the point any more. All the effort, the colossal effort, seemed pointless.

Often potential guests would ask, when pondering whether to come here, what we offered. The enquiry was based on the assumption that there was something important thrown in, something that could be used or consumed: therapy, or counselling, or some clever kind of cure. I never gave them the honest answer to the question, because it sounded too self-pitying or conceited. But what we really offered was ourselves. It was we who were being consumed. I don't want to sound melodramatic, because we were enriched by and rewarded for what we were doing. But it usually felt as if we were the finite fuel for the place. And now we were burnt up and burnt out. We were sustaining the community, but I knew it wasn't sustaining me or Francesca. The pressure of the place was often almost unbearable.

And it had caught up with me. I counted the pleats in the old curtain, working my way along the waves of the fabric because I couldn't get out of the chair. Fra came in with the laundry on her hip, but I was unable to move. This wasn't a panic attack so much as a shutdown. I was unplugged. Nothing moved me any more, and so I sat there unmoved. I needed to go somewhere peaceful and quiet. That's what everyone did here; they came to chill out and recharge. But it seemed to be at my expense. I had to get out, but this was my home. This was where I lived. I was trapped in a community of my own making. I had got what I wished for.

As usual in a crisis, problems mounted one on top of the other. The school Benny and Emma were attending failed its Ofsted review and was put in special measures. We noticed when we picked the kids up that there were parents with cans of lager and rollies in their hands. The school's weekly newsletter contained pleas for parents to stop swearing in the playground. Then, when trying to find the phone number for the parents of one of Benny's friends, we made the mistake of going online. The search results on the name revealed that the friend's father was doing time for GBH. This, I thought wearily, is where we've brought our daughters. Or where I'd brought them, because I suspected that Francesca resented me for dragging us into this mess. She never said as much, but her quiet resilience had a chill wind to it. She was melancholic that we were doing all this for strangers but that she was unable to be present for her best friends in Italy who were going through comparable crises: cancer, divorce, the death of a child.

The neighbour, Barry, was getting more aggressive. He would fire off his shotgun every time one of us was working at the edge of the woodland. It was no coincidence: he would spit abuse till our ears rang. Over the Christmas holidays we had, for fun, put up an Italian flag on the tree house. Shortly afterwards, unhinged Barry placed a dirty English St George flag on one of his trees, like a V-sign to the outsiders. He then picked a fight with one of our volunteers, a chap who was helping people to park on the outskirts of our woods during an open day. Barry strode up to him, took off his shirt and beckoned him with all his fingers, the universal sign of a thug spoiling for a fight. There was a scuffle and the police got involved.

I was trying to convalesce, but the crises kept coming. I stopped sleeping. Wandering around in the dark was becoming habitual. I'd get a brief gust of energy in the middle of the night, but by daybreak I'd be done in and feeling shattered again. I became noise averse, desperately trying to avoid shouting and banging. I was so brittle I worried about being snappy, so instead I tried to say nothing. And whilst this meltdown was going on I was still running the place, carrying on as usual: organizing jobs, cooking, cleaning, sorting out the crises and conflicts. I felt the reason I was so tired wasn't the work and the listening, it was the apparent uselessness of it all. It felt as if there was no end result. The self-harm and self-loathing, the boozing and using, the gambling and the rambling . . . they seemed to go on and on. People might stay with us for a few months but, really, they were no different when they left.

I was suffering acute compassion fatigue. I felt as if I had run out of energy, of motivation. I was so tired. Tired of getting in the mood on everyone else's behalf, of being hearty and energetic, and tired of being quiet and confessor-like when they needed to offload a lifetime's resentment and sadness. When I saw the guests in the morning and asked how they were, the replies were always monosyllabic and downbeat, if I got a reply at all. 'Yeah', they'd say, or just shrug their shoulders. The question was never returned. It felt as if I was constantly trying to ignite damp kindling, puffing on it to help get it on its way, but it would always peter out and leave me feeling dizzy from the effort. There were all these people in our family home constantly moaning and complaining, and I wanted to shake them and tell them to show some compassion themselves rather than always expect it and extract it from everyone else.

I longed for solitude or, even better, for old-fashioned family life. Man, when I looked back to how scathing I used to be about the nuclear family, about how it was just another gated community – and all I wanted now was to curl up on the sofa with my wife and kids and watch some really cheesy fifties musical. A few years ago I used to have, I thought, enough altruism for a whole village. Now I barely had enough kindness left for my own kids. I felt as if I was always impatient with them, telling them off for dropping crumbs or dripping wax.

My anger surprised me. I was so cross that people didn't listen. I felt betrayed and undermined. I was constantly getting it in the neck for no good reason. I had brought my family into this deprived place, and they were suffering the consequences. We were deeply in debt and whatever I found time to earn was only ever a dusting on a deep hole. I was so apathetic it would take me an hour to build up the energy to go to bed.

But something changed over the following weeks. As I rehearsed this angry monologue in my head, words coming as fast as my limbs were slow, I recognized phrases. It was as if I was echoing all the complaints of the guests we'd had here over the last two or three years. 'No one listens to me'; 'I get the blame for trying to help'; 'I'm ashamed I've let my family down'; 'I'm a poor provider.' We had teased gentle Rongo because he had once said he was going to lie down to get up the energy for bed, but now I was doing the same. The revelation was slow rather than sudden: I wasn't mending anyone because I was well and truly broken. I had fallen a long way and only then saw for the first time the fallen people around me: dear Jenny, so kind and wounded; Gerald, with his humour and shame; Ben, abandoned but brave. I saw the others with their scars and sorrows because of absent or unpredictable parents, because of a lack of self-control or the inability to stay still. I looked at them differently now, not with the gaze of the carer but with the compassion that comes from identification. Sorrow was what we had in common: wounds that were openings, entrances through which we could see, and identify with, one another.

For years I had thought that community gifted belonging, the holy grail of modern life, by asking us to give up belongings. But now I sensed that belonging comes also through being humbled, even humiliated. I wasn't even on the bottom rung of the ladder. I had been floored; we were all equal. It's only there that healing can take place.

Jean Vanier, the founder of the L'Arche communities, once said something that – whilst not absolving me of responsibility for this place – made me feel less wretched about dragging my family into this melee. 'We will only stay in community if we have gone through the passage from choosing community to knowing that we have been chosen for community.' I had always known, in theory, that this was a calling, that it wasn't something we, solely, had decided to do. But the notion that we might not be choosers at all, but chosen, came as a relief. It wasn't, perhaps, all my responsibility and all my fault.

I looked differently at the landscape too. The radiant beauty of the rugged quarry surprised me now. The elegance and poise of the animals was arresting. I watched one of our geese standing on one leg, the other thrust behind her like a ballerina. Her wings were outstretched like the figurehead on the prow of a ship. She held the position for a minute. I gazed at her, amazed that she was completely still. Her neck craned forward so that there was an almost continuous line between her orange leg and white neck. I sat still on Heartbreak Ridge and observed the murmurations of starlings: there was a high-pitched sound, like a stream. They flew directly overhead – it seemed as if there were thousands of them; they just kept coming – and it felt cleansing, like some kind of natural benediction. There was something joyful and exuberant about them. Their movement and noise seemed purely for pleasure, for their own entertainment. And as I looked up, the world was in black and white, a monochrome madness that had order to it. I wandered up to the pigs, thinking about Marty, and for once the animals seemed dainty, uncertain of their footing in the frozen, corrugated ground. The breath from their pink button snouts billowed in the cold air and you could see steam rising from their backs as they bowed their heads into the troughs.

I was reading a slim book about Little Gidding, the community that had inspired Pilsdon, which had, in turn, inspired us. In it, Robert Van de Weyer wrote that if someone 'can remain loyal to the community, for all its faults, then he will eventually start to look within himself for the source of what is wrong; and when this happens he will have begun the true task of community life'. The dangerous idealist tries to bend a community to his or her will, whereas the humble one allows the community to straighten them out. I began to think that I had expended huge amounts of energy trying to improve our tiny community, to make it open and honest, whereas it would have been so much easier, and tougher, just to be open and honest myself. I thought of all the reasons I was exhausted with our guests: the indiscipline, the blaming and gossip, the intemperance, the jittery nervousness, the addictive guzzling, the incessant internet browsing . . . and I wondered whether I wasn't guilty of some of that myself. There might have been a difference of degree, but we were all on the same spectrum. I saw myself as the source of what wasn't working. It wasn't a pleasing revelation, but it meant I could do something about it. In one way I was back in control, only in control of far less than I had thought.

I sat in one of the torn armchairs by the fire and told people how I felt. At first they were alarmed, I think: concerned that I was resigning, that my dynamo had given up and that I, like many people before me, was going to give up on them.

'You do look dish evil,' said Jenny, trying to be helpful.

'You what?'

'Physically,' she explained, 'you do look dish evil.'

'Dishevelled,' Gerald said gently.

'Exactly.' Jenny nodded.

The change in everyone was uplifting. Gerald, for all his apparent remoteness, sat down in another of the sagging armchairs and just listened. I had never seen him like this: in charge, offering counsel and kindness. I slowly realized that maybe his aloofness wasn't snootiness, as some people thought, but awkwardness at his position. He was embarrassed at being a recipient of generosity and now relished the idea of offering it. Jenny made me tea, told me to put my feet up and said she would do my cooking for the next few weeks. Ben, too, reckoned I should take it easy, and joked that he could be in charge for a while.

'What happens to us in the depths of the wood?' Hilary Mantel once wrote, talking about fairy tales:

Civilization and its discontents give way to the irrational and half-seen. Back in the village, with our soured relationships, we are neurotic, but the wood releases our full-blown madness. Birds and animals talk to us, departed souls speak. The tiny rush-light of the cottages is only a fading memory. Lost in the extinguishing darkness, we cannot see our hand before our face. We lose all sense of our body's boundaries. We melt into the trees, into the bark and the sap. From this green blood we draw new life, and are healed.

I felt as if I had gone deep into the metaphorical woods of ancient stories. I hadn't found the missing part of myself, as story theorists suggest happens; I had lost something. I wasn't sure what I had lost, whether it was control, or my need for control. Had I lost my temper, or finally got rid of it altogether? But I felt lighter at last. I felt as if I had put my family in the line of fire, but that they were safe. I was still completely committed but had also given up. I felt empty, but fulfilled.

It's late January again and the chickens are reluctant to come out of their coop in the morning. They don't trust the unfamiliar white ramp with its two inches of snow. Only the cockerel flies out as you open the door. All the colours have disappeared, and the woods are in black and white. There's no grass, no gravel; there are no flowers, only the meandering footprints of the wild-life in the snow. It's quieter too, strangely still. The kids make a snowman and one of the guys here turns him into a portly dude, with shades, carrot cigar and stick arms raised to the sky as if he's acclaiming some club anthem.

'How many for lunch?' someone shouts from the kitchen.

No one ever knows. The numbers change every day. Someone

goes shopping to Boots and never comes back. Trev, a rough sleeper from outside Wells, walks over for a warm meal and a hot shower. Eve rolls up with a dog. Someone else goes AWOL. We never know how many to lay for, so instinctively put out a couple of extra places. When you're cooking for ten anyway, one or two more doesn't make life too difficult.

The long table in the garden room was the most important part of the whole site. It was our symbol of hospitality. As someone at the Open Door Community once said, 'Justice is important, but supper is essential.' It was here that we shared all our meals, where we had our meetings, where the children did their homework and where many painful, profound discussions took place. Christine Pohl wrote in *Making Room* that there's a 'profoundly egalitarian dimension' to mealtimes; it's then that 'hospitality looks least like social services'.

So we had always considered our table the central metaphor of our woodland sanctuary. But we were using the one Fra and I had bought just for ourselves when we were first married – and we now needed to seat a dozen people. It was so narrow that you had to stagger the plates along either side, and it was only long enough because two leaves came out from under the main slab. They were never very solid and wobbled and dipped if you ever leaned on them with elbows or forearms. It had been a long-cherished dream to make a huge, sturdy table, something that would express solidity, stability and welcome. By now we were all becoming pretty competent woodworkers, but none of us had the confidence to attempt such a big task.

It was eerie how often someone arrived just as we needed them. Henry was an old friend of one of our residents and lived nearby. He had come round for a few volunteer days, equipped with all the latest tools and gadgets, and could turn his hand to almost any kind of carpentry. One evening he invited me round to his workshop a couple of miles away and I was overcome with envy: he had fifty or sixty chisels on magnetic strips, a whole wall of those tiny Ikea boxes, all carefully labelled. Everything was shiny, sharp, oiled and in place. He had a bespoke lathe, thicknessers, bandsaws, even a whole library about woodwork in the room next door.

'We need you to help us make a table,' I said, surprising myself with the bluntness of the request.

Henry nodded slowly. He had just had a career change, leaving a high-flying job in London to become a serious carpenter. He didn't need much persuasion.

None of our trees was mature enough to make a table three or four feet wide, so Henry and I went over to Interesting Timbers, a huge barn stacked high with every timber imaginable, all the planks spaced with slim batons to help them season. We enjoyed the sight and smell of the sawdust and all those trunks, slabs and planks, and climbed up on to stacks, pulling out anything with a strong grain. We looked at ash, oak and cherry, but in the end we bought three twelve-foot planks of sweet chestnut.

Together we designed a refectory table, one of those old-fashioned things with a trestle at each end and a long stretcher between the two. It was going to be ten foot by almost four and held together solely by pegs. We decided to use one of our own ash poles as the stretcher and involve all the guests in the construction process.

Over the next few weeks the table began to take shape. Henry and Eve cut one of the planks into the two trestles, giving each one wide feet from the offcuts. We decided to leave hints of bark on the other two planks and glued them together so that they were a mirror image of each other, the knots, bark and grain on one side reflected on the other. Once we had planed and sanded the join, you could barely see it. The trestles slid into two parallel runners on the underside of the table, held in place by pegs we made on the lathe. Each part of the process took many days, but it began to make sense. Henry had it all in his head, and the rest of us just followed orders. Everyone joined in: Ben and Jenny sanded all the surfaces for days, smoothing the edges and going back and forth with ever finer sandpaper. It was one of the first times Ben said something positive to me.

'I like this,' he said. 'Feel that, that's beautiful that is.'

He could work away without interruption, without someone telling him he was getting it wrong. He kept looking at the wood, feeling it and sensing how he had improved it. The tabletop now felt as smooth as cut marble, but warmer, more tactile.

I kept turning pegs on which we carved 'WHW', the abbreviation we now used for Windsor Hill Wood. The two 'W's were inside the top and bottom spaces of the H. I felled a sturdy ash tree, cut it to length and then chiselled away at both ends to make long tenons – the projecting end pieces of wood – which were supposed to slide through the mortices on the trestles. Henry was a perfectionist, never allowing any of us to be content with shoddy work. If the tenon didn't fit perfectly, my instinct was to reach for a bigger mallet and make it go in, but Henry would look over his glasses and tell me to be patient and methodical. Our carpentry sessions with him were like that: calming, but also instructive. You couldn't cut corners. You had to keep shaving off an almost transparent wafer of wood and then offer up the heavy trestle to the slimmed-down tenon. No go, so heave that trestle back off again, reach for the chisel, tickle it on the stone to keep it sharp, shave off another wafer and offer up the trestle again. And again, and again. It was slow, repetitive work, with the quiet chatter of Jenny, Henry and Ben in the background. When you made a mistake, Henry looked at what you'd done closely and evaluated it, and talked through what a loose joint might mean for strength or aesthetics. If it was a bad mistake, he would reassure everyone that this material was only firewood with aspirations. If it couldn't be part of the table, he said, at least it would keep us warm.

Each time we thought the wood was sufficiently sanded, Henry would insist it needed another going over. Days went by, and he still wasn't happy. It was like a walk in which the finish line keeps receding into the distance. But, finally, it was done. Fra gave it half a dozen coats of Danish oil, so the whitish wood turned a beautiful pale yellow. Then we finished it off with beeswax from our hives, thinned with a bit of turps. It looked pretty sensational, but we still hadn't put it together. All the bits were in various corners of Henry's workshop, and we had just assumed it would fit together. So we gingerly strapped everything on to the back of the pick-up, placing dust sheets and offcuts of carpets between the parts. The table was so long it went far in front of the cab.

But there was a problem. I'm always short of money and I hadn't filled up. The needle of the fuel gauge didn't move when I twisted the key in the ignition, but it was only a mile and I assumed we could make it. We didn't. The pick-up gave up just short of the house. Everyone gathered round to laugh and offload the parts of the table. It was a nervous time, assembling something that had never before been put together, and doing it all upside down. The stretcher went into the two trestles, which slid into their parallel runners on the underside of the table. Wedge-shaped pegs then kept the stretcher in place and the trestles rigid. Other pegs held the trestles in their runners; it just needed a couple of gentle taps from the mallet to hold everything together.

We turned it the right way up. The table was rock solid. We leaned on it, and pushed it, but it didn't budge. It looked huge. It was perfect for that space and for the ten-foot pew against the brick wall. It would, at a push, seat sixteen. For a long time we just stood around admiring it, ducking underneath to check bits we'd worked on or to compliment each other. Ben had a broad smile and was shaking his head.

'I didn't think we was ever going to get it finished,' he said happily.

'Didn't think it was ever going to get here without diesel in the tank,' Jenny said.

Benny and Emma were running their hands over the smooth surface and asking questions like why hadn't we taken off the bark, and why was it so big.

Over the next few years, the table evolved. I was concerned I would become absurdly protective about any stains or cuts but actually I enjoyed seeing how it changed: apart from going darker year by year, turning from yellowy-beige to sunset and beyond, it got cuts from where someone had stabbed it to get attention, stains where Jenny had spilt elderberry jelly, dents where Leo had bashed his metal cars. The girls used felt tips that went through the paper. Some of the beautiful bark fell off, and a longitudinal crack appeared in the ash stretcher as it dried out. It became a table that heard, and told, many stories.

Lee was a man in his forties with thick grey hair. He was under five foot tall and had severe learning difficulties. Physically, he wasn't quite right: his fingers had no middle joints, so he couldn't bend them, and his head was a slightly unorthodox shape. He was a noisy presence, a pathological attention-seeker. If he wasn't involved in a conversation he would interrupt or start doing something so daft that you would have to turn to him and deal with it immediately. He would light a newspaper in the middle of the room just to watch the flames, or play with the crook knives on his severely scarred forearms. He was from Manchester, and usually wore a coat or hat with the Man City logo. His accent was thick, and his standard phrase – which he repeated all day, and which always made us smile – was 'Were all right.' It was a line that seemed to express an indifferent shoulder-shrug, a reluctance ever to become enthusiastic. Sometimes the voice lowered at the end of the phrase, to suggest that something was below average; sometimes, rarely, the voice went up, to suggest it was just above average.

'How was that film you watched, Lee?'

'Were all right.'

'Did you like the pizza?'

'Were all right.'

'How were the pigs when you fed them?'

'Were all right.'

He seemed like a young boy to us. He was one of those people who had, presumably, been badly bullied as a youngster and now, in adulthood, had been so keen for approval that he'd been easily led astray and egged on by dodgy mates. He was an alcoholic but didn't really want to stop. He had only come to us because his gruff, exasperated father had sent him here, and Lee was now going through the motions. During one toe-curling meal he told us how much he missed his Special Brew and his laptop porn.

'What's porn, Daddy?' Benny asked. She always seemed to know when there was a subject that made people feel awkward and she would want to know why straight away.

Five-year-old Emma had heard talk of the laptop and wanted to show off her knowledge of computers. 'Is it to do with the inter-neck?' she asked, and everyone laughed at her malapropism.

'I suppose porn is kind of "internecking", isn't it?' Gerald said quickly. We laughed again, and left it at that.

The kids were constantly exposed to everything and, in a way, we were pleased. They heard stories about prison, war, drugs, death, divorce and everything else. One time, a guy was telling us about a book idea that had come to him in prison and Benny interrupted.

'You've been in prison?' she asked, wide-eyed.

'Yes, I was a bit of a naughty boy.'

'Cool,' she said, looking at him in a new light. You could tell she liked him more.

Encouraging our children to be accepting and non-judge-mental like that had always been one of the aims of this place. We were happy to have them surrounded by people who were born on, or had consciously moved to, the wrong side of the tracks. They were surrounded by conversations about all sorts of topics, and almost nothing was off limits. I realized, one day, how many adults we'd had discussing love, politics and religion around the table when seven-year-old Benny, her hair in bunches, stood up on the pew behind the new table to make an announcement.

'Everybody! Everybody!' she said, trying to get attention. 'I just want you to know that I'm a lesbian anarchist atheist.' She beamed and sat down again.

'What does that mean, exactly?' Gerald asked.

She giggled, and clearly had only a rough grasp on the concepts. But she had absorbed them somehow.

It wasn't always easy. Quite often one of the children would dash upstairs and we would follow, trying to work out what was wrong.

'Lee said,' Emma wailed once, 'that he wanted to give me a slap.'

So we reassured her, saying it would never happen, and that she was completely safe. Then I would go off to find Lee and explain to him how sensitive people could be.

Another time I followed Benny upstairs. She was more confused than upset.

'Dad, what does "psychologically dangerous" mean?' she asked.

'Why?'

'Lee told me he's psychologically dangerous.'

'Did he? What do you think it means?'

Her definition came pretty close, and once we had had a hug and I had given her a bit of reassurance, I headed off again to find Lee and tell him he was on his last chance.

There was nothing nasty about Lee; he was simply colossally tactless. He would say things that made the kids feel threatened or unwanted. One weekend he told them he was looking forward to Monday when they would be back at school and there would be some peace around the place. Benny went quiet and Emma shot upstairs again. That was the one thing that was guaranteed to press our buttons: when our kids were feeling excluded or pushed out from their own family home. It took a lot of energy to make them feel it was, first and foremost, their place, and that they were allowed to say if they were hurt or upset. It helped that we could slip into Italian when we needed to say something private to each other amidst all the noise; and it helped too that the majority of guests loved the kids and relished playing with them. In fact, they suffered more than we did from becoming close to guests who then left after a few months. Many times I had to explain to the kids that someone had gone AWOL, or hadn't come back from their weekend away as expected – and they would quietly cry, and pretend it didn't matter. That transience – the constant attachments and detachments – must have been really hard for them, especially as I assumed they might sometimes have wondered whether I too would fail to come back after a work assignment somewhere. I got into the habit of telling them, before I left, that I always came home. They would nod, listening, knowing they had to agree, yet I wasn't sure whether they truly believed me. Perhaps every child has that fear of parental abandonment, but our children's anxiety had a twist of experience to it. Their world was less reliable or trustworthy than it could have been, and they were struggling with loss and severance, both planned and unexpected.

Despite this, they were, on the whole, energetic, noisy, giggling children. They were part of the informal therapy. Most of our guests had struggled with turbulent or tragic childhoods, and when they got here many of them wanted to regress and be youngsters again. It was as if they needed to return to childishness to find, in time, a more measured maturity. I would often come in from an afternoon's writing to see a couple of grown men giggling as they blew bubbles with Leo, or concentrating as they did French knitting with the girls. There was no wall between the playroom and the kitchen, and there was always someone in the kitchen keeping an eye on things. It was at such moments that you glimpsed how this place worked, how everyone benefited from communal life: we were relaxed because someone was giving us a break from playing with the children; the kids were relishing wrapping these tough-looking men round their little fingers; the guests were happy because they could finally make candles, or play with clay, or bounce on the trampoline. The adults could be kids, and the kids could boss them around. Everyone got something out of the arrangement.

There were those, though, who weren't drawn to children. I

almost envied the detachment some guests had, their ability to breeze past the kids without getting drawn in. One morning I saw Emma rushing up to Maggie Purple with a snowball.

'I'm going to get Maggie,' she shouted, running towards her. Maggie was carrying food out to the chickens and was walking towards the coops. Little Emma slipped on the snow and fell hard on her bum. Maggie looked at her on the snow and walked past without breaking her stride.

'That's karma, that is,' she said, smiling.

The kids struggled to be heard sometimes, which only made them louder, which made me plead with them to quieten down. The level of noise around the place was one of the things I continued to struggle with. Fra and I realized we needed to accommodate the kids more at mealtimes, to listen to them and allow them, as much as everyone else, to hold court. Very often conversations were flying over their heads, so one day in late February I asked them what they most wanted to talk about.

'We want to talk about wee and poo,' Emma said, putting on her baby voice. She and Benny giggled, and reiterated the point.

'Are you sure?' I asked. 'You've got all these interesting people who could tell you about life, and you want to talk about wee and poo?'

'Yes, definitely.' Benny liked the control she had been given and wasn't going to give it back now. 'Right, everyone, who's got a good story about wee or poo?'

We glanced at each other across the table. Ryan, a man going through a messy divorce, caught my eye and looked as if he were asking permission to tell a lavatorial story. He had been with us a few weeks.

I shrugged and nodded.

'I don't know if I should really say this . . .'

'Don't worry about it,' Benny butted in, 'we've been badly brought up.' Everyone laughed at that, and Ryan was off.

'Do you know what a warm pocket is?'

The girls were wide-eyed now. They shook their heads.

'Well, I was studying in Liverpool in the eighties and I used to go to watch the football at Anfield in a student's overcoat. I had long hair and a long scarf. I looked a bit strangely dressed, a bit weird. So a couple of the rougher people in the terraces gave me a warm pocket.'

'So what is it?' everyone asked.

'Well, two men stood either side of me, put their cocks in my overcoat, and weed in each pocket.'

The girls giggled hysterically at the idea of adults pissing in a man's pocket. And Ryan smiled, shaking his head at the memory.

'When I was in France,' Gerald said, 'I was living on the fourth floor of this flat. One morning the landlord banged on the door, absolutely furious, and accused me of pissing off the balcony and into a convertible car down below. I had a heavy head from a night's big session and wasn't in the best of moods. I was outraged, thought it was a ridiculous accusation. But then, whilst I was talking to him and denying everything, I remembered snippets from the night before, and caught a memory of a beautiful jet of urine hitting that open-top car, and I realized it was me. I kept denying it, but he knew, and kicked me out that day.'

'Dad,' Benny shouted, 'can we wee out of our bedroom window?'

'Please, Daddy.' Emma seemed to think it might be a possibility.

From then on, it became an unusual tradition that the girls would ask any new guest if they had any amusing wee or poo stories. We now had an application form and took two references – I had got over my reluctance to ask probing questions, and thought that tough questions did more good than harm – but listening to those lavatorial stories sometimes gave us as good an insight into who a guest was as any answer they gave on that application form.

We were, as the girls had learned, in some ways a transient community: some guests stayed for a year, but nobody hung around permanently. However far down the line we were in terms of the creation of norms and infrastructure, we were often going back to the beginning and working through the whole process again: forming, storming, and so on. Each time a new guest arrived we got better at accompanying them through the typical stages of enchantment, disenchantment and realism. Whenever anyone left we had a big party, with lots of food and cakes and presents. Even those who had to be asked to leave had a farewell party. It had become a tradition that I wrote a nonsense poem, recounting all the funny things they had done since they had been with us – both the bizarre and the wonderful. It was a light way of reminding them what they had learned, and how they might have changed. In many ways we never knew who our successes were, never knew whether we had touched some-one or simply failed them. And it was always hard to judge the right departure time. Nobody wanted to leave, but we could often sense that after four or five months, which was the average stay now, they were beginning to resent the claustrophobia of a container that had previously felt cradling. It often felt as if our guests were maturing teenagers, desperate to leave but scared to do so.

Some people we never heard from again, but many decided to stay in the area, as if we were now their parents and this place their home from home. They would still come up for volunteer day, or for the odd meal through the week. Quite a few ended up getting jobs locally, working with friends of friends. Having that local diaspora of 'graduates' anchored us as well as them. It meant that new arrivals were reassured by old hands who had survived the intensity and conflicts of this place, and who even missed it now they were gone. They would roll up out of the blue and talk fondly of the 'old days' and how it used to be here 'back in the day', meaning six months ago. They would wander around, proudly telling anyone who would listen that they had planted this tree, or made that stool, or whatever. They had changed this place, they were rightly saying, as much as it had changed them. They would make suggestions. They were now offering support as well as receiving succour, giving our woodland community continuity and stability. And it meant the children weren't bereft of their extended family but still surrounded by their many uncles and aunts.

The thing that stopped the community feeling forever impermanent and ever-changing were all those volunteers, 'outpatients', well-wishers and respite visitors who came every Wednesday, or for long weekends, or week-long retreats. It would have been a slightly sad, sedate place without them, because they refreshed things, turning guests into hosts. Someone who had been feeling an outsider could suddenly be the insider, the person who offered tea and a tour. When they had been once, those visitors would come repeatedly, either once a week or, quite often, every other day. You didn't really know why they wanted to spend their days here and, as they weren't residential guests, we didn't necessarily ask. But all those visitors had the effect of making this a dynamic, rather than a dour place. They enlivened the house with banter and laughter and a new energy.

* * *

We had a dozen Petes: Recovery Pete, Little Pete, Pruning Pete, Poppy Pete, Mad Pete, Old Pete. Recovery Pete got his nickname because he was an evangelist for recovery. He was a tall man who had been a corporate high-flier and high-functioning coke fiend for twenty years. He would tell us stories about blackouts where he had woken up in some Scandinavian city without a clue how he had got there. I remember, the first time he came round we were doing the fencing. I was slamming the massive post rammer down on some fencing posts. He looked at it and smiled ruefully.

'Last time I saw one of those,' he said, 'the police were using it to bang down my front door.'

He told us the story of getting busted and getting clean, about making amends with his children and his family. He spoke about recovery the way an evangelist talks Jesus, or a fanatic talks footy. It was always on his mind. He couldn't get enough of it. He told us about going to NA, AA, CA, MA, SLA, DA, Al-Anon, and all the others.

'You should go to Anonymous Anonymous,' one of our other guests joked.

Missionary zeal, of course, is step twelve, the idea that one should 'carry this message' to others suffering the same malady. To keep it, as they say, you've got to give it away. Preaching sobriety helps keep people sober. Pete liked coming here as we had a constant stream of people in the early stages of recovery who needed help and support, and he was incredibly giving. He would drive down from Cardiff at the drop of a hat just to have a chat with someone.

Little Pete had come on an open day one time and had been coming back every other day ever since. Tall and skinny, he had a thin face and hair that had zig-zags shaved into the sides. He was the sort of lad who could do it all: angle grinder, chop-saw, engines, pigs. He always felt he should earn his tea, so I would send him off to do the jobs that had been avoided or forgotten. The kids adored him, shouting 'Pete, Pete!' as his motorbike roared into the woods. It looked like he was sitting on a sewing machine and it was so noisy you could normally hear him a good thirty seconds before you saw him.

Clive was another frequent visitor. A big eccentric man with longish curly hair, there was something about the way he dressed that told you he was offbeat: in his red trilby and yellow water-proof dungarees he looked like a children's TV presenter. He had a past as colourful as his clothes. He was an endearing combina-tion: strong but also quite fragile. There were plenty of others: Trish, Jeff, Sheila, Frank.

We finally found, too, a residential volunteer. I had received an email from a seeker called Gav who said he had given away his worldly possessions because he wanted to live only day to day and discover what love and compassion really meant. Despite that idealism, the email sounded grounded. He had worked on sailing ships for recovering addicts and troubled schoolchildren and he could turn his hand, he said, to almost anything. All he needed was a bit of time off now and again to see his girlfriend.

He wanted to come and volunteer, so we invited him down for a few weeks. He arrived soon after, having hitched a few hundred miles. He was tall and thin, with a large rucksack and an obvi-ously hand-knitted beanie on his head. Gav was loud, energetic and enthusiastic. He had a quick mug of tea and then asked what needed doing.

'We need to split and stack that pile of logs outside the right-hand log store,' I said, passing the axe to him from inside the workshop.

The idyllic sound of log-splitting filled the place. You can usually tell, just by listening, whether someone knows what they're doing and with Gav there was a regular smack of the axe on the block and the sound of wood fibres being cleft.

'What next?' he asked after half an hour. He was barely sweating.

'Have you finished the logs?' I asked doubtfully.

'Yeah, no worries.'

I peered over his shoulder up to the log stores and saw the pile, split evenly and beautifully stacked.

'Do you want a cuppa?'

'I'll crack on.'

I sneaked a peek in the workshop and he had already put the axe back where I'd got it from.

Every job I gave him was done speedily but carefully. He re-handled the froe, sharpened the chisels, fitted a fire alarm, replaced washers, laid the table.

We no longer worried that the problems with the neighbour were our fault. Dave, the car mechanic in town, told us that he used to live here twenty years ago and described Barry's bonkers abuse back then. Another man we met said that Barry had set his dogs on him. A woman we knew described him as a rural outlaw. Every local who came up here had a story about having been chased by him with a shotgun, or his swearing at them in the supermarket. Most tellingly, we were told that he used different names. He was, it was clear to everyone and, finally, to us, simply a very nasty piece of work, a complete wrong 'un. We nicknamed him Happy, after one of the dwarfs in *Snow White*, and began swapping stories about the latest absurdity by the sad, angry man next door. It was still unpleasant as the harassment continued, but it had a curious side effect on our community. Many people think that a community needs a common enemy to bring it together, to act as an external adversary. And often the slightly more unhinged communities demonize the outside world in return for cohesion and commitment. We never wanted such an enemy, but we did find that Happy brought us together and made us more determined to confront hatred with peace. He even provided us with a few laughs. The next time he tried to pick a fight with one of our volunteers, he chose the wrong man, squaring up to Scrap-metal Mark, who had been a boxer in the army and knew how to stand his ground. Barry had been put in his place not just by Mark but by Fra. Barry had pushed her too far, and once Fra blows, boy, she really blows. I watched her by the gate, her face taut and white, as she gave him both barrels.

'This is our family home,' she said, bouncing her index finger towards the ground, 'so don't ever trespass here again. Don't threaten us, don't harass us, don't intimidate us.'

Barry, the bully, was leaning backwards, surprised by the sudden and explosive indignation of his Italian neighbour.

Financially, too, things were far easier. We were receiving small donations quite regularly and occasionally big ones too. With one grant we had managed to buy a second shepherd's hut, meaning that the battered yurt, like an Old Testament tabernacle, now became our chapel. I was no longer subsidizing everything. One of our *consiglieri* acted as a treasurer, meaning that we could ask someone external to decide where the boundary was in that grey area between the community and the family. Francesca and I were going to supervision with a counsellor every month or two, allowing us to offload the frustrations and anxieties that went with running the community. We weren't exactly freewheeling, but it did feel as if the learning curve was finally levelling out.

The other thing that made a huge difference that spring was

the fact that on the advice of our *consiglieri*, we closed for a week. I had been opposed to the idea, arguing that hospitals don't ever close their doors; I also feared, I think, that if we shut people would never come back. But we accepted their counsel and for the first time in almost three years we had the place to ourselves. Guests went off to Pilsdon, or back to their parents or spouses, or into hostels. It was an extraordinary experience: the site felt strangely deserted, like a college outside term time. It reminded me of what it's like on those rare occasions when someone looks after the kids for a weekend. You can't believe how much time you have, how easy it is to walk from one room to the next. It was relaxing but hard work too, because we suddenly had to do every-thing ourselves – all the animals, all the logs, all the cooking. It was good to be reminded how much help we normally had. From then on, every nine months or so we would close up for a week and all have a short break from each other. Guests would return reinvigorated and, perhaps, more appreciative, and we, chilled and happy, were pleased to see them back.

We had become wary of parents asking us to look after their trou-bled children. It usually meant that they couldn't be bothered and saw us as a cheap option. Tom's parents were different, however. They both brought him down; they asked intelligent, concerned questions; they almost didn't want to leave him. They gave us their phone numbers and email addresses and urged us to contact them whenever we needed. They seemed, for once, like proper parents, the sort who were here because it offered their child something positive, not because it offered them a break.

Tom was a teenager from Birmingham who had been diagnosed as bipolar and was on heavy medication, including lithium. It made him lethargic and a bit chubby, the one condition exacerbating the other. He would sit in the armchair for hours on end, sometimes giggling at things on his phone but more usually staring out of the window. If you asked him to do something he would moan and groan a bit and stay where he was for half an hour. It often seemed like he was in a bit of a daze: he would stand in the middle of the garden room, scratching his stomach and asking, 'Where's the milk?' One of us would point to the rectangular white thing in the corner of the room and affectionately raise our eyebrows. The illness had knocked him sideways; and in the months before coming here he had been manic, then hospitalized, and later pursued by the police when he went on the run. His studies had been disrupted during his GCSEs and the guy was at a loss.

It took only a few weeks for Tom to become part of the place. We asked him to look after the pigs, and he faithfully fed them, gave them clean water and straw and everything else. The pigs were often the perfect animals for those down on their luck: big enough to seem serious, silent enough to keep secrets. He started cooking remarkably sophisticated meals, working all afternoon and following the recipe to the letter. But he was still at that age where he expected to be served, so he would prepare great food but then leave it all on the hob and go and sit down at the table, waiting for someone to bring it through.

'Tom,' Gav said, 'where's the grub?'

'In the kitchen.'

'Go get it then.' Gav laughed. There was something so amiable in Gav's manner that he could jockey people along without ever upsetting them. 'Part of the service is serving, right?'

'Suppose so,' said Tom, as he ambled back to the kitchen.

Tom used to make us laugh a lot. Being a teenager, he sniggered at every innuendo he could find – and he could find them anywhere. He was the master of the unsophisticated double entendre. But he also made us laugh because he came up with hilarious ideas that he thought were serious propositions.

'Did you ever hear,' he asked in his thick Brummie accent one evening, 'about that chicken whose head was chopped off in the US in the forties?'

'There must have been a few,' Ben said drolly, not looking up from his food.

'This one was called Mike, right?' Tom pushed on. 'His head was chopped off, but he lived for another year and a half. They went on tour with him.'

'Mike the headless chicken?' Benny asked, looking doubtful.

'Yeah, right,' someone else said.

'It's a true story,' Tom insisted. 'I reckon we could do something similar here as a fundraising exercise. Try chopping the heads off our chickens until one survives, then take it on tour as a circus attraction, like they used to in the old days. Make a bit of money for this place.'

'Can you imagine the reaction of the local farming community?' I said. 'They already think we're pretty wacky – and then they find out we've been beheading our chickens to make money in a circus?'

We were laughing now, not just at the idea of Mike the headless American chicken but more at the thought that Tom genuinely wanted us to hack through our beloved flock until one pulled through and became famous. And the more he asked, very seriously, if we could do it, the more we laughed, unable to believe he really meant it. The great thing about Tom, though, was that he never took offence. He loved it, loved making us laugh with outlandish ideas. That's why he quickly felt like part of the group. The more he made us laugh, the more we seemed bonded by the amusement.

But he would often have his low moments and you got glimpses of quite how doped up he was. He had so much medication to take each day that we set aside a whole drawer for his pills. He would put them in his palm – long ones, purple ones, round ones – and knock them back without water. I don't know if it was those pills, or his character, or his illness, but he was often pretty obtuse. I watched him having a conversation with Fra once.

'Where's the timer for the oven?' Tom asked.

'First left,' Fra said.

Tom's index finger emerged from his pocket and pointed at the row of buttons on the front of the cooker. It went from right to left and back to the right before hovering over the second right.

'First left,' Fra repeated, smiling.

The index finger went back to first right.

'First left.'

The finger travelled back to the left, then hovered over the second left.

'First left.'

He was the most lethargic washer-upper in the West, and there would be no hot water left once he had slowly washed, and slowly rinsed, every item under a running tap. During cleaning hour Tom would stand outside trying to shake the rug. But he did it so ineffec-tually that nothing happened – no shavings or dust left the thing.

'Hang it from that branch and give it a decent thwack,' Gav shouted.

It took Tom five minutes to position it where he wanted, and then he hit it so weakly that again nothing emerged. He might as well have tickled it.

But that was Tom. Once he had been here a few weeks we could tease him about how dopey he was, and about how much he expected everyone else to serve him.

'Is there any toast?' he shouted from the door.

'There is if you slice some bread and put it in the toaster,' Gav replied with a laugh.

'But I've got dirty boots on.'

'Take them off then.'

'Oh.' By now the double doors had been open for a minute or two, and the warmth of the room was dissipating as Tom sighed and groaned, sitting on the bench outside to take off his boots and complaining that there was ice on the bench and his bum was getting wet.

'Are there any mugs?'

'In the usual place.'

'Where's that?'

'The dresser.'

'Where's the milk?'

'Same place it was last time, you lemon.'

One night Ben came up to me looking disgruntled. He said I had been disrespectful to him. I tried to work out what I had done wrong, but he couldn't explain it.

'You've been off with me all day,' he said.

It was perfectly possible I had done something wrong, so I asked for an example. He just repeated his impression that I had been ignoring him, so I apologized for having appeared to do so and tried to explain how many balls were in the air.

'What balls?' he said, frowning.

'Things that need doing.'

People without three children and a day job rarely understood the demands. As I explained, he grew more angry and convinced himself that I was simply making up excuses for ignoring him. Something similar happened, if not most nights, certainly every week. Part of our job here was to allow people to let off steam: we needed to receive their anger and resentment, their furies and follies. It often felt as if we were drawing out a person's poison and although we were doing it out of kindness, the poison was often aimed at us. I always knew it was healthier when they were attacking us rather than putting us on a pedestal. When we were getting it in the neck for some perceived slight, we could work with it. It meant there was something emerging other than a sense of a guest's own inadequacy. And yet, when I was under attack, it took all my reserves of patience to accept their anger and sorrow, to listen to them without retaliating, defending myself or counter-attacking. I learned how to take the attacks and to make time to examine a person's irrational responses and reactions. Once you had taken their blows once or twice they came to trust you more and, sometimes, to realize that you weren't to blame. And when I was to blame for something, which wasn't infrequent, that was somehow healthy too, an opportunity to show them that I was imperfect and foolish.

I sat down with Ben and asked who else he thought had been ignoring him. He shrugged, smiling bitterly as if it would be quicker to say who hadn't. I let him talk unprompted. He listed all the times when his sisters, with no learning difficulties, unlike him, had been taken places, or offered opportunities denied to him; listed the times his mother had dumped him on distant relatives when she went off to her holiday home in Alicante. There was a visible rage inside him, but he didn't raise his voice or swear: he just kept that same habitual scowl.

We were constantly trying to bring these things out into the open, to allow guests to lose it with us so they could verbalize their pain. Only by allowing them the space to act out could we then sit down and discuss their patterns of behaviour and their reactions to things. But it meant there was a huge amount of emotional turbulence. It was as if our ship was permanently in choppy, if not very stormy, waters. I was always attempting to put down an anchor, only for the storm to pull us adrift. And those choppy waters were never clear but mixed with Zopiclone, Prozac, diazepam and endless other prescription drugs. I was aware that some people were so fearful they couldn't bear to be corrected. 'You're shouting at me,' I was once told, when I was very quietly, if firmly, reasserting a rule. There were quite a few people who put words into your mouth, not consciously but just because that's what they were convinced had been said.

Having Gav on board made a big difference; we were learning things from each other. He always spoke his mind; he didn't let things drift or go unspoken. He cajoled and joked. Watching Gav, I realized that many people responded to his vibrant drumming and were enthused by his energy. Others, though, found that confrontational loudness hard to handle, and I could see a slightly manic side to his quest. He was probing, questioning, reading and debating, with the result that some people who needed to unwind were being wound up. He taught me to hold my nerve, and perhaps I taught him to hold his tongue.

At times it felt as if we were making no difference at all to people's lives, possibly even doing more harm than good. In other periods, though, the change we saw made everything worth it. Jenny was still entertainingly scatty, but her skin had gone from paper white to rural ruddy. She used to cry extraordinarily easily, whereas now when she cried she would smile too and laugh bashfully: 'Am I overreacting?' She could hold her own and stand up for herself. She hadn't become a different person as such; she was still a fragile creature who, after cooking, would leave the kitchen walls looking as if the lid had been left off the food processor. But her eccentricities had been absorbed and appreciated. She knew she was loved, and she had people, not just a portly Jack Russell, she could love. She had a family.

Tom, too, was changing. He had come to us a rather mollycoddled youngest child and was slowly becoming a man. He was using an axe, using knives. He was cooking meals for a dozen people. Benny adored him and called him her boyfriend, which embarrassed and delighted him. She liked cooing, 'Tommy,' and practising her flirtatious pout. He, too, had his quirks: when Baxter peed indoors once, Tom cleaned it up with a pair of his socks, shuffling across the floor with them still on his feet. Half the trees in the wood seemed to have been smeared with peanut butter in his attempt to entice squirrels into range of his air rifle. His wheezy giggles interrupted us throughout the day, and we often couldn't work out how he had managed to construe whatever had just been said as sexual. He laughed like Muttley, so we nicknamed him Smuttley. He often fell over in the snow and usually roared with laughter when he did, shouting to everyone to look at how hilarious it was that he was lying in the snow again.

'Come on, Smuttley, get up, we're trying to move these logs!' Gav shouted.

'I can't,' Tom shouted back, his legs in the air as if someone were changing his nappies. 'I've fallen over again.'

From having been stigmatized at school, Tom was now fine with his diagnosis. It was what made him Tom. What happened to people was intangible. There wasn't a programme, there weren't any steps, as such. I would often set people challenges for the week, offer counsel or opinion. But the most important element was just living together. It made a difference that we had now been running this shelter for almost three years, and had just about worked out what we were doing. We knew the importance of the blend: not having five guests that were all, say, recovering addicts or ex-offenders, but having a mix of genders, ages, skills and problems. I had overcome my reluctance to lead and would tell people pretty bluntly what was what, even if I still had to pluck up my courage to do so. Most of all, we had realized that the best way to charge a flat battery was to jump-start it and give the motor a good run. If someone was lying in bed under a duvet of self-pity, I would help them out and get them working. We were making misfits feel important; telling them to work not just for their own sake but also for ours.

There were still plenty of nasty surprises. Ben had gone home for Easter and Fra decided to clean his room. We expected guests to clean their own spaces, but usually that meant it didn't get done. So she was wiping the bedside table and noticed coffee stains dripping down over the tops of the drawers. She pulled them out to wipe them too and found a lot of magazines. It wasn't pornography but extreme sadism: photographs of breasts smeared with shit and blindfolded faces covered in blood. There was humiliation in those snaps, as if the kick the viewer got wasn't carnal pleasure but violent revenge. For a lad in his early twenties, it seemed like a peculiar fantasy, and it really worried us. Sexual deviancy was one of the things for which we were always on high alert, not just because of our children but because many of our guests had suffered sexual violence in the past. We sat down with one of our wise advisers from the next-door village and she told us to trust our instincts. Our instinct was, very clearly, that we didn't want to have Ben back.

Asking someone to leave, or in this case telling them not to come back, was by far the toughest aspect of running this woodland community. We put a lot of time into planning departures and aiming for good endings. It was obvious with Ben that throughout his life he had been abandoned, ignored, evicted or had stormed out. So we would be repeating a familiar pattern in his life, and it would cause us and him much sadness. It was made harder by the fact that it wasn't a black-and-white issue. When someone is using or boozing here, the issue is very clear. As soon as I reach for the breathalyser or drug-testing kit, the person usually owns up, apologizes and knows the score. They go and pack their bags before I even ask them to. But this was more nuanced and was a tough call to make and to justify. On our sheet of dos and don'ts, it didn't even say 'No pornography on site' (something we would quickly add), so Ben could legitimately feel he hadn't been adequately warned. And I anticipated that the other guests would suddenly feel vulnerable, taking sides with Ben because they themselves felt less secure in their situation.

What made it even harder was that I didn't trust my own judgement. When you have to ask someone you really like to leave, you know it's the right call because it goes against what you want to do. But I had struggled with Ben for months: he had been grumpy, work-shy and gluttonous. He had complained about the contribution to our common purse, which was, I thought, cheap as chips. It now emerged, as I began to ask the right questions, that his occasional trips back to Plymouth had been to visit massage parlours. I didn't much like the guy, which was why I was suspicious of my instincts. But if there was any doubt about the safety of others, I had to act.

Ben took it fairly well. He didn't really want to be with us anyway, I thought: he seemed happy that I had said he should stay in Plymouth. That's where he wanted to be. It was his mother and stepfather who wanted him here, and they were livid.

'What do you mean?' His mother sounded intransigent. 'You said you would have him. He can't stay here. No way.'

'That's his home,' I said.

'But I've got other children to think about.'

'So do I. I've three children and four other guests.'

'But he'll drink all the time.'

'Then put down rules. Become a dry house. Give up alcohol, like we've had to.'

'We can't do that. It's the only way we can unwind at night.'

She went on and on. She was keeping me away from my own kids because she was trying to persuade me to look after hers. She tried to tell me that extreme sadism was normal; that the infliction of pain and humiliation wasn't so alarming. I heard a thud upstairs and Leo started wailing. I told her I had to go and hung up.

We saw it so often: parents who couldn't cope with their kids but who became furious when we refused to be free babysitters. Quite soon afterwards we decided we had to ask Lee to leave too. In many ways he was very similar to Ben: he had severe learning difficulties, was an alcoholic and a habitual user of porn. But I was fond of him: we had a laugh and teased each other. He was so thick-skinned you could coax him without fearing that he would get angry. There was always enough cheerful banter to oil the wheels. He had a degree of self-awareness and recognized that he needed help. But he continued to upset the children with his tact-lessness. They too were pretty thick-skinned by now. The older two were used to holding their own with some pretty tough customers. But with Lee they felt as if it wasn't their home, as if they were in the way. He was someone who was always desperate for attention and they knew they couldn't compete: they didn't cut their arms or have panic attacks. His needs were simply too great and we couldn't keep him here.

Like Ben, Lee seemed fine about it, which only made it sadder. He shrugged when I told him, as if he were used to disguising pain with indifference. He did, at least, know how fond we were of him and even if his stay had been short, it had been beneficial. He had felt cherished for once.

'It were all right here,' he said, looking around one last time before getting in his father's car. 'Were more than all right.'

Ben and Lee taught us our limits: that we could offer people a refuge in a period of crisis but not a permanent housing situation for a permanent condition. We realized that we could take referrals from parents only if their children were absolutely convinced they themselves wanted to be here.

But we still felt guilt at not being able to do more. Especially when, a month later, we received an email from Lee's father. Lee had died in his sleep. His father didn't say if alcohol or drugs were involved, but it didn't matter. I tried to picture Lee as I remembered him: short, ebullient, very much a Mancunian. His grey hair seemed odd on someone who came across like a little boy. He was always joking and jostling for attention. It seemed unbelievable that he had gone.

The forest floor is colourful again. There are primroses scattered around, their pale yellow flowers emerging from the centre of those rubbery leaves. Bluebells sway on elastic stems, making the purple pool appear to shimmer and ripple in the April breeze. Ramson – wild garlic – is sprouting all over the bank on the far side of the woods, those pointed oval leaves giving off a memorable whiff. The nettles, only ankle high, are just beginning their ascent. And, above, the trees exude gentle grandeur. The branches of the goat willow are full of powdery yellow pollen again and it's impossible to walk past without getting a dusting of gilt. The hawthorns seem bushy and tangled, that gunmetal-grey bark becoming pocked and rugged with age. The oaks are regal but smaller, their silhouettes against the sky appearing full of bumps and nodules.

Whenever there was a problem with someone, I would invariably take them for a walk. It was helpful to have a chat under the canopy, where we were dwarfed by trees. They put everything in context. The lyrical John Stewart Collis wrote in *The Worm Forgives the Plough* that when you've entered the wood 'you have really gone through a gate which is now closed behind you, and your ordinary world is shut out with all its noise and sorrow and care. Once inside, you seem to have stepped out of the flow of civilized time and to have entered into the peace of the ever-juvenile eternities of earth.' He wrote about the possibility of 'side-stepping' into happiness in the woods.

Everything in forestry is long term, measured in years and generations rather than in weeks or months. Some of our most erratic visitors were those who wanted everything right now: there was no gap between impulse and action, between desire and satisfaction. If they asked a question, they wanted an answer, and the right answer, right now. But in farming, as Wendell Berry wrote, 'limits are imposed upon haste by nature.' Trees, especially, are in no hurry. They have an indifference to the bustle and scurry in the undergrowth, aiming only upwards for the light. Nothing can be bounced by impetuous demands. There's a timelessness to this place that makes freneticism appear a bit absurd. It feels as if here you can finally shrug off the rush of modernity. Instead of feeling behind the times, or not where it's at, trees give you the feeling of being in exactly the right place. When you're sitting on that fallen trunk, which seems perfectly shaped as a seat, watching a robin watching you, there's a certainty that you're meant to be here, right now. You've been received and accepted by nature. Even the deer over there is acknowledging you, appreciating your slow-learned stillness.

That is what some of us felt here: a deep sense of belonging and bonding. And when I sat there with guests, they felt it too. There were still mobiles and laptops and cars around, but there were places in the woods to which you could retreat. They weren't tranquil or peaceful places: you only had to sit for a few seconds to hear the death drone of a fly as a spider killed it, or see a buzzard swoop on a field mouse, or glimpse a squirrel ring-bark a sycamore branch that would now die even more slowly than that flapping fly.

The woods can be a spooky place. It's like a horror movie sometimes, not just because of the dark but because there's an old railway tunnel here that's so long you can't even see the light at the end of it. It gets your pulse going; you know you're alive because you're seeing darkness and death. You can barely see the sky, and the seclusion, if not the claustrophobia, renders you twitchy. It always feels eerie here amidst the shadows of the trees and you're forced to confront your fears. This is a place to meditate on darkness rather than run away from it.

One of the great struggles for people here isn't the work, it's the stillness. Far more of our guests work too hard than not enough. They bustle all day, doing little tasks, anything to keep on the move. They tell me how much they've done, and I express gratitude. But I often ask whether they've sat down and confronted any fears. Have they sat in the woods at dusk? This was a place to take off the bandages, to remove the paper that covered the cracks. Back at the beginning – it seems a lifetime ago – I used to think that we were here to live alongside people and help them emerge from a crisis in their lives. But now, we've realized that what's hardest is simply to admit there is a crisis, to acknowledge it and sit with it. And what actually happens is that we unwittingly give our guests a whole series of additional mini-crises: the death of a runt piglet, a week without heating, a fox's slaughter of the whole flock of chickens, the painful expulsion of a guest, the personality clashes that build into loud rows or silent feuds. It would be wonderful if we could erase crisis from our guests' lives, but what we often appear to be doing is unintentionally presenting them with lots of additional little traumas and, hopefully, giving them the patience and perseverance to survive them. Perhaps that's all we manage to do: teach survival and resilience so that those bigger and more serious problems can be faced with courage and experience. I would love to say it's all healing here, that we cure and make whole. But more often than not we don't get much further than acceptance, recognition, even resignation. We just sit still in the woods and confess where we're at.

Year Four

'Men are free when they belong to a living, organic, believing community, active in fulfilling some unful-filled, perhaps unrealized purpose. Not when they are escaping to some wild west. The most unfree souls go west, and shout of freedom'

– D. H. Lawrence

It's autumn again, and the sun rarely gets above the treetops. It's filtered through the lace of bare branches. The trees are wearing their waistcoats of ivy and the place feels forlorn and dank. The birds are visible again, throwing beech leaves like Frisbees from their beaks, spinning them away in the search for food. Thirty or forty rooks descend en masse, shrieking and squawking as they come to steal the chickens' food. You can see isolated pheasants again, with their red goggles and narrow, white dog collars. Their bodies are the shape of an old-fashioned wine flask, their long tail feathers like an artist's quick brush-stroke, unfeasibly slim. One stands erect and squawks now, telling the world he's here. It feels cold but cosy once more: there are candles on tables, and the site smells of woodsmoke. In the house, there are hundreds of ladybirds, taking refuge in the warmth. The colourful infestation delights the children, who go around trying to entice the tiny creatures on to their palms.

The children picked up on everything that happened around them. They were like sponges, absorbing their surroundings, mimicking sounds and copying behaviours. It meant that we often glimpsed, through them, things we hadn't even noticed yet.

A young woman called Chloe had come to live with us. She had endured sexual abuse as a child and was an anorexic with both Tourette's and Asperger's. Within a week of her arrival both our girls were regularly pretending to be invalids, trying to outdo each other with bandages and pretend plaster casts. They were suddenly acting like cripples, walking around with an old pair of crutches and telling us, with smiles, how very ill they were. I wondered if, surrounded by so many wounded people, this was their way of getting parental attention – or if this was something they had learned from Chloe's very evident frailty.

Chloe was still in her teens and, more than any other guest, liked spending time playing with our children on the carpet: colouring in, doing jigsaws, messing about with Lego. It was as if she were their older sister, the one they looked up to. I watched them playing together and listened to their conversations. The kids begged her to come on the trampoline, but she said she had a spinal injury. They asked her why she wore long sleeves when it was so warm, and she told them she cut her arms.

'What do you mean?' asked Emma.

'I cut my arms.'

'On purpose?'

'Yes.'

She was tactful and honest. There was nothing wrong about the way she explained it to them. But I could see our little girls trying to work things out and longing to copy this new big sister. To them, cutting must have been a bit like shaving, and bandages and injuries a sign of maturity.

I washed up with Chloe that evening. She had rolled up her sleeves and I could see hundreds of raised white lines all the way up one arm. They were perfectly parallel, as if cutting herself was a discipline or ritual, a visual expression of how ordered everything could be. There were fresh cuts that had clearly been made since her arrival here.

We never duck an awkward issue, so I asked her about self-harm. Being Chloe, she was eloquent and forthright, deconstructing the habit at the same time as somehow justifying it. She talked about other incidents when she had been a danger to herself: not just starving herself but setting her hair on fire, and so on. She was a not uncommon combination of brazen and vulnerable, an external absolutist who was, inside, rather confused. There was an intelligence to her that had an edge of ferocity and a rigidity that wasn't just cerebral but physical. When I put an arm around her it was like hugging a block of ice.

Over the next few weeks her arm was like a barometer of how she was feeling: any time there was the mildest discussion that threw her off kilter, she would drift away and, I knew, cut herself. I once went into her room to see if she was all right, and she was there with dark blood flowing down her arm. It was her way of releasing tension or punishing herself. One time she cut herself so badly she spent the night on our sofa bed – it was the sort of emergency that meant we shared our side of the house after 9 p.m. Chloe's behaviour became, obviously, a bigger issue. She was unconsciously requesting constant attention: not just first aid, but conversation, reassurance and transport. Francesca was spending increasing amounts of time ferrying Chloe to doctor's appointments and becoming an almost full-time carer. We were always open with people about not being trained counsellors, or professionals, or staff in a therapeutic community. Fortunately, though, we were surrounded by people who knew how to handle such situations. One of the *consiglieri* on our management committee was a psychiatrist, a very smart, caring woman, and we described to her the situation with Chloe and asked her advice.

'You don't allow any violence, verbal or physical, right?' asked Jo, the psychiatrist.

We nodded.

'Do you think self-harm is violence?'

I could tell where she was going. 'It is, I suppose, but it's not threatening. It's not aimed against anyone except herself.'

'But it's still a form of violence?'

Fra and I looked at each other and gave a hesitant nod.

'Because I think you could make the case that if the woodland is a sanctuary where people are protected, they also need to be protected from themselves; and that if someone is constantly drawing blood, you need to intervene. She's hurting herself, and part of your challenge is to stop her doing that.'

'But self-harm,' Fra said, 'is her pressure release, and without it she might be even more unstable. It might make her not more balanced but even more wobbly.'

'Yes.' Jo nodded, acknowledging that it would probably make our life not easier but trickier.

A few days later I found myself sitting around the stove with Chloe. Raising the issue of her self-harm still felt as if I was being invasive, entering her own private world without permission. I tried, very gently, to say what we had discussed with Jo and asked her what would happen if she stopped the self-harm.

'I would probably cry more and get angrier.' She was crying now as she said it.

'Maybe you need to get angry. Sounds to me like you've got a lot to get angry about.'

'But I've never got angry. I never even had tantrums as a baby.'

'Does that sound usual?'

She shrugged. 'I worry about what would happen if I got angry.'

'What do you worry about?'

'That I'll hurt someone and you'll kick me out.'

'You're hurting someone already.'

'Yeah, but that's just me.'

'"Just me"?'

I told her that she could trust us to hold her anger, to contain it and live with it. As long as she was gentle with people around her right now, there was no problem if she got angry and upset about the past. This was the right place to take off the mask, to fall apart and put herself back together. I tried to find a tactful way to say that it might actually make her less spiky and judgemental if she let off steam more often. As things were at the moment, it felt like she was a pressure cooker with a faulty valve: other people would get scorched as she turned her scorn on them. I was trying to suggest she lift off the lid and let the steam escape.

We didn't know then quite how angry she would become, often with us; or how angry we would sometimes get with her. But she would end up staying more than a year and in that time she became like another daughter to us. And her previously habitual self-harm has never happened since.

Late one night that September I got a phone call from a priest in Wiltshire. He told me there was a former soldier called Marcus sleeping in his church doorway. He wondered if we had any space. I suggested he give the guy our number and we could have a chat. It was always preferable to suss someone out, even a little bit, before they came. Marcus didn't call; he just rolled up a couple of days later with his life's possessions in his backpack.

An ex-squaddie with a one-tooth smile, Marcus had a rich West Country accent: he said 'goad' and 'ode' instead of 'gold' and 'old'. He said he was a recovering alcoholic who had left home with nothing when his wife had told him she was expecting another man's child. He had wandered around the West Country sleeping rough until he heard about us. He was a warm, amusing, wounded man, someone who had a host of funny stories from being in the army.

Marcus was one of those people you had to ask to stop working because he went at it full tilt: he would crack on with jobs, loading huge logs on to the pick-up and cross-cutting, splitting and stacking them until sunset. But he would then complain about the other guests with 'slopey shoulders', those who needed to 'man up' and pull their weight. Because he had the military mindset that you never show weakness, he found it very hard to share what he was going through. He would talk about his wife, or his alcoholism, readily enough, but never what those things made him feel. Quite often I would find him weeping somewhere and try to listen to him, but he seemed embarrassed that he had revealed vulnerability and quickly stood up and got back to work. 'It's all fubar,' he smiled, hiding behind his barracks slang again.

Everyone who came here warmed to Marcus because he was so down to earth. There was nothing pretentious about him. He wasn't officer class – what he would call 'a Rupert' – but very much a private (he'd been briefly promoted to lance corporal, he told us, laughing, before being demoted for misconduct). He had the uncanny knack of being able to befriend anyone through his generosity and jokes. And he had an agricultural background, so local farmers enjoyed talking cattle and farm machinery with him. The mix here was always important – having a range of ages, genders, problems and backgrounds. Marcus definitely made sure that we weren't ever too hippie. He was tough and blunt. He didn't want muesli for breakfast, just eggs and bacon. He was so politically incorrect he had once failed a 'diversity' course at work, and we often had to yell 'Diversity!' at him when he was being tactless.

There were one or two alarm bells that I didn't heed. I've got a pretty well-tuned nose for the whiff of booze and once or twice I was sure I could smell lager on him. I normally breathalyse anyone who is suspected of drinking, but I didn't test him, as I thought that if he were an alcoholic he would have been bladdered, not just tipsy. We only realized months later how big that 'if' was. The other alarm bell was money. We had never been very good at making sure people paid their share in to our common purse, and Marcus kept coming up with excuses: he couldn't face contacting his wife, and she had his cards. He didn't want to contact SSAFA, the charity that offers assistance to veterans in need, as he was too proud to become a charity case. Months went by and he didn't contribute; he was contributing so much in other ways that we let it drift.

There was a boggy bit of ground that was a natural basin. It was mostly marsh grass and moss. It felt spongy underfoot and when it rained a large natural pond would cover the damp greenery. Kath's forest school was just beyond it, under the large horizontal boughs of an old ash tree. She and I had often spoken about creating a much larger pond, a place where her schoolkids could play amidst frogs, newts, and all the rest.

Kath knew a guy called Aaron who had a digger. She had been asking him to come round for months, but he had a busy job and a big family. Summer had turned to autumn and we began to wonder if Aaron was fictional. Then one day a chunky man with tattoos on his forearms rolled up with a neat digger on the back of his truck. He had a boyish face and smiled a lot. He didn't just dig a hole, he spent days sculpting a perfect oval and a raised pathway all the way around it. He would get out of his little cab to look at it from all angles, accepting a cup of tea and letting the kids sit at the controls. He was in no hurry, even though he was doing it all free of charge. He seemed pure Somerset: no rush, no greed, just earthy generosity expressed through the sharing of agricultural machinery. Aaron got so into it that we were left with an oval far bigger than we had expected: it was about eighty foot by thirty.

Being a quarry, there was no clay to puddle the pond, so we went for the less natural method, which meant buying a colossal pond liner. To protect it from damage, though, we needed huge amounts of old carpet. I phoned Dean, a carpet fitter who was one of our nearest neighbours.

'We need a lot of carpet, Dean,' I said.

'What's it for: hall, stairs, bedroom?'

'For a pond.'

'You what? You're not using my finest twist for a pond.'

I explained we needed to protect the pond liner, and that we couldn't really afford to pay.

'How much do you need?' he asked.

I told him the dimensions and he laughed. 'And you don't want to pay for it? That's a couple of thousand square foot. I could do a whole house with that.'

'But haven't you got loads of old offcuts you don't need?'

'I sell them as well.'

We seemed to have reached an impasse. 'Tell us what you need other than money.'

'A new woman,' he said bitterly. His wife had just left him for another man.

'I could do you some pigs.' There was silence, as if he were thinking about it, so I went into sales mode: 'I've got three Saddlebacks left. Beautiful dual-purpose pigs, good for bacon or pork. They're wormed, just ready to be weaned. They're lovely characters.'

'Three? What do they normally cost?'

I exaggerated slightly. 'About seventy-five each.'

'Pigs, eh?'

'Great pets, free pork. And think how much space you'll be creating in your warehouse, all that rubbish you know you'll never sell.'

He laughed. 'Okay. Come to the warehouse this afternoon and I'll see what we've got.'

Marcus and I went over in the pick-up and loaded up dozens of rolls of lilac twist and beige Berber. We did three runs until eventually the whole of the pond area was covered. It looked surreal: a patchwork of random colours and odd rectangles laid on the ground in the middle of the woods. Chloe and the kids lay down in it, sunbathing and pretending to swim.

A few days later a pallet arrived with a cubic metre of weighty pond liner on it. We put it on the pick-up and then unfolded it over the carpet, heaving it out in all directions. We cut off the corners and then wondered how on earth we were going to fill the pond with water. We worked out it would take roughly 50,000 litres. We didn't have a hose anywhere nearby, so it would mean either a thousand trips with the watering can or fifty with the IBC

– the huge cubic container we used to water the pigs – on the back of the pick-up.

Kath came round that afternoon as we were staring at the black hole.

'Why don't I talk to the Fire Brigade?' she said. 'You know Mark's a fireman? I'm sure he could persuade them to do a Monday night drill here.'

A week later, a dozen firemen rolled up. Leo was beside himself with excitement as the fire engine, something he had seen only on children's TV, was now in his home. He jumped up and down, shouting 'Nee-nah' at the rectangular vehicle.

They unrolled the hose along the ground and fixed on an extension. A few thousand litres of water barely seemed to make much difference: they just created a big puddle in the middle of the black liner. So they went back to the hydrant and got another load. They did a few more runs until the clear water was beginning to creep up the sides of the pond.

We conducted a bit of a charm offensive. Chloe and Marcus handed out hot dogs and slices of cake and cups of tea to the firemen. We showed them round and explained what we were up to. They met our other guests: a gaunt chap just out of rehab and another who had served two tours in Afghanistan. We thanked them for doing a job in a few hours that would have taken us weeks. There was a great deal of goodwill all round.

Within twenty-four hours we saw our first dragonfly skitting across the surface of the still-clear water. Within a week there were a dozen, plus damselflies and pond skaters. One quiet night, when I was sitting on the rustic bench we had made out of a fallen tree trunk, I saw a kingfisher. George, who was staying for a week, said he saw a heron, but he was so competitive I wondered whether he just said that to trump everyone else. Gav and his girlfriend, Rachel, placed squares of turf all over the exposed bits of black pond liner at the water's edge, and we began bedding in hundreds of pond plants: sedges, water forget-me-nots, loose-strifes, great wood-rush, water mint, creeping Jenny, marsh woundwort, marsh marigold, meadowsweet, great burnet, wild angelica, figworts, frogbits and starworts. Friends from town brought over buckets of frogspawn and various lilies.

'You know what it needs?' asked Marcus, smiling. 'A floating pontoon.' He was staring into the distance, as if remembering some favourite war film. Everyone liked the idea, and it sounded simple enough.

'Yeah, good idea,' Gav said.

'I'm full of those.' Marcus flashed his one tooth. 'Upstairs for thinking, downstairs for dancing.'

So we asked Scrap-metal Mark for a dozen rectangular fifty-litre containers. He brought them up, as usual, within a couple of days. He was better than Santa Claus. We strapped them to the underside of half a dozen pallets and bound the pallets together with some old planks that were clogging up the workshop. We put Expamet and chicken wire across the top to stop people slipping and then linked the pontoon to the shore with a wide plank. It was just the right width: wide enough to be a walkway but narrow enough to give a child a mild adrenaline rush as they tiptoed on to the bouncy pier.

More than anyone else, Marcus had spent hours creating the pond. He had helped out Aaron and the firemen, and everyone else. It was, in many ways, his creation and we let him decide what he wanted to do with it. But there were other reasons he kept improving it: he had promised to tell us his embarrassing army nickname only when it was finished, and he kept looking for new pond jobs to postpone the revelation. He wanted a fence all the way round, to make it safe for children, so that took a few more days, as we created a post-and-rail barrier.

'Now it needs a gate,' he said, so we made one of those.

'And now we need to make another bench.'

'Hang on,' said Gav, who always spoke his mind. 'The pond's done. It's finished. We want to know your nickname.'

'Yeah,' said Benny, standing on the pew in the garden room. 'You promised.'

'I'm not sure I can really say it in front of the children.' Marcus looked bashful, and looked to me for consent to continue.

I told him not to worry, so he told us the story. He recounted a tale of too much alcohol and a bet about who could get the most clothes pegs on their privates. That's why all his mates knew him as Peggy.

'Cool,' said Benny, delighted at how strange adults could be. 'Let's have a competition. Mummy, get the clothes pegs.'

'Not likely,' said Marcus. 'I was in hospital for forty-eight hours after that.'

So we decided to carve a sign saying 'Peggy's Pond' and placed it at the approach to the water. For years afterwards people would assume that Peggy was one of our elderly guests, someone who had passed away and was commemorated here in this beautiful quiet spot – or at least they did until Benny ran up to them and told them the rude story she loved about a man called Marcus who once lived here.

One of the big changes that autumn was simply organization. I had become exasperated over the years by finding pliers in the long grass or a screwdriver stabbed into a tree trunk. Everything seemed to be left lying around, and I would spend hours looking for, and cleaning, long-forgotten tools. Many people have garages and tool sheds in which they can't find anything, but at least they've only got themselves to blame. Here there were ten people grabbing things, manhandling and losing them. I did it myself, because nothing had its rightful place. To get anything from the tool shed you had to open the door fast and chuck something in before everything else collapsed on top of you.

Over the next few months we organized the workshop and tool shed. When I had taught in prisons, I had seen shadow boards on which the black silhouette of a missing tool was immediately visible. So we made one across the entirety of a workshop wall. It was black and white and you could see from twenty metres away if an auger bit or an adze had not been put back. Tony made endless wooden boxes for pop rivets, coach screws, bolts, nuts, washers, clout nails, oval-head nails, staples, handles, hooks – and all the other bits and bobs. Tom labelled everything, bursting into his usual smutty giggles when he wrote on one large box 'Random Screws'.

I walked past Chloe, who was painting, in big black letters: 'Tape Me'. By now we were so used to unorthodox behaviour that I wondered whether this was some kind of public appeal for domination. She caught me looking at it and laughed.

'It's going to say "Tape Measures".'

'Right,' I said, and we laughed.

We built pallet cubicles in Walnut Tree Bay for bits of tarp, flue, tiles and fencing. We made shelves, cupboards, boxes and drawers. Pretty soon, everything had a place and everyone knew where everything belonged. We began explaining to people on arrival the importance of putting things away and gradually they all started doing it. I knew the place had a different vibe when one ageing traveller rolled up for a few days. 'I've never seen such an organized community,' he said. I'm not sure he meant it entirely as a compliment, but it pleased me none-theless. I was secretly delighted too when I looked at a shelf a few weeks later to see that someone had written 'Boot Camp' on it in ballpoint pen. And I liked the fact that the person who wrote 'Boot Camp' was, I'm fairly sure, the same one who wrote 'Love You' underneath a beautifully painted bookshelf. People seemed to know that this was a place of both discipline and affection.

That autumn, a guy called Callum came to stay. A middle-aged Scottish man, he had lost his wife, job and home within a few months of each other. It was partly because he had been using, but he had also been diagnosed as bipolar, and after months of frenetic energy he was now deeply depressed. His monosyllabic replies were only just the right side of impolite. His whole face looked harrowed: his eyes were usually downcast and surrounded by the lines of a man who had clearly lived in the fast lane. I saw him sitting down outside, his elbows on his thighs and his head in his hands, whispering, 'Fuck, fuck, fuck,' to himself. I sat next to him and asked him what he was thinking about.

'My life,' he said, shaking his head.

We sat there like that for a few minutes, and he started telling me things about his old job, his cars, his holidays, his wife. It was the first time in a week that we had exchanged more than the bare minimum. He was crying now, a high-pitched whine coming out as he let it all go.

'The last few weeks,' he said, when his breathing had returned to normal, 'have been like the morning after the night before. I keep having flashbacks to all the embarrassing or daft things I've done. I've made such a mess of everything. I've hurt everyone I love.' The thought of it started him off again, and he began crying.

He often broke down in the middle of a job, or growled wistfully as he was working. I'd ask for his advice on things and he'd shrug, repeating the question and looking at me with a vacant, couldn't-care-less expression. With somebody else it might have been irritating but on the rare occasions he did say something, it was usually to express gratitude. He was just so low he could barely talk. I remember one exchange, if you can call it that, between Callum and Marcus.

'Callum, do you want a tea?' Marcus asked.

'Cup of tea?' Callum carried on staring at the ground, as if these words were reminders from a past life when things were better. And he was thinking about that life, not the tea.

'Callum?'

'What?'

'Do you want that tea?'

'Tea?' Callum repeated the question again, not replying.

A lot of people started avoiding him, because they just couldn't get through. He stopped washing. He didn't light his fire at night and would come in looking pale and wrecked each morning. He usually didn't fall asleep until dawn, and then, before he knew it, it was time to get up. He started giving away his possessions, a gesture that was both generous and desperate. Callum could see no future in which he might have needed his old computer screen, his plasma TV, his money. He hated himself for lacking the courage to commit suicide.

Another arrival that autumn was an old ambulance, donated by an Irishman we knew from town. It was a hefty van, a bit bigger than your usual camper van. We decided to turn it into a rustic library, full of classics, so that people had somewhere quiet to retreat to when the house got too rowdy. We wallpapered the whole inside with ripped pages from charity-shop editions of Shakespeare. As we were pasting up the pages, we shouted funny lines at each other.

'Great king, I am no strumpet!' Marcus called, laughing.

'Whatever.'

'How long within this wood intend you stay?' Tom asked.

'Good question.' Fra smiled.

Within a few days it looked beautiful: we had built a sort of chaise longue under the windscreen, half a dozen bookshelves, and a long desk that overlooked the orchard. All it needed now was electricity.

Callum and Recovery Pete started digging a trench in which to lay a cable. It would need to go through the chicken run with our small flock of fourteen birds. Digging a deep line in which to lay the cable wasn't easy – digging anything in this rocky quarry was always hard – but it was the kind of task you could happily do whilst chatting away to someone because it didn't, I fatally thought, require much concentration. I was finishing off something in the workshop just below, so left them to it. After a while I heard a really pained groan, and a few minutes later Callum came down with a pretty distraught look on his face.

'Everything okay?'

'I killed a chicken,' he said.

I was more worried about Callum than the chicken. He looked in pieces.

'We were just digging away,' he said, 'but they kept coming closer for the worms, and . . .'

This was just the latest example, for him, of ruining everything he touched. He couldn't even dig a trench without killing something.

I wandered up there, and Recovery Pete was looking

sheepish. Next to the trench was one of the hens, lying motionless. It had been hit by the pickaxe. Marcus was there now,
running along the trench with a club in his hand, trying to keep
the birds away from where the others were digging. It was even
worse than herding cats, as they flew up in the air, flapping
wildly at the energetic caveman.

We decided we might as well eat the dead bird, so someone
hung it up in the log store. But then Rachel, a vegetarian, went to
get logs for the house and was confronted by a mangled bird that
had dripped scarlet gunge all over the ash logs. She looked pale
when she came in. No one offered to pluck the bird, so I sat out
there in the rain, pulling the dappled grey feathers off my favourite Fenton Blue.

That evening we had one of those meals when nobody spoke
much. We were wet and cold and one chicken down. It would
have been miserable if it hadn't been for the kids. Leonardo was
talking now and had been watching *Toy Story* on TV. He loved
the Buzz Lightyear character, with his catchphrase 'To infinity
and beyond!' – only Leo misunderstood it and shouted, 'To infinity and the blonde!' It became his way of communicating with all
the adults. He would raise his tiny fist and shout, 'To infinity
and –' and we would reply '. . . the blonde!'

'Who is this blonde?' Callum asked. It was the first time I had
seen him smile in two months.

We often acquired things, or parted with them, with no money
involved. Our basic bartering didn't put anything between us
except goodwill. We called it 'degotiation'. It created ties and allegiances unmediated by currency. Plenty of people would do
favours for us and refuse payment; and so we would do favours in
return, or pass them on to someone else.

For all that, though, I was frequently amazed at how quickly the capitalist machine was recreated in our small community. Callum was very clearly cash-rich, and Marcus had nothing. One night I came into the kitchen to see Marcus peeling spuds, listening, as usual, to Christmas classics in the middle of September. He seemed perfectly cheerful, prancing around the kitchen in his apron as he sang along.

'Why are you cooking?' I asked. 'Isn't it Callum's turn tonight?' All the adults cooked one night a week.

'I said I'd do it for him,' Marcus said.

'Is he okay?'

Marcus shrugged, and I wondered what was going on. Callum had begun to perk up in recent days, and I wanted to check he was all right. When I opened the door to his room, he seemed fine, sitting in an armchair with his feet up on the table.

'You all right?' I asked.

'Fine. You?'

'Only Marcus said he was doing your night because you're unwell.'

'Not really. I said I'd give him a tenner to do my turn. Poor chap can't even afford his baccy, so I thought I would help out.'

'Right,' I said slowly, so he knew that his exchange with Marcus wasn't my idea of helping out. I wandered off to think about it, not sure that I wanted the richest to do the least work here as well as everywhere else. I chatted to Fra about it. We could see Callum making the point that he was creating employment, and all the usual bull.

We talked about it over tea. Marcus and Callum were happy with the arrangement, but I didn't like it and had to persuade them it was wrong. Before we knew it, Callum would be asking to pay more to avoid the menial jobs around the place.

A couple of weeks later Callum was 'on duty', which meant he was supposed to be cooking Sunday lunch for everyone. At midday he still hadn't emerged from his room, so Gav knocked on the door.

'Callum, you slacker,' Gav said in his cheerful tone, 'what are you doing about our lunch?'

Callum opened the door in his dressing gown. 'I'm going to take you all out to a pub. Big meal on me.' His eyes had that gleam in them, a look of defiance or mischief. The door closed again, and Gav and I exchanged glances, both shaking our heads.

Gav knocked again. The joy of having him around was that I wasn't the only one playing bad cop. The door opened, and Callum stood there.

'I think you should cook for us,' Gav said, straight up.

'I want to take you out for lunch,' Callum said, bewildered at the ingratitude.

'We don't want you to take us out for lunch. We would like you to cook lunch for us, the same way other people have cooked Sunday lunch for you for the last two months. You can't just pay someone else to do the work.'

'Why? What's the problem with that?'

'We don't want it to be bought. We would like it made.'

'You don't want a pie and chips, some lemonade, a decent pud?'

'Yeah, great. Love it. But we want you to make it, to make an effort beyond just putting your hand in your pocket.'

It was a good-natured discussion, and both Gav and Callum were smiling as they spoke, but it was a clash of cultures. Callum didn't get equality, and we – it was clear – didn't get capitalism.

But we influenced each other, and over the next few months Callum started enjoying his conversion to an alternative lifestyle.

254 | A PLACE OF REFUGE

From having been a high-flying businessman, he now wanted nothing to do with money, which was partly why he was giving it away to people like Marcus. He loved the allegory of the long spoons, in which the only way people can eat when they have long spoons is by feeding each other. It was an example of reciprocity and mutuality, which was completely at odds with the dog-eat-dog world in which he had lived. He scratched the words 'long spoons' on to the bonnet of his car. And he changed us subtly too. We realized we needed to be a bit more entrepreneurial, and he was always on hand to offer advice about how we could make 'a little earner' here or there. He still got revved up when there was business talk, even if the sums were tiny. We put more effort into selling our jigsaws, plants, produce, bird boxes and benches, and they all brought in a bit of income. We were, in a tiny way, becoming a social enterprise.

Little Leonardo was finally big enough to move out of his cot. Callum said we could take back our bed from the explosives chamber, but that would mean that Callum no longer had one. He said it was fine, and slept on a thin camping mattress on the floor. It looked uncomfortable and slightly skanky, and I got the impression Callum wanted it that way. He was still punishing himself. But the common purse was almost empty and couldn't stretch to buying a new bed.

We had a chat one lunchtime and I suggested we should build a four-poster. I looked around the table and it was like one of those moments in a film when the changing room is full of overweight, unconfident kids who are about to take on the fit bullies at their own game. There wasn't a chance we could do it. We had a slow-moving teenager, a recovering anorexic, an ex-squaddie whose idea of carpentry tended to be hitting six-inch nails into everything, a couple of volunteers who knew little about wood-work and troubled Callum.

I watched Callum as we talked through how we might do it. There was something about the look on his face that suggested he was up for it, something about the ludicrousness of us all making a four-poster bed that appealed to him. He was slowly coming round to the idea that he was, as he said, 'a crazy', and he admired a streak of craziness in others. He liked the daring in the idea. And I knew he would be an invaluable ally: I had watched him do odd jobs around the place, and you could tell from the way he held a shovel or handled a hammer that he knew exactly what he was doing.

'What's wrong with Ikea?' Marcus said.

'We could try Freecycle,' said Gav.

'There are loads of charity shops around,' someone else chipped in.

But in the end, everyone reluctantly agreed that we could make a four-poster from what was available on site.

The first thing to do was fell some ash poles. Gav and I took the chainsaw and wandered through the wood to a stand of tall, slim ashes that were swaying gently in the wind. They were densely spaced, ready for thinning, and Gav and I walked between them, looking up the slim trunks and trying to work out which ones would look best on a bed. The ideal was something with the diameter of a thigh, fairly straight but possibly with an interest-ing kink or twist to it. We reckoned the four posts for the bed needed to be about seven and a half foot long, so if we were lucky we would only need to fell a couple of trees. We chose the two we needed and felled one each.

We strapped the first one on to the saw horse and, with the back of a spade, we stripped off the bark. Green-and-white ribbons flew into the air, leaving the wet, slippery wood beneath. We then put the long lengths on the shave horse and used a draw knife to do some tidier stripping. Within less than an hour we had one beautiful, glistening pole. We did the same with the other three.

Having prepared the four posts, we needed four rails that would form the rectangle on which the mattress would sit. We felled another couple of slimmer trees and stripped them of bark. Part of the challenge was working with wood that was never straight or 'true' – everything had curves – and trying to create a horizontal rectangle was tricky. But there was something very peaceful about making a bed with no power tools. Through the week you could hear Callum tap-tapping the chisel, a first knock to take aim and a second to take the wood. It was an honest sound, and it echoed around the clearing outside the house. We had never seen Callum so focused, keen to get things right. And it was the kind of work you could do whilst chatting, so there was a background buzz of people stopping by to look and natter. It was industry in the old sense. Not perhaps efficient – no one ever accused us of that – but quiet and serene. It seemed to be one of those occasions in which, as Robert Frost wrote, 'love and need' are one, where 'work is play'.

We cut down some slimmer ash poles for the top rails of the bed. We found a couple of spalted alder boards (spalted means that the wood is coloured by fungi), with lovely waney edges on both sides. We were going to use them for the head and foot of the bed. Chloe spent hours sanding them smooth, rubbing them with ever-finer sandpaper in the sunshine. As usual, strange things happened. The chunky posts were a beautiful pale yellow and a female volunteer, Sophie, was patiently ragging Danish oil on to them. One of our male volunteers offered to hold the post firm for her, to stop the thing rolling. But he straddled it with one leg either side and held it with his hands, looking a bit like the Cerne Abbas Giant.

'There you go,' he said, nodding his head towards the post to say she could keep oiling.

'I don't think so,' she said, looking over to me for support.

'Anthony,' I said, pulling him aside. He hadn't seemed at all creepy to me, but there was something very odd about asking a young woman to oil a pole he was straddling. He acted all innocent, but I put him on another job, working with the men up by the log store.

We had decided to do an old-fashioned rope weave to support the mattress (the origin, I discovered, of the phrase 'sleep tight': it used to be a wish that the rope was taut and the bed firm). We bought a hundred metres of Hempex, a rope that looked like traditional hemp but was more durable. We drilled out sixteen horizontal holes in each rail and made two dozen awls (circular wedges) from an old broom handle. The last thing we needed was a tightener, a T-bar with a wide slit in the bottom of the vertical with which to wind the Hempex tight.

Callum and I took all the components into the explosives chamber and carefully assembled it. Throughout the project he had repeatedly said it wouldn't work. He was used to precision carpentry and reckoned our guesswork and optimism would never build a bed. But as we jiggled the rails into the posts, thwacking them together with the beetle, it began to take shape. The fact that we had made a few mortises accidentally skewed meant that the thing held together tightly, as it was under tension. The head- and foot-boards slid into their slots and we nudged oak pegs through all the holes. I looked over at Callum, who was still shaking his head.

258 | A PLACE OF REFUGE

When everything was assembled, it still rocked a bit. But as we began to thread the Hempex along the base, it firmed up. We put the rope in the slot of the T-bar, twisted the handles and, once it was sufficiently tight, we thwacked in an awl to hold it in place. We kept going like that, doing the whole warp and then threading the perpendicular weft over and under. It was much harder pulling it through the already taut rope, and once you got up speed you wanted to keep the momentum. Callum and I did it so fast we burnt the synthetic rope: it was like a cartoon in which one strand pings apart, not just once but all along the line.

'Oh,' I said, stopping to inspect the damage. 'Reckon it will hold?'

'I don't think anything about this bed will work,' Callum said, smiling.

The rope had only three strands, and one had completely burnt away with the friction of being pulled against itself.

'Put a mattress on,' Callum said, 'and hope for the best.'

We kept hitting in the awls, keeping the rope in place, until we had done the whole thing. Callum pushed hard against the uprights, which didn't budge a millimetre. Everyone came over to look and make approving noises. Like the table, it was one of those projects in which everyone had had a hand. The end result looked extremely elegant but also very natural, its strong posts little different from an actual tree trunk in appearance. And over the years I liked the fact that there were a few rough sleepers, used to kipping in doorways and cardboard shelters, who could enjoy the contrast here of sleeping in a four-poster. It was a bed that made people feel, if not regal, then certainly cherished.

It was more explicit with Chloe than with other guests that she wanted us to be her surrogate parents. She would sit on the carpet with our children playing games, or sit on the sofa with them watching programmes on the TV. She could spend hours colouring in; the only difference between Chloe and our kids was the almost obsessional precision of Chloe's colouring. She used to put on a childish voice sometimes when she hadn't got what she wanted. Like the children, she would impetuously interrupt when she wanted to say something, or storm off when things hadn't gone her way.

She had a great sense of humour and would make us all laugh. Whenever anybody had lost something, you could ask Chloe and she would run a systems check on her hard drive, and tell you exactly where it was. It was slightly freaky. When I got confused about which kid to pick up from which after-school club, Chloe would tell me exactly where I needed to be and when. Because she was so rigid and systematic, you could input the rules of our community and she would respect them, which was pretty rare round here. She was always punctual and precise. And because she was eloquent about what she needed, she improved this place with sound suggestions. Her antenna for bullshit was far more finely tuned than mine.

And we learned from her. She was thrown by any lack of clarity and often came to me to explain why she was confused by a grey area. She wanted everything in black and white: no metaphors, no nuance, just the rule and then complete consistency. It was good to be reminded of the need for precision and the danger of sending out mixed messages. She thawed too, and it became normal to put an arm around her or hug her as you would a child of your own. Many people mistook her for our daughter or an au pair.

But she was very troubled. Before coming to us, she hadn't eaten solids for months. She was fixated on certain numbers and would do things like turn round on the spot eighteen times, then eighteen times the other way. She had memorized the stock numbers in Argos and Ikea catalogues and insisted on us having a Gantt chart on the noticeboard so that she always knew who was coming and going. Her Tourette's meant that she would suddenly squeak or twitch when she was tense. In the morning, as I dragged myself out of bed at four or five o'clock to bank some writing, I would find a long epistle from Chloe in my tea mug, listing all the things that weren't as she wanted them. I would go to my office and, most mornings, receive a couple of long emails from her too.

We had seen it before: people who had lost control at critical periods of their lives could become extraordinarily controlling when they found themselves in a community. I recognized the symptoms in myself, as I cherished order and still struggled with the lack of control I had. But Chloe took it to a new level. She wanted everything geometrically perfect. She wanted to control portions, opinions, bookshelves, cleaning and everything else. And when she wasn't in control she became almost frantic, getting visibly worked up and winding everyone else up as well with her contagious anxiety.

She was so knowledgeable we nicknamed her Chloepedia, which was what, she said, they had called her at school. If you were talking about buses with someone, she would run down the corridor to give you, verbally not physically, the timetable. She was sufficiently bright to know that not eating had for her become an addiction, and that part of the addiction was the control it gave her over her own body.

'I've desexualized myself,' she once said to me. 'Not eating food numbs me. It means I have no sex drive and thus can't be blamed for anything physical that happens to me.'

But she began to come to terms with imperfection, with the idea that she couldn't control everyone or everything. She settled for 'functional dysfunctionality', which wasn't a bad description of what this place was like. We started to joke about the many conversations she had in her head:

'I want to continue,' she said to me one morning, 'the argument I was having with you in my head during the night.'

'OK,' I said warily, 'tell me where we're at. What have I said so far?'

We knew it was a joke, but a serious one. She was beginning to externalize, to bring out into the open all her anger and confusion. She blew up many times, but so did I. We got through it and became extremely fond of each other.

Callum, too, had changed markedly. We knew he was bipolar, and he had gone from being monosyllabic to manic, talking high-speed gibberish so fast you could barely follow what he was saying. From the crack of dawn to last thing at night, he would exhibit pressured speech. A lot of it was cosmic nonsense, about the galaxies and the universe, or extreme conspiracy theories about politics, quantum physics and banks. It would be a whirlwind of ideas and hunches, all folded in on each other at top speed. It was fun, in a way. After weeks of barely talking he was unstoppable, and usually very witty. He made us laugh and think. His whole face was different: alive, grinning, but almost taut with energy and excitement. It was like watching an old wreck of a car transformed into a lean racer before your eyes – but a car whose steering wheel seemed detached from the actual wheels. It went wherever fancy took it. Sometimes you just had to leave the room to catch your breath. Yet it was still Callum, and lurking beneath all the gibberish and exaggeration was the jester's wisdom: he was observing the absurdity of life and of humans from the point of view of a self-made pauper who had lost everything. And he was so blunt that he would always tell it how it was, or at least how he saw it.

We liked having Callum around, but the kids especially adored him. He was one of them: eating too many sweets, writing on the furniture, getting over-excited then suddenly dejected, being incredibly creative but quick, too, to lose concentration.

As winter came around, we decided we needed an outside loo. There was only one communal bathroom in the house, which wasn't enough. By now, Kath was bringing a minibus of school-children up here once a week for forest school; and whilst it was lovely to hear them in the distance, they certainly didn't leave our communal loo cleaner than they found it.

Instead of building a compost loo, we decided to construct a tree bog. It was designed by a guy called Jay Abrahams, and was simpler and smarter than a compost loo. (I won't go into too much detail, but you don't need to separate urine and faeces and you don't need to empty it.) You simply plant two rows of willow all around the base and allow those nutrient-hungry cultivars to absorb the nitrogen. The idea is that the willow acts as both a screen and a biomass crop, which you can coppice for firewood, weaving or whatever.

We spent many hours wandering around the site, looking for the perfect location. It needed to be sited somewhere that was both discreet and sunlit, somewhere near the various shelters but not, clearly, too close. In the end we decided on a bank behind one of the camper vans. It was surrounded by coppiced syca-mores and hazels, so was already pretty hidden, but was sufficiently south-facing for the willows to have light.

Herb, our friend from the nearby friary, came over, attracted by the idea of another eccentric project. He brought with him some decent planks of oak. Marcus and I went into the woods, scouting for some hefty hazel poles to use as the four main stilts for the block. Rather than a 'long drop', the tree bog is raised above the ground. Callum and Gav dug holes for the posts, battling, as usual, massive boulders that took hours to excavate. Eventually we got the four posts in place, but using green wood in the round, we again had to deal with the curves and knots of nature. Callum told us what needed doing to hold it together and keep it more or less square. Once the posts were rigid we stapled chicken wire on both the inside and the outside, creating a hollow into which we stuffed straw to act as a wick to dry out, and screen, the compost pile. We put the floor to the bog about a metre and a half above ground level and built a loo seat above that. Gav cut out a shapely oval in Herb's oak, and Tony made a hinged lid. To the right of the seat we had a box for the sawdust or ash you sprinkle in on top, to stop it smelling.

We had bought a lot of offcuts of western red cedar, Douglas fir and other species from a local sawmill. I chainsawed them to length, admiring the hairy, almost ginger bark on some of the planks. Gav and Marcus screwed them on to the posts, the curved bark on the outside. The whole bog was beginning to look a bit like a POW watchtower. Herb put on the roof at his usual speed, as Callum cut a plastic barrel in half to catch rainwater for the hand-washing basin. We built steps and a door and then started doing the finishing touches: a porcelain basin, a carved sign that said 'Busy' in red on one side and 'Free' in green on the other. We put up pegs for coats and hats, and Chloe drew an illustration of the tree-bog principles. There were towels, soap, a twistable bit of two-by-one as a lock. We planted about a hundred cuttings of willow in staggered rows all around the outside. It was very rustic

and very beautiful. One of our volunteers officially twinned the
bog with a compost loo in Cambodia. We carved a sign – 'Herb's
Bog' – on an offcut of his oak and had an unveiling ceremony
(pulling a tea towel off the wood) before Herb disappeared inside
for the inaugural fertilizing of the willow.

Gav and Rachel had hit the road again, moving to a care farm in
Dorset, but another high-calibre volunteer came to live with us.
After quite a few bad experiences with volunteers who brought
disruption and passive aggression, we had written a succinct
summary of the qualities required, not least the need to be
emotionally and physically robust. Kaitlyn was both, and much
more. A middle-aged woman who wanted a sabbatical from
work, she was an attractive, calm person. She brought a bit of
elegance to our hairy, muddy home. She was the only one who
would get dressed for tea, putting on earrings and lipstick.
Flowers would appear around the place and on the steps of her
little hut she lit candles and sang to herself. Her being here made
the place feel warmer, more homely. She was crafty in the creative
sense of the word, constantly making things with felt or rescuing
interesting bits of wood from the kindling pile. She had brought
up two children in a large community that looked after people
with severe behavioural issues, so she had experience and was,
thankfully, forthright about our needs as a family. She understood instinctively what Fra was going through as a mother; she
knew what it was like to share a husband with lots of other people.
In a tactful way, she was adamant that we had to look after our
family too, something our *consiglieri* had been keen to underline
each time there was a meeting.

The other thing about Kaitlyn was that she seemed to bring a
different understanding about groups. She would often say that

groups have an unconscious life of their own and that people communicate through their behaviour. Everything has meaning, she would say.

'It's not what's said that can be harmful but what's not,' she told me once. 'It's not what's on the table but what's kept underneath it that can cause problems in groups. You've created this wonderful, incredible space where things can be talked about, but you still need to make sure things don't get segmented and separated. Things need to be joined up.' As she spoke, she would slowly rotate her fingertips on her thigh, as if playing chords in slow motion on a guitar.

Kaitlyn somehow managed to bring things to the surface. She would watch behaviour and comment on it, not necessarily critically but out of curiosity, with a sense of enquiry as to why something was happening. She was very observant. For example, there was something that, for months, had really riled me. Every morning we would meet up around our big table at nine o'clock and discuss what jobs needed doing. By then people were expected to have had breakfast and be dressed and ready for work. The working week was pretty gentle and since I usually started work four hours earlier – writing in a freezing hut at 5 a.m. – I was really irritated when people weren't ready to start their working day by nine. If they were ill that wasn't a problem, but often Callum would saunter in at nine thirty, saying something daft like he had got stuck in traffic.

That morning we were sitting round the table: Fra, Kaitlyn, Chloe, Marcus and me. But by a quarter past nine Recovery Pete and Callum still hadn't shown. I could feel myself going gently barmy, because this happened every other day.

'I don't understand why they can't get here for nine,' I said, shaking my head.

'Perhaps they don't know they have to be,' Kaitlyn suggested.

I couldn't comprehend it. 'Everyone knows we start at nine,' I said. 'It's on the website, it's on that laminated sheet there by the communal laptop, it's on the noticeboard, it's one of the first things I say to people when they say they want to come here. I can't understand how we could possibly be any clearer about what the expectation is.'

'Then maybe they're not hearing it,' Kaitlyn said quietly. 'And there's a message in there. If they're not meeting expectations, there's a reason. Why don't you go and ask them to join this conversation rather than us talking about them in their absence? After all, this is about them not being present.'

It was an example of her wanting things to be joined up. You don't sit in a room getting frustrated with people and slagging them off. Better to involve them in your frustration. It was such a simple, obvious suggestion, and already I could feel my irritation subsiding. I went and woke them both up, and they came in five minutes later, bleary-eyed.

'We didn't want,' I said, almost calmly, 'to be sitting here talking about you in your absence. We were talking about you because you're rarely ever here for nine, and we're wondering why.'

Recovery Pete, bless him, said he didn't know he had to be. I frowned, shaking my head. I reiterated what I had said before, that the timetable was written in bold on the website, on a large sheet of paper in the middle of the room, that I communicated it verbally as soon as people arrived.

'I just didn't know,' he said, and I believed him. He looked bewildered that we were irritated. 'I don't remember you telling me. I've never led a disciplined life. If I see a boundary, I put my head down and charge.' He laughed. 'If someone gives me a time-table, I ignore it. I always have. I just don't hear instructions.'

We all smiled affectionately, because he was being so honest about his failings. I caught Kaitlyn's eye, acknowledging that she was right: that some people just don't hear it, however explicit you are. Callum was different. He knew the score, he just consciously ignored it. He apologized, and I apologized for getting wound up, and we got on with it.

There were, I thought, two reasons why someone would ignore something as basic as the work timetable. For some people there was an element of 'Screw you', as if we represented some kind of authority they wanted to challenge. But far more often, I thought, it was the opposite: because we tried to make it relaxed, people didn't think there was any organization here. I knew we could be laid-back only because there was a rigid timetable and a disciplined rhythm. But some people saw just the laid-back bit and didn't see the discipline that enabled it. I told Callum my theory that stress comes from chaos, and that we were only calm because things here are ordered, and punctuality was part of that. Since then, I've been even more explicit about the timetable. Everyone understands that I'm a stickler for timekeeping, and that it's a sign of respect to be on time for communal work. When he left six months later, Callum presented us with a giant clock, a teasing symbol of my insistence on punctuality.

'Why is it so huge?' a bemused Benny asked him.

'Because I couldn't find one any bigger,' Callum said.

Kaitlyn didn't let things go unnoticed. Another time, we were having our weekly house meeting. We tried to keep it no longer than an hour, talking about people on the horizon, jobs, housekeeping, rotas, money, and all the rest. We had overrun and I was keen to crack on, but something that had been said had made Chloe extremely uncomfortable. Because of her Tourette's it was very easy to know when she was anxious: she shrieked and corkscrewed her body. We ignored it, perhaps because of impatience to get on with things, or politeness at not wanting to draw attention to it. But everyone was aware of it, and Kaitlyn wouldn't leave it unacknowledged.

'Before we finish,' she said softly, 'can we talk about what's just happened? I notice something has upset you, Chloe, and would like to give you the opportunity to explain what it was.'

Dear Chloe always struggled to open up one on one, let alone in a group. But she managed to explain what had irked her. She shrieked loudly again as she spoke, interrupting herself with a wail: the contrast between the scream and her whispers was very marked. But she explained herself, and now we weren't ignoring her but listening and empathizing. At the end of the meeting, instead of being upset Chloe was almost on a high, happy that she had managed to explain why she was thrown by an innocuous comment about calories. It was all thanks to Kaitlyn, who wanted everything, as she always said, 'to be put on the table'. The way she did it was admirable. There was never a trace of prying or manipulation, only a gentle, understated invitation to reveal what was really going on under the surface. It meant that we all started examining how we were feeling, reacting and behaving, and consciously tried to empathize with others when they shared their deeper selves.

I was constantly walking a tightrope between becoming too authoritarian and being insufficiently strict. We never wanted this place to be a lock-down rehab, where phones were confiscated and rooms searched. It had to be a relaxed place that worked because of individuals' own responsibility. But because we were easy-going, there was always behaviour that we considered unwise or even damaging and which we had to discuss and discourage. A soldier who was severely traumatized by his time in Afghanistan would play 'shoot 'em up' games on the communal computer, staring at the screen as he gunned down his enemies in quick succession. Callum would place bets at every opportunity, jumping up from the table mid-mouthful to look at the screen and see if he had won big. Chloe frequently disappeared into her room to weigh herself, checking if sticking to that day's calorie calculation had knocked a few ounces off. I knew it was compulsive behaviour which needed to be addressed. Other people noticed it too. Someone who had really absorbed the message and serenity of 'The Big Book,' came up to me one morning and said that there were dangerously addictive behaviours in the house. I had let it drift for too long because I really didn't want to restrict people's freedom. I didn't want to add to the already long list of things guests could and couldn't do.

What was interesting was their relief when I put my foot down. The soldier seemed to relax when I said that shooting pixellated people was inappropriate to someone with PTSD from warfare. Callum nodded and said that was fine. Chloe agreed that I could confiscate her bathroom scales.

I was sure it was the right thing to have done. And yet I was uneasy. With each passing month we seemed to have more rules: not just no drugs, alcohol or violence, but now no pornography and no gambling. We had often been diddled by smooth talkers who had asked us to lend them money, so we now said there could be no moneylending on site. There was a danger that rather than being a friend I was becoming some sort of enforcement officer. And even if I wanted to enforce such things, when do you intervene? How do you know when someone is placing a bet on their phone, or watching porn on it? How do you decide when weighing oneself is healthy and when it's unhealthy? It might have been relatively easy to become an enforcer if these people had been clients in a professional setting. But they weren't: they were companions with whom we had three meals a day. They played with our children. We sang and laughed together. It felt like I was breaking a spell when I stepped away from them and said, austerely, that something wasn't on. I always dreaded doing it, and I'm sure my discomfort was very obvious.

But afterwards it usually seemed that the person concerned, and everyone else, didn't feel restricted or deprived but somehow liberated. It was as if the safety of this space had been reasserted and that chains had been not imposed but removed. It gradually made me more confident about intervening and more relaxed when doing so. I was learning how to lay down the law in a way that was, I hope, liberating them from compulsions.

The other reason I had always been wary of becoming the enforcement officer is that I had glimpsed how easy it would be to warp the most well-meaning community into a cult. It's something we often joked about, not least because one of the soldiers who had previously stayed here gave us a load of military fatigues, so we all wandered around the woods in identical desert gear, looking like some weird Somerset militia. But although we laughed about it I could see how quickly – even with the best of intentions – we could become a cult, persuading people to cut ties with friends and family, or to empty their bank accounts into ours. Plenty of the people who came to us were longing to sever ties with their past lives, to throw money, perhaps even themselves, at us.

Fra and I could understand, sadly, the advantages of cutting ties. We had often seen people here start to recover, only for their recovery to be torpedoed by a partner, parent or friend who actually wanted them just the way they were before. People like

Tracey, Anna and Gerald were frequently destabilized by irate and irrational phone calls, the accusation being that they were dossing in the woods and should come home.

It was hard, too, to say no to money. Callum, an entrepreneur addicted to gambling, felt that he was like a substance abuser and needed complete abstinence. He wanted to give away all his money, and he wanted to give a lot of it to us. It wasn't straight-forward, though. As a community, we certainly needed the money. We had always run this place on a shoestring, and he was offering us a few thousand quid. But we knew he wasn't in his right mind and could later, quite rightly, accuse us of taking advantage of his vulnerable state. Something similar was often offered to us: whether because of self-hatred, gratitude or even enlightenment, guests wanted to give us presents, to offload possessions, to divest themselves of worldly stuff. I fretted about how I could be sure, as I limited their freedoms, persuaded them to resist phone calls and accepted gifts, that I wasn't becoming a cult leader. Especially as, when people asked how it worked here, I now half joked that Fra and I were benevolent dictators and that if anyone doubted our benevolence they were free to leave. It felt more honest than pretending that we were a cooperative or completely consensual. Many were relieved at the newfound clar-ity: rather than every new arrival being allowed to rattle the cage, to shake things up incessantly with their own suggestions, it was a more stable place.

The fact that Marcus, after three months here, still wasn't paying into our common purse was becoming increasingly problematic. He felt guilty, I think, that he wasn't contributing like everyone else, and so worked longer hours. But then he would come in and find people asleep in the armchairs and feel resentful.

I decided to contact SSAFA. A local woman offered to come round, but Marcus was having none of it.

'I don't need no support,' he said proudly. 'Them guys what got limbs blown off in Helmand need it, din 'em, not me. I don't want to be no charity case.'

'But Marcus,' I trod softly, 'in some ways you already are a charity case. There's nothing wrong with that. But it should be clear that that's happening right now.'

'How do you mean?'

'Well, everyone else here is paying for your food. That's fine, we're all happy to do it. But I think people might be miffed if you turn down SSAFA's support out of pride, when that pride costs us, not you.'

He frowned, and I could see him getting steamed up. 'Don't like what you're saying,' he said.

'Listen, Marcus, pride's not necessarily a good thing. It gets in the way of receiving graciously.'

'Don't want to be no charity case,' he repeated.

'But you are already, brother. We all are in some way.' I didn't want to labour the point, and I certainly didn't want to make him feel bad, but I was amazed that he hadn't wondered how we had fed him for the last three months. It seemed we had been so cautious about not making him feel like a charity case that we hadn't made it sufficiently explicit what had been happening. Now he knew, he didn't like it at all. Money, as it so often does in communal living, had come between us.

I told him that someone from SSAFA was due to visit next week, and he said he would think about it.

'I've already thought about it, Marcus. That's why I've spent a lot of time arranging their visit.'

He nodded, as if he had understood something he didn't want

to. He said he needed to go home, to pick up his Land Rover and his dog. He was going to face his wife, he said. So the next day I drove him to a nearby dual carriageway and lent him a jacket. I turned the car around and waved at him as he stood there with his thumb out on the slip road. We never saw him again. The days went by, and we kept expecting him back. Then, slowly, we realized he had slipped away. As days turned into weeks, it was obvious he had gone for good. It wasn't even a bad ending; it didn't feel like an ending at all.

It takes a long time for a group of people to get their heads round that sort of abandonment: not just the children, who didn't understand it, but everyone who had lived with him and shared deep experiences over the previous few months. It felt like a mystery and we couldn't resist speculating as to what had happened. The imminence of the SSAFA meeting had made him do a runner, and we wondered whether it wasn't just that he didn't want to be a charity case but perhaps he had never been in the army in the first place. SSAFA would have asked about his regiment and his service history, and if he hadn't been in the army he would have been rumbled very quickly. A friend sent us a post on the Diggers and Dreamers website warning communities about a blagger who was doing the rounds pretending to be ex-military but who was really an ex-con. He used the name Marcus, among other aliases. Another friend, who had met Marcus here, said he had rolled up at his place in Suffolk a few months after he had left us and had shared a few beers, like any non-problem drinker. Perhaps, we wondered, not only had he not been in the army; perhaps he wasn't even an alcoholic. Plenty of people resist the label, battling for years against the idea that they're powerless over drink; Marcus, perhaps, had done the opposite: had invented his alcoholism to gain entry here and enjoy the company and simplicity for a few free months.

But they were all guesses. We didn't know who he was. I had really liked his ruggedness, his mixture of manliness and sadness. I thought I had the measure of him, thought he had a good heart. But perhaps I was completely wrong, my judgement askew. It was one of those moments in which the person before you goes up in smoke and there's nothing to grasp hold of any more. We all yearned for an explanation or a reason, but we had neither. We tried to contact him, but he had fallen off the radar. We didn't really feel duped so much as confused. It wasn't the first or the last time it happened; for all the safeguards we put in place, what we were doing was so inherently risky you could never eliminate that confusion. We even wanted, bizarre as it might sound, for this to be a refuge for chancers too, a place where they, as much as anyone else, could be themselves.

Two years have gone by since Marcus left and we still sometimes wonder whether he'll roll up, flashing his one-tooth smile. If he ever comes out of hiding, we'll walk out to greet him on the path and welcome him home.

It's bitterly cold again, and we're getting through the wood stores at an alarming rate. Back in the summer it took months to cut, split and stack all the firewood and now we're burning two or three barrows of it a day to keep the house, and the huts, warm. It's like a meal that takes hours to prepare and minutes to eat. The woodland feels skeletal. The ivy's green leaves are the only ones left in the woods. They hug the bare trunks, their glossy triangles glinting in the weak winter sunlight. Throughout the day I can hear the clunk of wood chucked into the metal barrows and often see a silhouette shuffling towards a shelter. You can hear the sounds of guns from nearby shoots. The clouds seem bruised purple as they speed south.

The pond is iced over, and the children enjoy walking down there through the frosted grass and skating on the excitingly thin ice. They throw sticks to break it, but the sticks just skid, twisting on the surface like the detached hands of a clock. When the snows come, they come hard, covering everything with a foot of beauty. We all go tobogganing in the field behind the woods, the one with the river at the bottom. The thought of that river gives everyone a rush of adrenaline as they career, out of control, towards it. People get snowballs in faces and laugh and argue. We build a large igloo one day, using plastic boxes to make huge bricks of packed snow. It looks like an old-fashioned conical beehive as it rises to a peak at eight feet. We all crawl inside the opening, lighting a candle and watching the eerie light flicker on the compressed grey snow.

That January, a young woman called Sara became our new residential volunteer. She was an urbane agrarian, a back-to-the-lander who, as a horticultural therapist, believed in the healing power of gardening and of contact with the soil. She began improving our horticultural operation, which until now had been, at best, low-key. The greenhouse became a warm potting shed, and – having decided to accept Callum's rather large donation – we ordered a forty-foot polytunnel. We built new raised beds with sawmill offcuts; they looked rustic with waney-edged boards up to waist height. Sara sowed thousands of seeds and within a month there were dozens of trays with emerging seedlings in perfect straight lines. Emma adored Sara and would faithfully bring her any finished loo roll so that they could use the inner tubes of cardboard as sowing pots for lettuces.

I had always liked that line of Bernard of Clairvaux: 'If you are to do the work of a prophet, what you need is not a sceptre but a hoe.' It seems to express the notion that real revolutionaries are grounded and humble, rooted in the particular rather than aspiring to recognition and glory. I didn't think we were prophets, but we were certainly doing our share of hoeing. We were beginning to live by the labour of our own hands.

We would spend days pickaxing new plateaus, which Sara would convert into soft-fruit beds or herb gardens. We doubled the number of gardening tools we had and spent a small fortune on importing compost into this stony quarry. We built compost bays and filled water butts with comfrey and nettle as a natural fertilizer. We gathered horse manure from local stables and left it to rot. Quite soon Sara was selling a dozen plants every Wednesday, slowly earning back much of the money we had spent on infrastructure.

Putting up the polytunnel, however, took months. It arrived in February in thousands of unlabelled bits, and the instructions were unfathomable. We couldn't decide where to put it, as there weren't many clearings with sufficient sunlight and we didn't want it right outside the front door. For weeks all we did was look at the clearings and the hundreds of bolts and bars and scratch our heads. We spent days laboriously turning the soil and manuring one site, only to decide – for all sorts of reasons – that it was wrong. We eventually decided to put the polytunnel down by the chickens. Exhausted with rotavating by now, we brought the pigs down to do it for us. They quickly got their tough snouts stuck in and turned over the turf.

We were beginning to build links with various local and national charities: we would either contact them on behalf of a guest who was leaving us or, more commonly, would receive referrals from them. Some of the most common referrals we got were soldiers who had been discharged and were struggling with disability, addiction or PTSD. One day I got a call from Veterans Aid saying they had a soldier who desperately needed somewhere to go. He didn't have any physical injuries but was an alcoholic and had been profoundly traumatized by several tours in Iraq and Afghanistan.

When Darren turned up a few days later he still looked like he was in the army: he was clean-shaven, had polished boots, a buzz cut and a shemagh – the Afghan scarf – around his neck. His limbs were long and skinny. He was muscular in a lean way, and his arms were covered in tattoos. He shook hands like he wanted to show you how hard he was. His face was angular and tense: he wasn't the kind you'd want to meet on a dark night. He was only in his twenties, but he looked both wired and exhausted.

I think he suspected we were all hippies, and he sounded pretty offhand about the idea of staying with us.

'What's the SOP round here then?' He was looking over my shoulder.

'Sop?' I asked.

'Standard Operating Procedure.'

He spoke in an array of military acronyms. I told him the way things worked, and he sounded fine with that. I made it clear that we needed him, that I liked having soldiers around because they were usually strong, hard-working and – most of all – punctual.

'What about the hound?' He jutted his chin towards his car window, where a Staffordshire bull terrier was showing off its pear-shaped jaw.

'Is it trained?'

He sneered, as if it were a stupid question.

'You want a trial week,' I said. 'The dog can have one too.'

He decided to give it a go and grabbed an oily green pack out of the boot.

Fra was, understandably, worried about the Staffie. The dog looked pretty ferocious, the sort that you hear on the news has ripped off a toddler's face. But it was called, incongruously for a hard man's pet, Daisy, and was a soppy, sweet thing. And once Darren had let us all know how hard he was – biting Daisy's ear hard when she misbehaved – he softened too. Sitting beside the fire at night, he began to tell us bits of his life: how he had grown up in Devon and had only discovered his stepdad wasn't his real father on his thirteenth birthday. He didn't really know who his father was but liked the idea that his old man had been a gangster, since his stepfather's car had once been torched. Darren had dropped out of school at twelve and was by then already drinking hard. He had joined up at seventeen, and within a year was out on patrol in some of the fiercest war zones in Basra and Helmand. Although he had left the army two years ago, it still felt as if he were clinging to it: wearing fatigues and a knife on his hip, and borrowing the air rifle to 'slot', as he said, some rabbits. His boot polishing was almost obsessive-compulsive, and he had a double-edged attitude to the army: he loved it, saying life only made sense to him in the army; but, at the same time, he hated what had happened to him. He had lost almost all his friends, and those who hadn't died in Helmand had committed suicide since coming home. He had been drifting ever since leaving the army: he had been married to a girl for six weeks before discovering, he said, that the kid she had claimed was his wasn't. He went and lived with another woman who got jealous of his dog. He discovered Daisy had wounds and bruises because the woman was hitting her with a frying pan.

'There's stuff from the war burnt on your brain you won't ever get rid of,' he said to me one of the first days he was here. 'That's why so many soldiers commit suicide – because they think it'll never get better. Or they drink to blot it all out.'

Every other day, something happened that made us realize how traumatized he was. If a door slammed, or the girls accidentally popped a balloon, Darren would swear furiously and start shaking. He wouldn't be able to eat or talk for a while, and none of us could really get through to him. He would get terrors at night, reliving moments from the war in his sleep. When he came in the next morning he looked white and brittle, as if he had spent the night with ghosts. We had to ask the men who came to excavate one of the caves on site to stop using explosives in case it set Darren off again.

He swore so much that I had to reiterate the rule that there was no swearing in the house. So sometimes he would run out of the door with little Daisy chasing after him, and you could see him with his hands cupped around his mouth as if he were sneezing. The first time it happened I went up to him, putting a hand on his back. I thought he was being sick as he jerked convulsively. But then I heard what he was hissing through his teeth: desperate, unstoppable expletives.

He certainly wasn't easy to live with, but everyone was fond of Darren. He was tough, but – though he pretended he wasn't – very vulnerable. Although he had left school at twelve, he was smart and eloquent. We realized that one of our challenges was to nudge him into becoming a civilian, because he was still too attached to military garb and slang. He was clinging to a past life and if we were to be of any use to him, we needed to make him comfortable in civilian clothing and settings. For a while we called him Sarge, his old rank in the army, but stopped because it was a throwback to a life he needed to leave behind. He was still using army acronyms all the time: talking about setting up a VCP (vehicle checkpoint) on volunteer day or calling the garden room our PB (patrol base). When someone got mildly hurt cutting some kindling, Darren yelled for a CROW (combat replacement of war). So some of us started using and inventing our own acronyms and abbreviations to keep up.

'VPL in the kitchen!' Callum would shout.

'What the fuck's a VPL?' Darren would shout back.

'Stop swearing, Darren.'

'Just want to know what a VPL is.'

'Visible panty line.'

Later, Sara asked us not to disturb her as she was PTM. Darren looked confused, assuming it was something feminine.

'Pretending to meditate,' Sara expanded, laughing.

Over the next few weeks it felt as if we were softening him. One day, when we were in the middle of coppicing, I saw Darren with his arms around a huge ash tree.

'Look!' I shouted. 'Darren's become a hippie tree-hugger like the rest of us.'

Everyone looked up from their work and laughed at the sight of the tough nut, who was undeniably hugging a tree.

'I'm just checking its fucking girth, you morons,' he snarled back.

'Yeah, that's what you say to all your women, right?' Callum laughed.

Before you knew it, they were both insulting the other's mother, ratcheting up the insults each time until the laughter stopped and it looked for a second as if they were going to come to blows. They both had billhooks in their hands, and I was about to put myself in the middle of them. But Darren seemed to admire the fact that someone could give as good as they got, and he started laughing again.

It was always hard to know when you were safe to tease Darren affectionately and when it would send him off in fifth gear. There was a local woman here, one of our middle-aged volunteers, who had taken quite a shine to him. A few women seemed to want to mother him, and he didn't mind. This volunteer, Ruth, was a holistic healer and took Darren round to her therapy room to 'unblock his chakras'. This was a man who, when Fra and I had got back from our monthly supervision, asked us if we had 'boo-hooed like babies' with our supervisor. So the fact that he had gone to unblock his chakras, with what we thought was more than a hint of attraction on one side, if not both, presented an opportunity that was too good to miss. For weeks he had been teasing us about being hippies, and here he was, going off to lie on the couch of a pretty, alternative lady. At dinner that night, we tried to get the words 'blocked' and 'chakras' into every sentence we could.

Whenever Darren went to an AA meeting he gelled back his hair, polished his boots (again) and sprayed deodorant all over himself. He looked a bit like a spiv, and Maggie looked at him with disdain: 'I reckon there's a gay Italian man inside Darren just trying to get out.'

Darren shot her a glare but smiled. 'Better than having one on the outside trying to get in.'

But other times it would go horribly wrong. I wanted Darren to help Sara plant out some of the seedlings. I thought an activity that required precision, sensitivity and patience would be a good discipline, and I knew that Sara was tough enough to handle him.

So one morning, as we were sitting round the table, I suggested it. He flew off the handle.

'I'm not planting no fucking vegetables,' he shouted, pointing his finger at my chest. 'Don't give me pussy work, because I ain't no fucking pussy.'

He went on like that and the more I tried to talk him down, the more agitated he became, swearing and threatening. It was as if he had a demon inside him: he told us he would 'open up' the next person who asked him to plant fucking vegetables. He had crossed a line, and I took him outside and told him very clearly where the line was. He didn't like it, but he understood rank, and I pulled it hard. I told him he couldn't swear in the house but, much more seriously, he couldn't threaten anyone. This was a safe sanctuary, and there couldn't be any verbal violence. I told him to go inside and apologize.

'I don't never apologize,' he said, staring at me.

'If you can't apologize, you'd better leave.'

'You're not serious?'

'Just go inside and say sorry.'

He looked at me in disbelief. I had had years of experience of persuading our kids to apologize. Sometimes it would take an hour, but life stopped until they said sorry. Darren was, by comparison, a pushover. He sat down and stared at the trees. I listened to him say his piece, about how he felt we were trying to change him, to neuter him somehow: stopping him swearing, and stopping him wearing military fatigues, and now suggesting he do 'pussy work'.

'Real men work the soil,' I said. 'Throughout history warriors have also been gardeners.'

'Bullshit.'

We argued the point for a while, and I told him that real men also know when to say sorry. Eventually he went inside and made a sincere apology, and we all agreed that he didn't have to do any gardening.

Spud was another of the local rough sleepers who was hanging out with us. A rotund Geordie, he had been referred to us by a local charity. He had lost his job because he had shattered a couple of vertebrae falling off scaffolding. His driving licence had been taken away for drink-driving and his woman had dumped him. For a month now he had been sleeping rough in a barn outside town.

Darren and I went to see him because Darren had offered to help improve his shelter. We walked across the field behind the hospital. One minute it felt like you were in the centre of town, and the next you were right out of it. We jumped through a collapsed stone wall and alongside a hedge until we came to a ruin, a stone barn with no roof. The 'door' was a hole where the fireplace used to be. Spud had a fire going in the corner, which was blackened by smoke. There was a cheap blue tarp held in place with string and breeze blocks. It flapped in the wind, making an irritating noise that must, at night, have been even more annoying. But there was something romantic and elemental about the place: the view was incredible – you could see across fields to the valley below and then up the other side, where the sheep were white dots. I was pleased Darren could be useful, adjusting the tarp, using bungees to make it tight. It was good that, as well as having people come in, we were also going out to them.

Spud started coming here to help out. One sunny March morning, Darren, Spud and I were coppicing. I had done a lot of the chainsaw work the week before, and it felt like a completely new clearing in the woods: there were bare stumps everywhere and eight-foot logs scattered around the site. Already it felt like nature was moving in. A nuthatch, upside down, was studying us from behind his wraparound shades. We could hear the drilling of a woodpecker. It felt fresh, almost like spring. We had billhooks and bow saws and made a pile of good straight hazel for rustic furniture and another pile for firewood. We cut off the bushy brash and laid it in a tangle on top of the beige tree stumps; within a few months these stumps would send up two dozen shoots and the brash would stop the deer and rabbits grazing on the regrowth.

Spud was showing video clips on his phone to Darren. 'Come on, Spud, we're working!' I shouted.

Darren had pulled out his phone now, and was showing Spud a topless photo someone had sent him.

'Come on, fellas, give us a hand!'

'Look at this.' Darren wanted to bond by looking at a stranger's boobs. 'Almost as big as Spud's, aren't they?'

'Easy,' Spud said, coming towards us with a log.

It went on like that for an hour: trying to coax them to work, to put away their phones, to enjoy the noise of nature rather than that of another YouTube clip. And then, quite suddenly, we heard a helicopter getting closer. It didn't just fly low overhead, it banked and circled over us repeatedly. It seemed only about sixty or seventy foot above us, its blades making even the snowdrops back off.

I looked for Darren and he was standing with his back to a thick ash tree. He was white and hyperventilating.

'Darren, you okay?'

He didn't say anything but looked at me in terror. The helicopter circled for another ten seconds before banking sharply to the right and pulling away. Darren swore at it for the next five minutes. He had slid down the trunk now, so that he was sitting on the cold ground.

I walked him inside and got him a cup of tea. He sat in the armchair, his thousand-yard stare fixed on the past in Helmand. He couldn't talk or eat, and just sat there looking catatonic.

He was still sitting in the chair when Benny came back from school. She looked at his drawn face and decided to write him one of her letters. To guests who didn't know her that well, Benny could come across as an ice queen: she would ignore you a lot of the time, strutting around the place looking snooty, as if she were a model on a catwalk. When you called her, she would put her fingertips on her chest and say, mock-diva, '*Moi?*' But when she saw someone in the deep end, she would quietly write them a letter that could move them to tears. She wrote a little note in her neatest handwriting, and then showed it to me:

'Dear Darren,' it said. 'I'm sorry you're sad. I really like having you here because you swear so much. It's really cool. Love, Benny.'

That's all it was, but it melted him. I watched her take it over to him and he read it, smiled broadly and gave her a hug. After that, he cheered up a bit and played Scrabble with the girls. They all tried hard to use the square tiles to write swear words.

Fra, meanwhile, had phoned the local airbase to complain. They of all people, she thought, should realize that soldiers with PTSD need to feel safe, and not pursued by low-flying aircraft. The complaint got passed up the line, until she got through to the helicopter trainer, the guy who set the flight path. It turned out it was an old friend of ours and that he had asked the pilot to circle over our woods because he thought our kids would enjoy it. We laughed about it but then spent days dealing with the fallout. The next morning Darren came in looking shattered.

'Fucking flashbacks, man,' he said, looking dejected. 'Like it's not bad enough seeing your mates dying in front of you once. I've got to watch it again and again. All through the night. I had a mate, Charlie, who had everything below his waist blown off by an IED. I had to carry the half-body two miles to where a helicopter could land. And when I laid him down, waiting for the chopper, there wasn't fear in his fucking eyes, but resentment, like, 'Why wasn't it you?' Charlie had a wife and kids; I only had the whisky to live for. And now I wish I had died out there, had a death with honour and valour, rather than this fucking agony of surviving completely unscathed.'

'Not exactly unscathed,' I butted in.

'There's not a scratch on me,' he said.

'Not on the outside, but you've got your scars.'

He nodded slowly. 'My scars are their scars. I can't get my mates out of my head, that's what does my head in. They're there all the time, their guts hanging out on my lap, another slotted through the throat and squirting blood at me like he's a fucking water pistol. Another mate, he was told he'd have these flashbacks all his life, and he topped himself. Why not? Fifty years of this, I would rather die today, I really would. Can you imagine fifty more years of this shit? After fifty years I won't have the flag on the coffin, the last post, all that solemn send-off stuff. If I survive, I'll become an embittered old drunk, with a funeral attended by a couple of whores and a landlord collecting debts.' He stared at the fire, his angular face tense. 'It just doesn't make sense. Peace is harder than the war. All I want to do is get back to warfare. At least there you knew what you were doing. There was the adrenaline of having people shooting at you. It was a high, a fucking trip. You're terrified but excited. Nothing gives you that hit: no drugs, no drink, no bird. And it's harder to adjust to coming out of the army than it was fighting the war. When you get back, you don't even understand what it was all for: like you've been fighting to protect the citizens of a country who just want to break into fucking Foot Locker to steal trainers.'

Here, the most unlikely people found common ground. For weeks Darren and Chloe had barely spoken. They didn't have much to say to each other: he was a highly strung and fairly misogynist soldier, and she was a well-educated cosmopolitan teenager. But Chloe was listening to Darren talking about PTSD and suddenly they discovered they had something very serious – terror and trauma – in common. I just listened as they discussed triggers, therapies and coping strategies. From that evening they got on better. They still didn't have much in common, but they had a newfound respect, and empathy, for each other.

Darren was still wound up when we were talking about what jobs to do the following morning. The advantage here was that there were always plenty of grunt jobs that were perfect for anger management. I gave him a splitting axe and showed him the large pile of cross-cut logs.

'That lot,' I said, pointing at the pile, 'split to this size,' I put my hand in a circle, the size of a thigh, 'and stacked there.'

'Got it.'

All morning we heard him growling as he brought the heavy axe on to the logs. We could hear the lovely rip of wood fibres coming apart. At about ten he broke his first splitting axe. I gave him another, and within an hour he had broken that one too. By the log stores there was now a carpet of split logs. He hadn't stacked any, he had just walked around the clearing swinging like some warrior from the Dark Ages. He got through three axe handles by lunch, but by then he was sweating and serene.

'That's the best stress relief,' he said, smiling.

* * *

A week later Sara came walking up the slope, saying that Harriet
had had her new litter of piglets. We all downed tools and walked
over, some of us running in excitement. I felt terrible: I had calcu-
lated she was due to farrow in three weeks' time and hadn't
wormed her, or put down more bedding, or checked her milk, or
disinfected her ark and her teats. When we got there, it was bad.
There were two dead piglets outside the ark and two more inside.
They lay there on the hard, frosty ground, completely still. Inside,
five were still alive.

Clive was experienced with pigs, and he took charge. He told
us to pick up the carcasses, keeping an eye out for Harriet the
sow, in case she didn't like it. They felt barely heavier than a wet
flannel. We put more straw in the ark and made it cosy. Harriet
settled down, and we put the surviving piglets on her teats. I was
sighing with guilt, worrying about how I had let her down. We
had never lost so many.

'Don't worry,' Clive said. 'Where there's livestock, there's
deadstock.'

The morning's trauma wasn't over. We had a bonfire going to
deal with the brash from our coppicing and Clive said we should
burn the dead piglets. We got the fire roaring and then put the
poor things on the flames. Darren came round the corner and
went white. He hadn't had much sleep anyway, and his eyes were
burning more than normal. He ran off into the woods and I heard
him retching. He came back a few minutes later, wiping his mouth.

'I smelt burnt flesh and it took me right back there,' he said. He
was staring into the distance again. 'I had to pick up dozens of
bodies after a botched air attack on an Afghan village. They had
"phossed" the whole place, and me and my mates had to go and
pick up all the civilians: babies, toddlers, the elderly. They were all
crispy. The place is a FOB now.'

'What's that?'

'Forward operating base. Makes me think they did it on purpose. It was a Taliban-infested town, so they torched the lot.'

It was often like that. There we were, enjoying the sunlit spring in a Somerset woodland. You couldn't hear any traffic. It was quiet and peaceful. And yet, at the same time, it was tormented and troubled. In the midst of the calm, there were memories of terror. People got the shakes. It was quite a contradiction.

I knew, by now, what the deal was: we were giving away our peace and, in return, absorbing the anxieties and negativities. We were sponging up bad energy as best we could and found great satisfaction in the hard work and the strange exchange. By that spring, though, Francesca had hit the same buffers I had twelve months before. She had been a full-time carer for Chloe for almost a year: driving her to countless appointments, staunching wounds both literal and metaphorical, getting caught up in the contagious control-freakery of the anorexic. Her sense of stability and centredness had been slowly eroded and she subtly retreated, in an attempt at self-preservation. She was still ever-present, but wary now. It began to feel, she said, as if the community were continuing alongside her, not around her any more. It was a parallel place, in her own home, but held now at arm's length due to acute compassion fatigue. She decided to look for part-time work, something to give her a role away from here.

'I don't know how you do it,' she said to me wearily one evening. It didn't sound like a compliment; more as if she really wanted to know not how, but why.

People frequently asked us how we coped, how we survived despite dealing with crises day after day for years on end. Personally, I felt that attempting to absorb the stresses and sorrows of our guests was a duty, part of a spiritual discipline. And perhaps that, in some ways, made it more manageable: duty is a comfortable yoke, a burden that gives as well as takes away responsibility. We had given up on any notion that things were within our power, that we were doing the work of curing or heal-ing, and that too was liberating. We were, I hope, offering compassion, service and basic attendance, but not because we were ourselves well or superior; we were serving and carrying and, hopefully, sustaining. But we felt we had a way to process, or redeem, all the negativity and sadness: going to chapel twice a day, squeezing out the sponge and finding a source of peace and refreshment, far more than we needed for ourselves. Regardless of what people believed, we were inviting them to chapel too, maintaining together a rhythm of prayer and reflection. It meant we were receiving, and giving away, what wasn't ours. And that made us feel, in normal circumstances, not drained but somehow refreshed by the work. Often we didn't even feel as if we were doing the work at all. We were vessels, just jars of clay. The trou-ble was that vessels got broken, shattered so that the pieces couldn't be found. That's where, I think, Francesca was, cast down but not destroyed.

I watched the bonfire, wondering how I could help her find her missing fragments. The smoke was being levelled by the wind, the flames flattened and sucked through the orange brash. A few minutes later it seemed to be going out and people reached forward to prod the fire. You didn't know where it would catch next. It subsided, seeming finished, but suddenly crackled again, a cleansing pyre of autumn leaves in springtime. The purple crocuses that had just pushed through looked like mini champagne flutes lined up on a grassy tray. It felt as if we were at some sort of surreal party, the kind that never ends; and, as everyone knows, it's often the host of the party who enjoys it the least.

That spring, a man called Ricky had been referred to us by a local charity. He looked a bit like a pirate, with large rings in his ears and tattoos all over his arms. He was missing lots of teeth but wore a plate with dentures, so his smile – compared to the rest of him – looked surprisingly new. He was a rugged-looking man, the sort you know has lived hard. He always wore a black biker's jacket and creased-up jackboots. But he was also strangely camp: he winked at you when he laughed and had glasses that made him look less macho.

He wasn't one of those people who told you their whole life story as soon as they arrived, but he wasn't closed or evasive either. Over the next few days he talked a bit about his life: how he moved to India in the sixties because his mother had started a relationship with some sort of aspiring guru. The relationship didn't work out, and Ricky and his siblings drifted around London and Somerset for years. 'We used to look for food in bins,' he said.

He had children – two young boys – who he hadn't seen for years. He had been sleeping rough, having had his beloved camper van conned from him by an ex, or so he said. He had always been an odd-job man, doing electrics, carpentry, plumbing, engines, and everything else. Within days of him being here he started doing stuff we had been meaning to do for years: he rewired a lamp, made a new gate, re-handled all the axes Darren had broken, re-handled a hammer and a mallet, sorted out the energizer for the electric fence, fixed the pick-up and filled it with four gallons of diesel he found in the other camper van. All day long he was tinkering around, slowly improving the place. He made a cutlery tray and a present for Leo and sorted out a few bikes.

But Ricky had been a loner for so long that he barely noticed other people. He got up from the table and wandered off for a fag as soon as he had finished eating. He didn't clear up, or wash up, or make tea. After a couple of days I mentioned it to him, but he frowned and went silent. He was a growling, surly presence, holding you hostage by giving the impression that he was ready to explode at any minute. I became tentative about confronting things I knew were wrong. I kept mentioning, during every meal, that we all needed to help clear up, but he turned his head sideways in anger, as if I were asking him to wash my socks. And at the end of the meal he still managed to slip away when my back was turned, back to the workshop for a fag and some oily labour. It wasn't deliberately thoughtless: he just hadn't thought at all.

He was extremely uptight about paperwork. We tried to help him sort a few things out, but any time he needed to fill in a form he would become tense and critical, blaming everyone else for the absurd complications he himself had created. When we were doing the polytunnel, he was even more stressed. It was as if he could only demonstrate his worth if he could get the hoops perfectly vertical and the crop bars immaculately horizontal. No one else could work with him, so I became the monkey to his organ grinder, following his terse commands.

'What makes you so anxious doing this?' I asked him, but he didn't reply.

Although things were often tough, we were frequently laughing. One afternoon in June, Callum had lost his temper and had taken a sledgehammer to a pallet. There were splinters and nails everywhere and he looked at me sheepishly as I walked past. 'It just fell apart in me hands,' he said, using the familiar catchphrase.

Various other sayings had become habitual. Francesca and I would often say 'Good morning' to each other in the evening, as that was the earliest time we'd found to stop and say hello. Leo would go up to burly men, holding out his fists and saying, 'You're in big chubble.' Once he had got one laugh, he kept trying for more. 'To infinity and –' he would shout, raising his right hand.

'– the blonde,' Callum would reply from the workshop.

Leo, recognizing Callum's voice, ran off to see his beloved 'uncle'.

Leo felt things so keenly but didn't yet have the eloquence to express himself. 'I really, really, really . . .' he would say.

'What?'

'I just really, really, really, really . . .'

'What?'

And he would scream and run away because you didn't understand him. You would find him disconsolate somewhere, his forehead resting on his forearms.

One guest, on leaving, accidentally packed Leo's beloved Batman cape with her clothes. For a few days he was distraught and we reassured him that she was going to post it back. But when her homemade envelope arrived it had come open and there was a letter in it but no cape.

'Somewhere in Somerset,' Callum joked, 'there's a postman going round in a toddler's Batman cape.'

Although we tried to avoid people becoming romantically involved, one day I found a bra up by the ambulance. I hung it on the corner of the log store, where it blew in the wind like some strange white flag, waiting – like Cinderella's glass slipper – to be claimed by the right-shaped person. There were now all sorts of things around the site that were awaiting the right-shaped person.

Someone had wandered off with my adze, so I hadn't quite finished a stool I was making, and it had only one, not two, buttocks scorped out. The one-buttocked stool sat in the workshop, awaiting the magic one-buttocked guest.

We organized a woodland Olympics that summer: we had a rock putt, a log jump, welly whanging and a tug-of-peace. Callum invented a ball game that was a combination of badminton and ping-pong – called bad pong– which involved playing ping-pong with badminton rackets. New arrivals were always a bit shocked when we asked them if they fancied 'a game of bad pong'.

Even when there were house discussions, as there often were, we still had a laugh. At one house meeting it was getting a bit heated, as we were discussing whether certain people were pulling their weight. Bridget was back for a fortnight and was coming under the cosh a bit. She defended herself by saying that it was her input that had given the willows around the tree bog a one hundred per cent success rate.

'It was your output that helped too,' Ricky quipped.

Another time Sara asked us all what our favourite vegetables were, so that she would know what to plant in the raised beds and polytunnel. Darren nodded his head and said, 'My favourite vegetable is steak.' We all laughed, and he realized his mistake. 'No, hang on,' he said, 'I mean chips.'

Having Darren at the table was always a laugh. One evening, the girls were handing round melon and Darren looked at it, frowning. He put some on his plate and tucked in, picking it up in his fingers and starting at one end. He crunched through the outer shell, grimacing as he munched on it.

'Bit tough, this one,' he said.

A few days later, Spud came by looking sheepish. I wondered

what was wrong, and he took me aside. 'Anyone know how to saw?' he asked.

I frowned. We were living in a working woodland, so it seemed like a strange question. 'Saw?'

He pulled out a mangled, dirty teddy. 'This is Ted,' he said. 'His scarf has come off.' He showed me a bit of ripped fabric.

'Sew?' I said.

'Aye, saw,' he said.

At that point, his mucker Darren came in and starting roaring with laughter at the idea that Spud, the tough homeless man, had brought round his teddy to be fixed. As Darren was laughing Spud made it worse by saying, 'Aye, and he needs a bath and all.'

Darren shrieked at that, pointing at Spud and calling him a soft northerner.

By now the kids had come in, and they were smiling at the scene. The unshaven man they had seen for the last few weeks was suddenly one of them, a kid with a cuddly toy, and they warmed to him from then on.

We often laughed at ourselves too. One morning I told everyone I had to get over to Castle Cary.

'What are you doing there?' Darren asked, suspecting I was slacking.

'I've got to pick up an old shed and a Welsh hermit who's coming to stay.'

'Only here,' he said, smiling.

I was at a lunch for my mother's birthday ten miles away when Sara phoned. Darren had lost it. He was running around wanting to top himself. He had a rope and was looking for a tree. I drove back and arrived to find that Sara had been chasing Darren through the woods. She had locked up the air rifle and hidden the carving knives. Darren had bid farewell to everyone on Facebook – where else? – and one of his old army mates had phoned and told me that if Darren committed suicide whilst he was with us 'it'll be the end of you'.

We sat Darren down and listened to him. He couldn't see the point: all the struggle and fight, the drive to earn money and feed children, just to die in the end. He kept saying that he was an 'evil cunt', that God had turned his back on him. He said he had a mask of nice, kind Darren, but actually he was a killing machine, a bastard who had shot people up.

Callum listened, recognizing the feelings of pointlessness, but he put Darren right: 'I reckon you're the opposite. The outside is the tough nut, but inside you're a kind bloke.'

'I haven't got any GCSEs, or any A levels,' Darren said. 'Haven't even got a trade. My trade is death. And the shooting isn't the worst bit: seeing someone in the scopes at 300 metres, pulling the trigger and seeing a puff of red mist is nothing. It's when you're knifing someone up close, hearing the gurgle, the noise of the life leaving them – that doesn't ever get out of your head. It's burnt on there. It's two years since I got out, and it doesn't feel any better. I just want to finish it all.'

I couldn't leave him, so I put him in the car and took him to my mother's birthday. I parked up outside and explained that it was a family do.

'I get it, best behaviour.'

'No swearing?'

'Why the fuck not?' He laughed.

But he was well behaved, sitting on the floor playing cards with the girls and chatting to my folks, who had put their drinks away.

A week later, though, he was gone. He was out all Thursday night and came in boasting that he had got laid. By then Daisy, his dog, had crapped on the rug in the garden room because she hadn't been let out. Darren was always telling us he was irresistible to women, but when I checked out his story, it turned out that he was just in a pub with Spud, getting pissed.

'Listen, Darren,' I said. 'I don't understand why Francesca or I should clean up after your dog when we're rushing to get the kids to school, and all because you got pissed last night.'

'I only had one drink,' he said.

'Really?' It sounded extremely improbable for a man who came to us saying he was an alcoholic.

'You calling me a liar?'

He picked up Daisy and stormed off. He had decided to go and live above a pub that offered accommodation to war veterans. That's where he had been drinking all last night. His car sped off, kicking up mud and stones as it went.

It made me very melancholic. For all his bluster, swagger and swearing, he often came across as a lost boy who wanted a father figure. I was, briefly, that figure, but I had pushed him too hard and he had stormed off. Darren had made the place edgy, probably too edgy. But he was switched on and driven. I didn't like bad endings, and this one was definitely bad.

But later that afternoon Darren came back and said goodbye properly. He hugged everyone and stood there, slightly embarrassed at all the emotion going round. He had already been drinking.

By then we were used to successes and breakthroughs. Chloe had smashed up her scales with a sledgehammer as a ceremonial farewell to her eating disorder and had gone back to university. Ricky had got a job, and the YMCA had found him a flat in town. Jenny had got clean and gone home. But it was fairly common, too, for a stay to go sour and to end suddenly. And when Darren left we once again asked ourselves if we weren't, in trying to do good, causing more harm or hurt. We wondered whether we had challenged too much, or not enough. Each bad ending was like that, making us question ourselves and what we were doing and leaving us with as many regrets as memories.

June. A local farm had a few orphan lambs and so we offered them a couple of piglets in return. We loaded two of the pigs into the pick-up, covering them with the old chipboard table-tennis table. The farm was up on the plateau of Priddy, and there were lambs everywhere in the fields, legs straight but divergent, like someone struggling to walk on stilts. We unloaded our pigs and chose four lambs. They were only a few days old and their wool was in tight curls like a new carpet. Compared to handling the pigs, they were easy to pick up and move: docile and cuddly. They were beautiful beasts, with knobbly knees and ears like horizontal ovals.

We put them in the orchard at dusk and they skipped around merrily. We warmed up some milk and the children fed them from the bottle, amazed at how strongly the little beasts could suck.

'You were worse,' Fra laughed at Emma as she was pulled forward by a lamb.

Over the next few days they grew fast. They would watch us with their jaws moving sideways, looking like insolent teenagers chewing gum. But they also bleated loudly and ran up to us when we entered the pen. You only realized how grey their coats were when you rubbed it and glimpsed the layer of pristine white fleece beneath.

One night when we were feeding them we noticed that Sam, who was normally a greedy feeder, was backing away from the bottle. He was hugely bloated, bulging unnaturally on both sides.

He was moving uncomfortably too. There was clearly something very wrong. We put all the lambs inside the shed and I went and googled 'inflated sheep' (which is another thing you shouldn't put into a search engine). We called a friend, who told us it was a common ailment but could be fatal if not dealt with immediately. She told us to fill a large syringe with a mixture of oil and ground ginger and force it down poor Sam's throat. We did so, and then watched for half an hour, hoping Sam would froth a bit at the mouth as he expelled air. Sam kept raising his tail, but nothing emerged. We called another friend, a woman with seven hundred lambs, and she suggested crushing up an antacid tablet, such as a Rennie, and mixing it with water. We did that and, once again, forced it down the lamb's throat, but still the poor creature just stood there, apart from the others, its breathing becoming ever more laboured. Later, the others lay asleep in the straw, using each other as pillows. We assumed, sadly, that this was the end. Maggie's dad said that you could hold the lamb's nostrils and breathe hard into its mouth to try to move the blockage; or butter a gloved finger and put it inside its anus to unblock it; or cut an incision near its hind legs and then suture it up again. The last of these sounded absurd, but it is apparently a common remedy. An hour later, having lacked the knowledge or the courage to cut the animal, we went to bed, not expecting to see Sam alive in the morning.

When I woke up the next day, I went immediately to the shed and there, bright as usual, was Sam, back to normal dimensions. It was as if a balloon had been deflated; he was bouncing around with the others. All that day, every time one of us approached the orchard Sam bounded up to us, as if in gratitude. And then we would watch him run off, kicking both legs – fore and aft – in the air at the same time, like a gymnast doing aerial splits.

* * *

Sharing our meals was one of the most important aspects of life here. It brought us together, whatever our differences. But meals were often difficult times. We've lived with carnivores, vegans and vegetarians, with a woman who had a wheat and dairy allergy, and another who was allergic to eggs, nuts and cocoa. We had had guests with food phobias who couldn't touch cheese, or bear the sight of bananas or ketchup. We usually had one or two people with eating disorders living with us. Cooking for all those needs was hard enough, but the actual eating time was even harder. There was one man who sounded not unlike the pigs as he snuffled everything in sight. A recovering anorexic would find it even more difficult to eat to the soundtrack of his grunting and munching. We had an over-eater who ate incessantly to allay her loneliness.

It was clear that most of our guests had never sat round a table as part of a family. Conversation was often inappropriate, and people grabbed whatever food they could as fast as possible and sloped off as soon as they had finished. We didn't just have to teach the children basic table manners, we were teaching almost everyone the very basics: we wash our hands, we start together once we've given thanks, we clear the table together when everyone's finished. We pass, share, offer. We savour rather than scoff. We refuse what we want for the benefit of someone else.

The symbolism of food, of course, goes very deep. For many it is associated with love, and the way some people showed love for our children was by showering them with sweets. Or guests felt unloved if someone didn't save the last slice of cake for them. For those with eating disorders though, food represented not only calories but also a whole host of other complex issues. Sheila MacLeod wrote in *The Art of Starvation* that 'in observing the behaviour of the slimmer and the anorexic, we may read the same text, "I want to lose weight." But the subtexts differ. Whereas the slimmer's reads, "I want to be a sexually attractive woman," the anorexic's reads, "I want to shed the burden of womanhood." Slimming is basically a matter of vanity. Anorexia is much more a matter of pride.' Not eating food isn't only about shedding weight, MacLeod wrote, but about shedding responsibility.

I was always aware of the stresses, as well as the pleasures, of mealtimes. Part of the problem was that eating increases anxiety for anorexics: those who starve themselves produce less noradrenaline, which means that their anxiety levels drop. Once they start eating again, their anxiety levels rise, which sometimes reinforces that perilous correlation between serenity and starvation. Not for the first time, our simple rules were making people more fretful and nervous than if we had allowed them to pursue their habitual coping strategies.

There were other aspects to living with people with eating disorders. Basal ganglia, situated at the base of the forebrain, are responsible for perfectionism and compulsion. They are over-firing in anorexics, meaning that they're often ferocious instillers of order. Sheila MacLeod called it a 'general sense of superiority, which can only be described as moral ... the subtext reads, "unless I impose some form and order on life, I shall lose control, chaos will ensue, and life will become meaningless."'

Everyone living in a community struggles with the lack of control over their lives and their environment. There's always a subtle battle over who will take command. But anorexics sometimes took that urge for control to a new level, alphabetizing the spice rack, offering a commentary on your cooking, reading ingredients obsessively, insisting that everything be done their way. Anxiety can be contagious, as can bossiness, and it often took epic amounts of patience to accept being bossed about by a guest who critiqued everybody's cooking.

Francesca and I worried about the way in which the kids grew picky, mimicking adult food issues. Once Benny shivered and said she couldn't touch cheese, and we were very alarmed. There was, however, a fairly simple solution. In the words of one of my heroes, the Italian aristocrat and communitarian Lanza del Vasto, we needed to 'find the shortest, simplest way between the earth, the hands, and the mouth'. When the children were being fussy, I would take them out for a walk in the woods. I couldn't ever persuade them to eat lettuce sitting at the table, but it was hard, out in the wild, to stop them munching the leaves or flowers we found: Jack-by-the-hedge, ramsons, borage and nasturtiums. They would make infusions of the leaves of ribwort plantain to cure coughs. I would show them St John's wort or heal-all or yarrow, and we would experiment making lotions and potions. If they didn't eat during meals, we took them for a walk afterwards, letting them pluck plums, pears and apples from the various fruit trees. Benny would hoof tomatoes from the polytunnel. They would race around the clearings, picking wild strawberries and bitter raspberries. It didn't matter if they didn't like stuff and spat it out. They were learning that food and medicines were all around them, that eating could be an adventure rather than a chore, and that nature was a far more elegant provider than the supermarket.

Sara was an expert not only at growing kilos of produce, but also at foraging for everything the woodland had to offer. In the months she was here we made nettle soup, wild garlic pesto, elderflower cordial, hazelnut flour and medlar cheese. We pickled unripe seed pods from the nasturtiums and ate them like poor man's capers. We painted a sign at the entrance to the polytunnel, a line from Wendell Berry: 'The soil is the great connector of lives . . . without proper care for it we can have no community.' It was high summer by then, and all Sara's gardening was coming to fruition. In the polytunnel there were dozens of impossibly glossy aubergines, dense clusters of tomatoes, cucumbers hanging like spiky salamis, chillies so pointed they seem to warn of danger. Colourful peppers hung like balloons at a party. Peas bulged like knuckles in their pods. You could barely see the soil in the raised beds because of the courgettes, cabbages and chard. The flat peltate leaves of the nasturtiums rose all around the borders, interrupted only by the rich orange flowers. All over the place there were Californian poppies, sweet peas and marigolds, giving colour to the usual greens and browns of our home. The girls shook seeds from the dried-out poppy heads and used them to bake bread.

It was a happy period, partly I think because the children felt central to the place now, not squeezed aside. They were getting old enough to hold their own. They were, in their own way, sowing, harvesting and cooking. Their lives were now happily aligned with Windsor Hill Wood rather than overshadowed by it; they enriched it, and vice versa. As I watched them passing round their slightly burnt poppy-seed bread, Sara reminded me that the word 'ecology' originally meant nothing more than the study of the home. We had discovered, thanks to her, an environmentalism that implied wilderness but also domesticity. We were tending, weeding and nurturing not only all of Sara's veg but also ourselves. We were growing, and growing together. As Masanobu Fukuoka, the Japanese philosopher–farmer, once wrote, 'The ultimate goal of farming is not the growing of crops but the cultivation and perfection of human beings.'

The lifestyle here was wholesome for the children, but it was truly healing for the many guests. Even dour Ricky, before he left, had come up to me and said he was feeling 'hale'. It was an odd, old-fashioned word to use, but it seemed right somehow. It means both healthy and whole, as if one's divided or hidden sides have come together. It's a bit like the Italian description of being *tutto d'un pezzo*, all in one piece, completely coherent. And that's what living communally often feels like: you come out of hiding, with all the shame and embarrassment that can cause, but as you live with others you realize there's no reason for that shame, that in the open it melts away and you can be yourself at last.

Year Five

'Human beings will be happier – not when they cure cancer or get to Mars or eliminate racial prejudice or flush Lake Erie – but when they find ways to inhabit primitive communities again'

– Kurt Vonnegut

Summer is on the wane again. The leaves have turned brittle, and the birds are playing musical chairs on the branches, circling around before suddenly descending to compete for the perfect perch. Everything in the polytunnel has gone soft and mouldy. There are puddles all over the pitted drive, and muddy wellies line the walls of the garden room once more.

Francesca has found a part-time job as a teaching assistant at the local school, and her absence, three days a week, changes the feel of the place. It's still a family home, but not like it was a few years ago, when everyone was here all the time. Now Francesca, Benny and Emma head out to school, Leo goes to nursery, and it can feel – in the day at least – a tiny bit more institutionalized. I no longer have Fra as a sounding board during the day, someone to talk to about one crisis or another. And so many things happen from one day to the next that Francesca can sometimes feel outside the loop, unaware of what's happening or who's coming.

But as we get used to it a new balance emerges. Gav and Rachel and their dog come back to live with us. They had spent a year on another community farm but although it had been more comfortable, they felt it was a place where issues were ignored rather than discussed and they decided they preferred being here. It was great to have them back. They were a highly skilled couple and a laugh too, always seeing the funny side of absurd situations. Their presence here made life much easier. Rachel was quick-witted and tough (we nicknamed her 'the nutcracker'); Gav had been a skipper on boats for years and was a natural leader. He was great at encouraging, cajoling and challenging the troops, and it took a huge weight off my shoulders to have someone else in that role. I didn't mind at all relinquishing aspects of leadership, but over the next few months I found myself displaced from a territory I didn't even know had been mine. Gav often spoke of the Buddhist vows he had taken – a vow of truthfulness, a vow never to kill living creatures – and the moral high ground was always his. Heck, I thought ironically, that's my terrain. Now I was getting a taste of my own medicine. A different person was on the summit and I was having to accept someone else's exacting idealism. In the messy compromises of communal living, Gav often let us know how we all fell short. But it was good to be challenged, and he had a generosity of spirit that was striking. At one point, one of our guests was having quite a go at him, as she felt she was doing more than her fair share. It was getting pretty personal. I could see Gav under the cosh and assumed he would retaliate. But he simply said, 'If you're ever feeling that way, just ask me. I'll always help out if I can.' He had completely disarmed the situation, like an Aikido artist stepping backwards to dissipate an assailant's force.

* * *

A man called Simon was referred to us by a rehab centre and was brought down by one of the staff there. He looked a bit like Shaggy from *Scooby-Doo*: tall and thin, with a straggly beard. He didn't like wearing his false teeth, so his mouth looked like a rubber band, elastic and shapeless. He amused the girls by showing them how he could gurn, pushing his bottom lip well over his nose.

'How do you do that?' Emma asked, astonished by his strange face.

'I got no teeth.' He smiled at her, flashing his gums. 'You know what my ambition is? One day, I want to eat an apple again.'

The girls looked at me, amazed at such a simple goal. I made a note to try to help him fulfil it.

Simon wore a hat all the time and his hands were covered in scabs and sores. His nails were gnawed down hard and he drank huge quantities of coffee. He had the open vulnerability of a man who had been taken advantage of all his life. He told me early on that he had been raped by a priest when he was in care, and told me too of all the times he was exploited by his alleged friends on the streets. He had the facial scars of someone who had been in quite a few fights.

'Me, I were sleeping rough for twenty years. Twenty years until I went into rehab. Couldn't sleep in a bed for the first month there. Had to stay in me sleeping bag.' He had a thick Yorkshire accent. He told me of his daily grind for two decades: look for dry cardboard, then fag ends, then booze, then food.

He had bad shakes. Not because of the DTs but because of some neurological disease. Sometimes he shook so much he could only put sugar in his tea by holding both his arms completely straight, one hand holding the spoon, the other holding that hand and steadying it. When he passed you a cup of tea it was the same: he had to hold it low at the end of a straight arm so as not to spill it.

I spent quite a few days trying to help Si sort out his paperwork. He had no form of ID, no bank account, no birth certificate, nothing. His wallet had been stolen on the streets a few years ago and since then he had got by without anything. So he and I were filling in forms, but it was almost impossible.

'What was your mum's maiden name, Si?' He was rolling a fag as I filled in the forms.

'Don't know.'

'Her unmarried name? Do you know what she was called before she married your old man?'

'They weren't married.'

'So what's her surname?'

'Don't know,' he shouted at me, annoyed at all the questions.

I waited, letting him enjoy his fag. Then I asked him about his memories of his mother. He hated her, he said. She left him in that home, where all those things happened to him. He told me about his abandonment.

I tried again. 'Do you remember her date of birth?'

He shrugged.

'Father's date of birth?'

He shrugged again. 'He were a bastard, an' all.'

We gave up, and left it for another day. Without some form of ID he couldn't get a bank account, so he couldn't get a cheaper phone deal and all the rest. But although he was so wounded, he was quick-witted and kind. Whenever I was showing a new guest round, Si was always the one who made them a cuppa and took them off for a fag and a chat.

'We've got lots of odd jobs,' I would say to the new guest, trying to make them feel they would be useful.

'Aye, and plenty of odd people too.' Si would gurn, pulling his deliberately demented face.

He always sided with the underdog, wanting to talk to whoever was lost or lonely, never the key worker who had brought them down. Si gave them bags of basil, tomatoes or eggs, frowning angrily if they ever demurred.

'Si,' Maggie said one time, 'you can't give away all our communal produce.'

'You calling me a fucking thief?'

'No, Si, come on. I'm just asking you to leave some for us.'

It was the first time I saw a flash of his anger: not sneaky, but explosive. His face was contorted in fury and he jabbed his finger towards Maggie. I tried to calm him down, explaining that the problem arose because he was generous and kind, not because he was a thief. But he was offended and wanted to go on the counter-attack.

He wasn't easy to live with. He was aggrieved at tiny things: he showed me an insect bite, staring at me as if it were my fault and for which, to show him affection, I apologized profusely.

'You're not going to sue me, are you?' I joked.

His face broke into a smile, and the real Si came out: 'Pointless suing you, you ain't got no more than me.'

At heart he was gentle, concerned about the welfare of all the animals and guests. He was on his phone the whole time, spending silly amounts of money checking up on his erstwhile fellow travellers, telling us about who was clean, who had relapsed and who had died. He talked a lot about how much he worked, about everything he had done: watering the plants, letting out the chickens, doing the washing-up. He told you about it not because he was boasting about how hard he worked, I think, but because it made him feel a part of the place, integral to something.

But like many people here he had no distance between impulse and action. As soon as he had an idea or invitation, he wanted to act on it, meaning he was easily distracted or turned. There was no planning, only improvisation and impetuousness. He had no constancy or concentration, only chaotic spontaneity.

One night he was shouting outside our bedroom at eleven o'clock. I ignored him, but the shouting only got louder. I put my head out of the window, and there was Si, looking desperate.

'Got to send a text,' he shouted. 'Ain't got no credit. Give me your phone.'

I quietly explained to him that it could wait until the morning. But Si couldn't wait. He had to do it right that minute. I wearily chucked him my phone and watched as he huffed and puffed, his shaking fingers struggling to hit the right keys.

It happened again and again. He had to do things immediately, without delay. If the doctor had an appointment in the next hour, he dropped everything and expected you to too. When someone invited him somewhere, he wanted to be taken to the train station. His fury if you refused was almost frightening.

'Si,' I said each time it happened, 'you need to plan things. You're cooking tonight, so you can't go. And you're in charge of the chickens, so you've got to close the coop up at dusk. We need to organize comings and goings in advance; that's why we talk about them in our house meetings every week.'

His mouth was set in a wrinkled circle. He didn't like it, and I noticed that there was an aggression to his urgent, desperate demands. His insistence seemed nearly violent. Even little Leo had learned to delay gratification more than Si. That had always been part of our job here: to teach people to put some distance between desire and satisfaction. But I was doubtful that people

Si's age could really learn how. A few months with us couldn't correct a lifetime of bad, or no, parenting. His life had always been so hand to mouth that any suggestion that he delay gratification must have seemed to him as if there were a danger of starvation.

Francis was referred to us by a local charity in October. A round, red-faced man, we were told he was an alcoholic. But once he got here Francis said he didn't have a drink problem, he was emotionally abused by his wife, which gave him anxiety issues. He was troubled by all the oars his friends were putting in, offering advice and gossiping. After a few days, he said that it was only here that he didn't feel infantilized and nagged, which sounded complimentary but rang a distant alarm bell in my head. He was expecting us to be always on his side.

Francis didn't like to waste anything, which made him an unusual cook. He would put anything in the pot that needed finishing and then throw in colossal quantities of garlic. He was the only one of our guests who would use the pig's ears, the trotters, the heart and the liver. If something was a bit high, or had a greyish mould on it, Francis said that was all the more reason to eat it quickly. If there were hairs or lumps, Francis would chuckle and say that they gave the food 'purchase'.

'It'll be fine,' he would say, smiling at our squeamishness.

'You know the vampire thing is made up?' Maggie asked in her no-nonsense voice. 'You don't have to put in this much garlic.'

There was one memorable meal when he didn't want to make breadcrumbs out of the stale bread, so he simply sliced an old loaf into thirds and plonked the cubes of hard bread on top of the cauliflower.

'What's this?' said Benny, looking at the three lumps of burnt bread, each one the size of one of those furry rear-view mirror dice from the eighties.

'Breadcrumbs,' said Francis. 'It'll be fine.'

His catchphrase captured his easy-going nature but also hinted at an innate placidity, at the fact that he felt nothing needed to be done any better. He was as far from a perfectionist as it was possible to be. And each time I tried to point out that a job might need a bit more work, he always came out with his catchphrase and a shrug: 'It'll be fine.'

Over the next few months, Francis became a boulder that I just couldn't shift. There was a stubbornness in him that foiled every attempt to work together. He slumped in the armchair most of the day, an immovable object. It felt passive and uncreative. It was as if sitting down were a form of protest: 'I will not be moved.' None of the jobs he was asked to do got done. It seemed easier for him not to try than to risk failure. There was a passive aggressiveness to that task avoidance, even if it was not conscious. He always had an excuse for not having done something, just as there was always an excuse for him having got bladdered. I would listen, then get bored of listening because what he was saying didn't really make sense. I wasn't sure whether he even believed his side-stepping reasoning. Each time I tried to grab hold of a sentence and suggest it wasn't right, he would have moved on elsewhere and would be dodging me again. I felt like I had a little boy in front of me, someone who took the credit for things he hadn't done and no responsibility for the things he had.

As usual, the flashpoints were mundane but telling: little domestic disagreements that told you all you needed to know about someone's behaviour. We begged Francis not to invite any more friends around unless we, as a community, had agreed to it.

We asked him to pull the plug after washing up so that we didn't have to put our arms into cold, dirty water; to empty the Hoover into the bin not on top of the rose bushes, where we would find shreds of rubber bands, clumps of hair and all the other crap that comes out of a Hoover bag . . . but none of it sank in.

The irritation gurgled in my guts. I wish I could have been more seraphic but sometimes that kind of irritation can only be calmed by expressing it out loud. I trusted it too. Irritation tells me when things aren't right. With Francis I communicated that irritation, allowing it to emerge slowly and with precision.

'Do you understand what we've asked you to do?' I asked him, as I pointed at the clumps of Hoover innards on the woodland floor.

'Yes.' He nodded.

'And you know we've asked you these things many, many times before?'

'Yes.'

'Can you explain to me why you're still not doing them then?'

His explanation went round and round, and inside out and back to front. I found it all, intellectually, fairly fascinating. Some people are convinced they are doing the right thing even when they're blatantly doing the opposite of what has been asked. It's simply impossible to get through to them. There's a deafness that is insurmountable. We tried all the usual tactics: we asked Francis to repeat what we had said after giving him clear instructions; we drew his attention to agreements we had made; we put them in writing; we asked him to give his word. Most importantly, we gave him a forum in which he could disagree, so that jobs didn't feel imposed but were agreed communally. None of it made much difference. There was a strange edge of defiance about him. It would have been so easy to empty the Hoover into the small bin in the kitchen, but Francis would walk out amongst the trees, much further away, to dump the contents there. What it meant I didn't know, but it was a statement and I wished I could understand it.

I found myself enforcing the rules ever more strictly, not because I enjoyed doing so – it was, actually, one of the most tedious aspects of being in charge – but because those rules were the means through which an individual's personality came into focus. I was fairly inflexible because that stopped anyone slipping out of focus, getting blurry and evasive. And so I watched Francis with fascination, unable to comprehend why such an intelligent man was so dishonest with himself. Perhaps, I thought, he felt no one had ever sought his consent, so he disagreed internally and found fault with every instruction. Perhaps it was a power thing, prompted by the desire to be in charge and on top. It might have been disempowerment by contagion: according to him he had been continually disempowered, so he now lacked the oomph to get things done. He was even disempowering others, sharing his sense of worthlessness. Francis had developed the habit of sneering at Si, one of our more fragile and unstable guests, belittling him frequently in a jokey but slightly unpleasant way. It was as if, after having been picked on himself, he could now get his own back on the most vulnerable.

One day, we were talking about writing an equal opportunities policy.

'Look at Si,' Francis said. 'He's all the evidence you need to show that we allow diversity.'

'What's that supposed to mean?' Si asked.

'I'm joking.'

'The fuck are you talking about?' said Si, his toothless mouth pulled into a tight circle.

'There you go,' said Francis, holding his palm out to Si, who was now livid. 'You see? We allow all sorts here.'

I stepped in and tried to calm things down, appealing to Francis to wind his neck in.

It was tiring trying to keep everyone in line. And however explicit we made the rules, people were still trying to swerve around them for the most absurd reasons. Max was still coming every Wednesday. For months he had been asking me for money, and we had told him repeatedly it was the one thing we couldn't give him. One Wednesday he asked us, again, for a fiver.

'We don't lend money,' Gav said.

'But,' he looked at me with his calculating expression, 'I've put three pound in your donation tin this summer.'

'Have you?'

'All I would like' – he spoke incredibly slowly, as if he had to concentrate on each word, 'is one pound twenty back so I can go down the pub and buy myself some cheesy chips.'

We gave the guests a very simple set of dos and don'ts and tried to demonstrate the calm meadows that lay beyond obedience. I had done enough incompetent livestock handling by then to know that shoving from behind was a pointless task. It was better to show the rewards in front: a life free from addiction, free from resentment, and so on.

But obedience required listening. That was the etymology of the word: it meant to list towards. And before we could begin to encourage obedience, we had to invite people to listen. Many would interrupt within seconds, stutter 'buts' before you had finished your first sentence, raise fingers as a sign that you needed to stop. There was an impatience to express themselves, to defy what they thought you might be about to say, whereas listening implies a kind of submission, a laying aside of our own will and our own words. It requires an acceptance that someone else has something worthwhile to say. All of which, I felt, could be taught only by example and by demonstration. People had to know that they were being heard, not silenced; that they were being obeyed, not just obeying. It was an act of humility for us too as we submitted to their complaints and commands. We showed compliance and contrition. And very slowly the lessons were learned. We used to talk about 'well-being' in our Tuesday house meetings, but it took so much time that we decided to have a separate 'well-being meeting' after cleaning hour on a Thursday. That weekly meeting was essentially a long group therapy session in which people spoke at length about how they were feeling. As someone spoke, all the others were silent and concentrating. I felt inordinately proud of our guests. Many people who had, only a few months before, been verbal pugilists now sat with their eyes closed, nodding slowly as they listened deeply to the pains of someone else's life.

Si was obsessed with cleanliness, often berating us if the bathroom wasn't in order, or the chicken coop hadn't been cleaned out. 'It's bloody disgusting,' he would say with fury. Many of the other guests would get upset at the ferocity of the criticisms. It felt as if he were subconsciously trying to shame us somehow.

'Simon,' I said, 'I don't think any of us need to feel ashamed.'

He disagreed, and continued talking about dirt in the plughole or crap in the chickens' straw, which was kind of par for the course.

'Listen,' Fra said to him gently, 'if you want us to clean something, that's fine. But just ask us, remind us, that's all you need to do. If you get so angry, you'll upset people.'

It didn't really sink in, and many of the guests were now on edge, constantly worried they would get an earbashing from Si about how dirty they were. It was easy for me to put up a palm and say calmly to him that I refused to be shamed by him, but others with already low self-esteem found it far harder.

There was a possessiveness about Simon too. Every day he took over a new part of the operation, so that it became his job to pick up the post, to water the polytunnel, to distribute scraps to the chickens, and a dozen other little tasks. He was, I noticed, fixated on fairness, trying to give all the birds in the flock exactly the same proportion of leftovers.

These things became apparent only over the course of a few weeks or more. It took time to realize that a one-off was becoming a pattern, and even more time to understand why it was happening. I'm not an analyst, but I guessed that having lost control in his past, Simon was now desperate to control all he could. And his disgust at the dirt was presumably related to acts perpetrated on him in his youth. Perhaps that's too reductionist, but it seemed plausible, especially given his reaction when his compensation was finalized. Si was part of a group of abuse victims that was suing the Catholic Church. A solicitor from Yorkshire had driven all the way down here and we knew a settlement was in the offing. Then one day Si came into my office and slumped in the armchair.

'It's come through,' Si said.

Si was always worried about money, getting incredibly fidgety if someone owed him a couple of quid or if he lost a coin down the back of a chair, so I assumed he would be relieved, but it was the opposite. He felt worse now.

'It's strange,' he said. 'They've given me all this money, but I still feel as if something's been taken away.'

'They stole your childhood,' I said.

He nodded, and told me about it again. I've often been taken aback at the visceral antipathy of many people towards Christianity. But listening to Si I could understand it completely. He had profound wounds which had been inflicted by men who were supposedly devout. How could he – who had led a life on the streets, always on drink and drugs – ever be reconciled to a religion, or even a quiet, contemplative existence, when he had been so harmed and hurt at the hands of a priest?

'I saw all my forms,' he said. 'They reckon I've got something called PTSD.'

We talked about it for a while, until he decided he needed a bath.

'I feel dirty,' he said wistfully.

Our links with the local community were becoming deeper. Various tradesmen who had given us a hand over the years, and been tipped handsomely in sausages and eggs, were now friendly when we had a guest who was leaving here and looking for work. We were fully a part of what Ivan Illich, the Jewish-Catholic priest and social critic, once called 'the vernacular economy'. Various housing associations commissioned rustic furniture from us, so we made benches, chairs and raised beds. Those commissions gave us a bit of income but, more importantly, new friends, who heard about what was going on a mile outside town. We usually tried to involve some of the residents of those estates in the creative process, so they would come up here and have a laugh. Their help also meant that residents felt like creators rather than merely recipients and that, strategically, they would look after the new furniture, not spray or torch it.

One local school asked us to make an outdoor chair for their playground. Clive and I walked up to the plateau, where there was a good cubic metre of wood: it was the base of a double trunk that was so huge I had left it where it was a couple of winters ago, thinking that one day it would come in useful. It was bigger than I remembered, and we struggled to shift it at all. When we peered over the edge of the plateau, there was another ledge twenty feet below.

'Let's roll him down there,' said Clive.

So we inched the lump to the edge of the plateau and shouldered it over the edge. It picked up speed and went like a boulder falling down a canyon in a western, bouncing on the small ledge below and keeping going. It smashed through the two horizontal rails of the pond fence with a loud crack and then splashed into the middle of the pond, causing concentric waves, which spilled over into the soggy grass. Clive and I laughed.

'He seemed so heavy up there. Didn't think he could move that fast.'

We took off our clothes and dived into the pond. A year since we had dug it, it was now full of cream water lilies and yellow irises. There were dragonflies and damselflies hovering only a foot from us, as if affronted by our invasion. We waded towards the massive lump of wood and floated it to the edge. We then pushed it up the bank, on to dry land, and stood there in the sun, drying off.

Maggie came over the brow of the hill and saw us standing there in our pants.

'What are you two doing?' she asked, laughing.

'It's not what it looks like,' said Clive. 'We had a bit of a problem with gravity.'

'Pulled your trousers down, did it?' Maggie smiled. 'I thought I'd heard all the excuses there were, but that one's new.'

Clive pointed to the broken fence and Maggie nodded, smiling at another absurd situation.

Clive spent the whole day carving the double trunk, using a chainsaw, then chisels, then sandpaper. By the end of the day the wood had become a smooth throne. It was so ergonomic that it felt as if the wood was cradling you as you reclined into its curves.

As I was admiring it, Clive started telling me about a new project of his. He had designed a modular shelter for disaster relief. He showed me photographs of the prototype, a beautiful onion-shaped shelter with a flue emerging from the centre. The door was hinged at the top, like an old DeLorean car. He wondered whether he could bolt one together here and use us as a sort of shop window for his nascent business. Our chapel was still Morag's old, almost disintegrated yurt. The canvas was shredded in places and it had turned from bright white to algae-green. So the idea of a new – and watertight – structure was exciting. It looked eccentric but stunning. It suited Clive and it suited us. So we thanked him and accepted his offer.

Weeks came and went, and Clive fell off the radar. It often happened: people would come up here almost every day and then suddenly we'd never see them again for months or years. He phoned occasionally, promising he would be round tomorrow, but it never happened. Autumn cooled into winter, and still there was no sign of our shiny new shelter. Then one week in early winter it all happened. Clive spent days bolting together curved panels made of hemp, balsa wood and green resin. We placed it above the pond, and a chap nicknamed Badger built a spiral staircase up to the entrance out of – of course – pallets. Clive fitted a woodburner and the door. We put straw bales around the inside walls, so that eight or ten people could comfortably sit there, and threw woodchip all over the floor.

YEAR FIVE | 321

From the outside it still looked like Cinderella's carriage with its brown bulging panels. But inside it looked like a farmyard chapel, just as Ted Hughes described the place of his ancestor, Nicholas Ferrar: 'pigs and hay/ filled a church oozing manure mud/ from the porch.' On the matt-black woodburner sat the same cowbell we had been using for years.

We still sat in silence twice a day, some meditating, some praying, some just being still and listening to the incessant birdsong – irregular and jarring, but sometimes incidentally harmonious, like the sound of an orchestra warming up. I couldn't have survived here without those periods of quiet. So many people rolled up, coming in search of a peace which we often struggled to find ourselves, that I began to understand those community leaders who retreat, who almost hide away in an attempt to preserve themselves from being torn apart in a slow, centrifugal disintegration. There was so much wailing and gnashing of teeth, so many people and children around, that often the place didn't appear calm at all. But then, sitting in silence alongside half a dozen others in that round shelter, it all made sense somehow. The tranquillity returned and recharged you. We shared the silence, and understood each other once more. Sometimes someone would say something, a thought or a prayer, but often the only noise was a rabbit shuffling around the sedges or a bird landing on the water.

Francis was always there. The relationship between us had become very strained. I felt we were recreating the impasse that existed in his marriage: he thinking I was cruel or abusive because I thought he was stubborn or lazy. But in the chapel we seemed to put all that aside. The fact that we were there together meant we were still committed to being here and to each other.

* * *

It was probably because Gav and Rachel were here that the place became more directional. Rather than simply giving people a peaceful situation in which to work, relax and reflect, we consciously started accompanying them through their personal development: not only listening, but offering sometimes forth-right counsel; not only empathizing but also, when necessary, challenging. I realized that until now certain guests had been frustrated that they weren't more prodded, weren't given a programme to follow or a clearly illuminated pathway along which they could progress.

We started man-marking guests, as it were, each one of us mentoring one of them with weekly conversations, setting them tasks and challenges. We used anything we could: non-violent communication, psychodrama, art therapy, the Enneagram (a model of personality types), in-house AA meetings, relaxation classes, anger-management sessions. We brought in counsellors and therapists, found AA and NA sponsors, took them to SMART Recovery meetings and drove them to job interviews, hospitals and eating-disorder clinics.

Gav and Rachel 'got tight', as they say in football. They didn't leave any space for someone to turn and sneak away with the ball. Firmly but compassionately, they would make sure their mentee was being honest, was listening, and that they were following the programme that had been devised for them. They were both a decade younger than Francesca and me but in many ways far more competent. One of Gav's closest mates had been in rehab for the best part of a year, and Gav had learned a lot about what is addressed in rehab, be it defiance, evasiveness or dishonesty. He and Rachel both had an emotional intelligence that was off the scale. I would often watch them get straight to the heart of the issue in our Thursday well-being meetings. There was one time when Francis was saying he was fed up with people accusing him of being stubborn.

'I'm not stubborn.' His hand sliced the air. 'No way.'

'Francis,' Gav said quietly, 'is it a criticism you've heard before?'

'All the time.'

'Who's called you stubborn?'

'My wife, my friends, my work colleagues, you lot . . .'

'But if it's a criticism you've heard so many times, why not listen to it?'

'Because it's wrong.'

'Says who?'

'Me. I know what I'm like.'

'I'm sorry, Francis –' Gav was still talking softly – 'but it sounds to me as if you're not listening to anyone around you. If so many of the people in your life have said the same thing, why not accept that they might have a point? Why be so defensive about it?'

What was intriguing was that Francis was pretty wise about everyone except himself. We often had cyberchondriacs here, people who diagnosed themselves with all sorts of illnesses solely through internet research. One of them was Rosie, a confused, fey woman who had convinced herself she had had undiagnosed Lyme disease for the last twenty years. I hadn't pushed her on it, whereas Francis led her by his questions to unpalatable conclusions.

'Are you open,' he said, 'to the idea that you don't have Lyme disease?'

Rosie smiled painfully. 'No, not really.'

'You're not open—'

'I'm an open person, but—'

'– you're closed on this one?'

'Well, an applied kinesiologist confirmed that it was Lyme. The relief, then, the sense that someone understood me—'

'Is it understanding you want more than the diagnosis?'

'No. Well, it's both. But—'

'Has Lyme become a friend for you? Is it a diagnosis with which you have a relationship?'

'It just all makes sense: I get tired in the early afternoon, soon after lunch. There's an anger – Lyme Rage – that is typical of the disease. I've got painful knees.'

'Don't we all have those symptoms?' Francis asked.

Every day we were having these hard, hopefully healthy conversations. It so often came down to the notion of openness: was someone prepared to be open to a new idea, however much they resisted it? And that openness was part of discovering a completely new narrative to their lives: they needed a new story of themselves to live by, to become an alternative character in a different drama. Often, of course, it didn't happen. Sometimes we were dealing with people who were so mentally unstable, or simple, that you couldn't reason with them. There was one chap who spent hours each week trying to get through to Highgrove to give Prince Charles his advice. Another was hearing so many other voices in his head that ours was just one more to add to the mix. One guest had brain trauma from a car crash and just didn't quite function in a normal way.

Dan was one of the people it was hardest to help. He complained that everyone had failed him in his life up till now. It was beguiling to hear that he thought we wouldn't let him down, that we were different. But of course we too quickly fell short of his expectations. Every time he was given an opportunity to open up, to engage in a discussion about his well-being, he brought down the shutters with a hefty bang. He didn't want to talk about it; it wasn't a good moment; he wasn't in the mood. We got the feeling that, like Diana, he wanted to remain misunderstood. That way, perhaps, he could retain his sense of dislocation and complain about it. I knew from his references that there had been some extremely dark stuff in his past, but he never wanted to talk to me or anyone else about it. I could understand that and suggested a counsellor. That too was rejected. Things would stay the way they always had been, he said. Which begged the question of why he was here at all, and why he was taking up a place when we had a pretty long waiting list.

Some of the others found his attitude incomprehensible. They were frustrated with his knee-jerk intolerance and negativity. He hated animals, he said, and thought books were pointless. It felt as if we were trying to light a fire and each time Dan would come and pour a bucket of cold water on it. Nothing seemed to satisfy him. There was no gratitude, curiosity or flexibility. He seemed stuck in a rut and resented anyone offering to help him out of it. He felt patronized if we were solicitous, and ignored if we weren't. I knew he was grumbling incessantly to someone else. He preferred the security of his rigid resentment to the uncertainty of openness. There wasn't a chink in his emotional armour.

Dan made it pretty clear he couldn't care less about healing or wholeness. He just wanted somewhere safe to charge his batteries, and he was doing that by plugging them into us and, it seemed, sucking the life blood. It was draining.

But it meant there was, at least, a connection. He must have known he was plugged into a sustaining current. He wasn't unaware that this place was safe, and that he was gaining something by being here. Sometimes you had to let someone simply be, allow them to follow the programme, do the hours and watch what happened. Results were never guaranteed but just because they seemed far off or improbable, you couldn't unplug someone or set them loose. Because that, I'm sure, is what he was expecting. He was waiting for us to reject him; perhaps that's why he was pouring cold water on us before we poured it on him.

What was noticeable with Dan - and it was something we saw repeatedly - was that he preferred a gruesome security to the uncertainty of something better. It was entirely understandable. He had had almost no security all his life, and his profound pessimism dissuaded him from risking the little that he now had: he was living in a one-bedroom council flat that he hated. He was, he said, surrounded by bad memories, worse neighbours and the noise of all-nighters. It was a place - his words - of pushers and thieves, of aggression and intimidation. But he couldn't leave it. He had a home for life, however miserable. There was no way he would ever get clean living there, I thought. I heard myself echoing the politicians' line about the 'benefits trap'. And it was a trap that pulled him back in. One day, he just walked off site and didn't return.

I used to feel slighted when those things happened, but Herb, a friend and one of our *consiglieri*, often reminded us that we weren't a treatment centre, that we couldn't fix people and hope to put everything right. Sometimes all we could do was give someone a brief sunlit period in their lives, a rest from torrid reality. We were granting space, nothing more. We couldn't force people to give up grim certainty for simple insecurity and vulnerability. We just lived alongside, offering someone a bowl and a bed, giving them time, work and responsibilities. They might respond; they might not. Any amelioration might be temporary; it might be permanent. All we could do was keep creating and recreating a sanctuary, inviting people inside and allowing them to participate in that continual process.

What happened months, or years, after people left was telling. Dan and I often speak on the phone now. I think he knows that this is one place that didn't let him down or reject him. If that's all he takes away from his months here, it's not bad. Other guests, who left in a huff or on a whim, come back, marvelling that we're still here, still doing the same things with similar people. There's a predictability here that they don't get elsewhere. Alice and Stew came back out of the blue the other day, three years since they had left, and found an unchanged rhythm. They were amazed that we're still doing cleaning hour at the same time on the same day; still going to chapel at the same times; still having the same discussions about money, washing-up, and where to put all the blasted wellies. Gerald, who I had breathalysed and asked to leave a long time ago, got in touch over Christmas and told me he had been dry for two years to the day and that he was grateful we had kicked him out and forced him to hit rock bottom. I'm not sure it was much of a compliment, but we had a laugh, and I teased him about how he, the archetypal cynic, had become a grateful, meditating elder of the recovery community.

Often the news isn't so good though. A few weeks after my chat with Gerald, I spent the whole day dealing with a familiar emergency: trying to work out what we could do with a former guest who had relapsed so badly they were in hospital. Only this time Tracey couldn't be found, because she'd discharged herself from the ward and headed back to the off licence. Everyone assumed we'd take her back, because nowhere else had she ever been sober so long. But we were full, and we didn't like being bounced into a decision. Her partner and friends and her AA sponsor all called, and of course I conceded that we'd find space somewhere. Tracey was delivered a day later, looking purple and pickled. She was shaking and tearful and embarrassed and scared, and despite everything I was glad she was back here. We hugged and sat and talked. But within minutes she was blaming other people. Her

328 | A PLACE OF REFUGE

father was unkind to her. Her partner didn't understand what it was like. I could feel my irritation mounting. She was still, after all this, in denial.

That Christmas, we again had a full house: our usual guests, a couple of volunteers, plus half a dozen others from town who either didn't have, or didn't like, their own family. Many just didn't like Christmas. We brought another table into the garden room so that we could seat twenty, and exchanged eccentric charity shop presents. One of our volunteers gave Callum, who was back for a few days, a T-shirt that said, 'I hate being bipolar. It's awesome.' There was something touching about a couple of men of the road wearing yellow-and-green party hats and pulling crackers with over-excited children. I used to think we were offering these fellas something: company, roots, shelter, whatever. But now I wondered whether they weren't having as much effect on us as we were on them. I didn't romanticize their slickered, scarred lives, the fights and frozen nights. But they were living completely in the present. They were delighted with the smallest gifts – new gloves, or a new torch – and their gratitude was contagious.

It felt as if things were getting easier. It was always challenging, and tough, and exceptionally hard work, but it no longer felt as if the boat was being rocked or torpedoed every day. Fra was back to herself. There were many things that made a difference, but one of them was detachment. Counsellors are trained experts in detachment, in the analytical, unemotional examination of problems, but they don't live with their clients day and night. Theirs is a clinical environment, whereas here we're together all the time, often from the crack of dawn until we collapse in bed at night. Contact with guests isn't intermittent and at arm's length but constant and intimate. Combining love with detachment was an exceptionally difficult skill to acquire. It took Fra and me years to learn – and we learned the hard way, without training but after buckets of experience. Over time, though, we realized how to be close and empathetic to people without becoming destabilized, how to let them explode without getting shrapnel all over ourselves.

For years I had been trying to practise a sort of self-emptying, a letting go of everything. The most profoundly spiritual people seem almost transparent, like a window through which light comes in. They never interrupt, or impose, or confront. There's nothing to block out the light. It's what theologians call kenosis, an attempt to evacuate the self, to create sacred internal space by removing the will, the desire, the ego, the hunger, and all the rest. Trying to empty the self had been an incredibly hard discipline, and not just because I'm a particularly wilful person. Kenosis in a community means biting your tongue so much that it bleeds. It implies a continual and metaphorical washing of feet. And it often feels as if you're not just washing feet but frequently getting kicked by them whilst you're at it. I had sometimes confused self-emptying with retreat from leadership, meaning the place became a free-for-all and we saw our favourite things get broken or stolen, people jump into the vacuum and fill a space I was trying to vacate.

But as the seasons went by I came to notice that attempted selflessness had the great advantage of meaning decisions were never emotional or knee-jerk. Boundaries and expectations were respected because people realized this place wasn't an ego trip. I wasn't asserting myself, but only the rule. And the rule, people knew, worked. The free-for-all was replaced by something far more rigorous, and the rigour felt right because it wasn't imposed by some man with a messiah complex.

The paradox was that in emptying ourselves as far as possible we had managed to maintain our sanity in this strange and sensitive psychiatric unit. In the early years I used to get frustrated if things went curly with a guest, if they disappeared or fell off the wagon, or whatever. It would feel like we had failed, as if someone else's behaviour had been an illustration of how incompetent we were. Whereas now I realized their disappearance or relapse wasn't our responsibility or our failure. I wouldn't get angry with an individual for their erratic behaviour and, more to the point, I wouldn't be proud when someone got clean or well. We were still deeply sad when things went wrong, or hugely grateful when they went right – but solely for their sake, not ours. We didn't feel we were to blame, or to credit. It didn't feel as if we were even doing the work any more; we were just providing a context. It meant that without diminishing the love here, there was also something dispassionate. I no longer got all wound up, tangled in people's traumas and dramas. When someone had a go at me, I listened and tried to understand what was going on. When there was a ticking bomb in the house, rather than panic I found that I could quite frequently, and calmly, defuse it.

All the anger and rage and sorrow that was poured out in our house wasn't a burden any more but a blessing. We felt privileged to have somewhere to hold the pain. We didn't want to cure it, or deny it, just to contain it. To provide a place where it could be expressed and examined. I was simply trying to help people put things in the light and if I were in some way transparent, that might help let the light in. None of which should give the idea that I was always serene. Everyone who lived here for more than a few days could attest to the fact that I still got cranky or stressed. I would often be not a window but a brick wall.

* * *

In early January I saw Francis having the kind of conversation with Rachel that looked serious. I sidled up, just to check that everything was okay.

'We've got a bit of an issue,' said Rachel, smiling.

'It'll be fine.' Francis shrugged.

He had checked the muslins that were wrapped around the hams hanging in the lean-to. Inside, it now looked like one of those cellars in Emilia-Romagna with teardrop hams hanging from the roof. It even smelt the same: a musty, slightly mouldy aroma. Francis said that one of the hams appeared to have maggots in it, and he had cut off the affected meat and put the maggot-ridden muslins in the washing machine.

'Only problem,' Rachel said, 'is that Francesca's clean underwear was in there.'

So we all tore around for half an hour, trying to sort it out before Fra got home from the school run.

Max was still coming up on Wednesdays and making us chuckle. He broke two sledgehammers in one day when he was breaking up some rubble for foundations.

'Just fell apart in me hands,' he said, knowing our catchphrase.

But then he phoned me up a day later. 'I just wanted to ask,' he said in his slow-motion Somerset accent, 'if you've re-handled them sledgehammers, as I were hoping to come up and break some more stuff.'

Max didn't mind what he broke – handles, rocks, rules – as long as he was smashing something up. And behaviour that was outrageous now made us smile as much as seethe. Another Wednesday, Max was sitting at the table. He put one finger against a nostril and exhaled sharply, sending snot on to his lap. Then he swapped sides and cleared the other nostril.

'Max,' Gav said sharply, 'use a tissue.'

'Don't need to,' he said slowly.

'No, brother, you do need to.'

By then we all had the giggles. Leo was trying to copy what he had seen. The more we laughed, the more Max tried to justify himself, which only made us laugh more. He smiled sheepishly, enjoying the attention and the fact that he had cheered us up.

Brian was in his late fifties. He had a round, gentle face and looking at his cheery mask, you would have no idea he had recently attempted suicide. His family had told us he was profoundly depressed and had been on anti-depressants for most of his adult life. Brian said he was fine. 'No problem, no problem,' he kept saying. He dressed slightly shabbily: ill-fitting tracksuit bottoms, an oversized woollen hat on his head, trainers with the soles coming loose. He limped around the site – he had just had a hip operation – looking for things to keep him busy. He kindled everything he could lay his hands on: the boot remover, a high chair, the leg of an axe block, some teak Gav had been keeping for years. When I tried to explain that these were useful objects, he smiled and said, 'No problem, no problem.'

'Brian, it is a bit of a problem actually,' Fra said. 'You're smashing up things we want to keep. You're burning things we need, that we use.'

'I understand, okay, no problem, no problem,' he said automatically.

Brian enjoyed filling the log stores as quickly as possible. He ordered the books in alphabetical order and wiped down the surfaces manically. We tried to suggest he stop, that he just sit down and enjoy the calm, but he couldn't keep still. I wondered whether it was his medication that made him so jumpy. One of our experienced drug users said it was just like watching someone on speed. It was as if he had akathisia, a restlessness, a kind of physical complement to his verbal incontinence. When Brian came to our chapel, to sit in silence, he kept fidgeting, sniffing, coughing and muttering until his self-control evaporated and he started talking to himself. We used to do a 'feelings check' at nine each morning, a one-word description of our state of mind. Brian's one word normally lasted for ten minutes.

Talking was what Brian did all the time. He wittered on, telling you stories, jokes and observations. He would tell you about food offers down the Co-op, about a man he had chatted to in another shop, something he had read in a magazine. He waylaid everyone. His need for interaction was pathological, so even if you were walking away he would call after you, pulling you back into his orbit. The more we tried to retreat, the more he sank conversational hooks into us, reeling us back in. He would burst into my shed three or four times every afternoon, never knocking.

There was a great loneliness about Brian. He had a wife and children, but his wife had decided their marriage was over and his children had grown up. He craved company and companionship but didn't know when it was appropriate. We gave him explicit boundaries – never come into the shed; only go in the kitchen after 7 a.m. – but it made no difference. It was almost as if breaking boundaries was his form of self-assertion. He would still burst in and recount something he had read in the *Sun* or heard on talkSPORT. I was working in my shed at five o'clock in the morning when he came in to ask for a pencil.

'Brian, do you remember what we said? I'd rather not be disturbed when I'm working.'

'Yes, but I need a pencil.'

'At five o'clock in the morning?'

'I'm doing the crossword.'

There wasn't a boundary he could respect. It was very explicit that we didn't share the phone, because of some huge bills in the past, but Brian would answer it, almost racing us to get to it first.

'What's going on?' I asked him afterwards. 'Do you remember that the phone isn't communal?'

'I thought it might be an emergency.'

'What gave you that idea?'

'Well, it was ringing.'

He would claim he was honest because he would faithfully tell you in retrospect all the boundaries he had disregarded.

'I'm going to be honest with you, because I'm an honest person. I used your phone a few times yesterday.'

'Being honest –' I closed my eyes to maintain my patience – 'means not breaking a boundary in the first place. You're not being honest if you're telling me which ones you've ignored.'

'I didn't ignore nothing, I'm telling you now. I'm being straight with you.'

We went through a revised sheet of dos and don'ts with him, explaining very slowly what it all meant. It affected everyone, because where we had flexibility before – allowing people to use the phone occasionally, or come into the office when they really needed – we now had none. Brian went from being a chancer to a lawyer, talking in grandiose terms about documents, policies and everything else. He even congratulated himself on having introduced some clarity.

'It's good that's clear now,' he said.

'Brian, it's been clear for years. We haven't decided anything new.'

'As long as it's the same for everyone,' he said, as if he were being picked on.

He was exhausting to be around. The incessant bustling meant that no one could be relaxed whilst Brian was fretting around them, tidying and ordering. He buggered one guest's keyboard by dousing it with his personal stash of anti-bacterial spray. He bleached the bath before he got in it, and managed to get bleach in the washing machine so that Rachel's clothes came out with strange pink streaks on them. He would put boots outside in the rain, and batteries in the cat food, just to make sure things were tidy. He used tea towels to mop the floor. He put personal note-pads and books in the recycling. Late at night he would empty the petty cash tin, count it, call me in to show me what it totted up to, then tell me he was going to put it all back again.

His intentions were good. He was a lovable bloke. And it was ironic that we had spent years trying to encourage tidiness – and now we had someone who couldn't stop tidying. I knew that manic tidying was probably a sign of inner turmoil, and it was hard to criticize him when he was trying to be helpful. But he was causing chaos. If you put a cup of tea down and turned your back, it would be washed up. Wood was piled so high in the boiler room you couldn't even get at the boiler. It meant that the place was feeling incredibly restless and noisy, not least because another of the residents was an affable, but astonishingly loud, American.

'Didn't I tell you,' he shouted to me one day as I tried to find his volume control, 'that my mom calls me her little foghorn?'

So we decided on a strategy that would put stillness at the centre, not the periphery, of the project. We suggested two peri-ods of silence in the house itself, or at least in the large garden room where everyone hung out. Until nine each morning and between two and three after lunch were now quiet times. It wasn't a strict silence, as people could still whisper hellos and quick questions, but the centre of our home now, at last, felt a bit like a library. People who wanted a noisy breakfast came and joined our kids in the kitchen and those who wanted to read, or write, sat next door in the communal calm. The key point wasn't silence, but stillness. We asked Brian not to tidy or talk in those two periods each day. He couldn't bustle or natter.

It took months for him to understand the deal. He still came into my office unannounced, or started wiping down surfaces as we were all sitting reading during quiet time. But eventually we managed to get him to a point at which, inevitably, the real troubles came to the surface. Instead of saying, 'No problem,' he started talking about his problems: about the end of his marriage, his being sacked from work, his upbringing. Before, he had been almost evasive about the reason he was here. Everything was fine, he would say. Now, though, he let the mask drop. It was a mask he had clearly worn for years and, once it came loose, it was as if he didn't know how to behave any more. There was suddenly an emotional honesty to him that was unchecked and, as expected, we became the targets for some of his pain. He told us that he felt unheard; that we weren't keeping the place in order; that he was confused. We took it, knowing that blame is a way to discharge pain. In many ways, I thought I heard the emotions of a scared boy being recounted by an eloquent adult. He went from saying, 'No problem, no problem,' to having so many he didn't know where to start. He would weep in our well-being meetings. And even though his anxiety was sometimes aimed at us, the fact that he was being blunt, and open, was a relief. It was easy to warm to him now. There's a story that the American children's entertainer Fred Rogers always carried in his pocket a written note of something he had once heard from a social worker. It seemed so relevant to Brian: 'There isn't anyone you can't learn to love once you've heard their story.' And the point wasn't just that Brian, hopefully, felt our love, but that he was able to go easy on himself as well, that he was able to look in the mirror with affection and fondness.

Brian started seeing a counsellor once a week. Despite his sadness, we laughed with him a lot.

'I'm going to do a sponsored silence,' he said one night at the table.

There was uproar as people rushed to offer him money.

Simon was getting harder to handle. He seemed to be getting less, rather than more, stable. He was so used to being taken advantage of that being disgruntled had become a habit. He moaned a lot, his mouth pouting like he was chewing both cheeks. He stared at me over his broken glasses one morning and said, 'I think I'm going to tell that counsellor she can fuck off. Can't afford sixty quid a month. Just can't afford it.'

He received far more in benefits than I was able to earn in a month and I didn't think it was sensible to stop seeing the counsellor when he was spending so much on tobacco and phone calls. I told him so, but he just repeated that he thought she should fuck off.

'She's trying to help you, Si.'

He got so wound up that he didn't want lunch. 'Don't want owt,' he said, his stock phrase when he was fed up. He would often shout at people from a hundred metres away, expecting them to drop everything. He got furious when he asked Francis to cut some lettuce but it wasn't done immediately, three hours before dinner.

Then one morning it all went pear-shaped. He was livid that no one had filled up the kettle for him and that the sugar pot was empty. He stormed into the kitchen at 6 a.m., effing and blinding. There was no instant coffee, so he made a cafetière, thumping the plunger down so hard he showered the whole area with brown liquid. He made a pot of tea then broke the pot. More effing and blinding, and accusing everyone of letting him down, of not pulling their weight; his face was contorted into a picture of pain and fury. One of the guests, who had been a victim of violence, was visibly flinching, her head moving away from Si as he crashed chairs on the floor.

I had seen him like this before, and he was already on his last warning. I knew I had to ask him to leave and it made me extremely sad. This was a man who had every reason to be furious about what had been done to him: abandoned by parents, abused by a priest, cheated on by his wife. He had played his part too: losing touch with his children, living on the streets for years with multiple addictions. And despite that, he was a good, kind soul. He was the one everybody remembered. 'Say hi to Simon,' they all said when they wrote after a visit. 'Give Simon my love.' Whenever people came here with their parole officer or social worker, he always offered them tea, talked about tobacco and the streets and the like. He identified with all the lost souls, and he made them feel normal, welcomed, cared for. He gave them a roll-up, or a stamp. He let them make a call on his phone. It was hard to think of an underdog more 'under' than Simon, and that made people here feel they had an ally, someone who knew what they were going through.

But I couldn't let him stay. One of our few rules was no physical or verbal aggression – and Simon was truly frightening when he lost it. He was vulnerable, but so were all our guests – and they felt even more so when he was shouting accusations and insults.

He knew he had blown it. I'd given him a warning before and he knew he couldn't do it again. He came and saw me afterwards and sat with his head in his hands.

'I can't stay here, can I?'

'No, Si. No, you can't.'

He sighed heavily. He started chopping his palm through the air as he recounted the injustices of the sugar and the teapot. I interrupted him and told him it was irrelevant.

'I know,' he said, stroking his shaggy beard with his scarred right hand. 'You can't have that behaviour.' He laughed ruefully. 'I'm back on streets then. Back to the sleeping bag on the pavement.'

I was aware of the emotional blackmail in these conversations. When we had to ask people to leave, they sometimes accused us of making them homeless, or chucking them out on to the streets. I could have told him that he had made himself homeless, explaining that actions have consequences, but I didn't. He knew it already.

'I've dug myself a big hole now.'

'There are two ways this can happen,' I said to Si. 'You can pack your bags and storm off now, ranting about sugar and teapots. Or you can stay until the weekend, and have a farewell dinner and presents and hugs and goodwill.'

'I want one of your nonsense poems too.' He smiled.

'We've had plenty of nonsense, eh?'

'Aye, have that.'

'If you leave on good terms, then you can come back in the future, come back for volunteer day, or a respite holiday, or what-ever. You can decide how you leave. I far prefer the second option.'

He nodded, looking at me with no discernible resentment. 'I liked it here,' he said sadly. 'I really liked it here.'

'We liked having you here.'

After each departure we would try to process stuff, chew over what had happened, what we did wrong and how we could have done it better. We tried to remember who had said what to whom, what the reaction was, how we had handled it. I'm not sure we ever got much wiser. Anything we learned was solely through experience and getting things wrong. We realized the obvious: that those who didn't go through the extremely basic procedures (filling in an application form, say, or coming on the day they said they would) were likely to be the problematic ones who would create chaos later on. We no longer felt we had to take the very neediest in society. We began to blend them with some of the more stable sorts: someone between houses or jobs, someone who was simply lonely or sad rather than recovering from a heroin habit and a five-year stretch in Belmarsh. We told people it wasn't okay to come here until they felt able to tell the whole group why they had come. We realized that people had to accompany us, rather than vice versa.

So much happens. A chap called Ian has gone for a walk and comes back stinking of whisky, so I ask him to leave. Francis falls and dislocates his shoulder. The bees have swarmed. One of our guests has been arrested in town for firearms offences, having waved a BB gun in Screwfix in what he calls a 'reverse hold-up' (he had given them cash and was demanding a receipt). Ten piglets have been stolen. Quite often there are two or three incidents before breakfast and I have to give Fra a bulletin before she takes the kids off to school. Often someone you think has been here a couple of months has only been here ten days. There are so many dramas that I've already been through more with guests than I have with most of my closest, though far away, friends. Hygiene is still a problem. One day Fra finds a plaster in the last slice of bread. Someone, I discovered, has been peeing in the kettle in the shepherd's hut. Another guest has been using our

frying pan as a litter tray for his kitten. As happens in all therapeutic communities, we have an episode of shit-smearing. We
keep going through the crises, through the pain barriers.

Perhaps because time appeared different here, or because nature
never seemed in much of a hurry, we had learned patience, allowing things to come to us rather than rushing after them. We
waited for things to happen: for the willow structure to take root,
for the vine to come to life, for the return of the brutally hacked
roses. I had come to appreciate Francis's sedentary approach to
gardening. 'Give it time,' he always said. I was so frequently
outwitted by slow-moving slugs it sounded like good advice. We
knew the moods of the seasons now: the mellow cosiness of
candles and fires in midwinter, the exuberant bustle of late spring,
the indolence of high summer and the industry of the long
autumn before the dark and cold returned. 'I do like the seasons,'
Max said to me once. 'They're a right good idea, they are.' We had
found our circadian rhythm here, waking when it was light and
sleeping when it was dark.

Freddie was a thin, wan character who hadn't washed or shaved
for a few months before he arrived here in the spring. With him,
it was as if there was no one home. He looked blank and bored.
He stood vacantly in the kitchen and, like Tom, couldn't work out
where the fridge or dishwasher could be. He didn't ask either, just
stood still and stared. The lights had gone off inside. In the workshop I asked him to hang up a mallet next to the others on the
tool board, but he shuffled along the line of tools – the froe, the
adze, the auger bits – and couldn't identify the mallets.

'To the right,' I said, and he turned slowly, like he'd got a crick
in his soul.

In the end, I took it from him and showed him where it lived. He said nothing. At lunch, he ate dry bread. Even the most hardened guest was looking at him with sympathy, unable to get any sort of reaction from him. We offered cheese or salad or omelette, but he just munched on his white bread, staring at his lap. He was on anti-psychotics, and I wasn't sure how much that slowed him down.

'He's less than monosyllabic,' Maggie said to me.

To begin with, all he could whisper was 'yes' and 'no'. After a couple of days he would say short sentences, looking at the floor timidly and whispering so quietly you had to ask him to repeat what he had said. When we did have brief exchanges, he told me he needed to come here because he had to find his voice again. He had retreated so far into his shell he didn't know how to get out, he said.

For that first week, one or two people were wondering why we had Freddie here. Any rational community would have said, 'No, thanks.' But others thought we could help him, that he was going through a crisis, and that he might emerge from it by being here. After a trial week, we told Freddie he could stay as long as he needed.

Slowly, he began to speak in full sentences. He looked us in the eye. He smiled and started to make jokes. I would see him wandering around the pig pens, patting the broad sows and talking to them. He would sit with us in the chapel. The children took him by the hand down to the pond to look at the tiny frogs, the size of a fingernail, crawling through the damp moss on to dry land.

He began to open up to us, explaining about the breakdown he had been through. He had taken too many recreational drugs and was eloquent about his paranoia and delusions. He had been, he said, full of anger and pain at the idea that he had no free will, so kept doing things to prove that he was free. For a few years he was a sort of ascetic wanderer. He walked and hitched thousands of miles without money, getting as far as Moscow before turning round and heading back. He had done the same round much of Africa. He had smoked too much weed, and began to get paranoid, thinking that his expressions of his freedom were in fact being forced on him. 'They were expecting me to do it,' he kept saying. He had hoped to be enlightened but had sunk into darkness. When he stopped travelling, the whole experience of years as a wandering beggar caught up with him and he collapsed into a silent stupor.

It was clear his brain was still struggling. He was holding an apple core one day and looked over to Gav.

'What shall I do with this?' he whispered.

'What do you want to do with it?' Gav smiled.

'Get rid of it.'

'Put it in the compost then.'

'But that's in the other room.'

'Put it on your plate then.'

'But that's the other side of the table.'

'Well, hold on to it then.'

'Okay.'

So he held on to it for the next half-hour until he finally got up and put it in the compost. He hadn't been joking; he simply didn't know what he should do with it and didn't want to do something that required any effort.

I watched him over the next few weeks, never sure when to indulge or when to challenge his eccentricities. He would spasm a lot, shivering and raising his shoulders.

'What's going on, Freddie?' I asked him as he rocked

backwards and forwards, his arms wrapped around his torso like he was sitting in freezing snow.

'My ego's inside out,' he said in a strong, normal voice. 'People can see inside me, see all the shameful things. But it's not me. I'm being made by everyone else, being manipulated, hypnotized by aliens.' His explanation went on for a long time.

Other times he would stand in the kitchen and contort his body into extraordinary shapes, almost like a clown or a comic.

'What are you up to, Freddie?' Emma asked.

'I play this guessing game with myself. I get into strange shapes and have to guess what it is.' He leapt into the air. 'This is a one-legged hippo in a disco.' He laughed manically. 'Can you see it?'

'Can we play?' Benny came up.

So all three of them twisted into shapes and guessed what the shapes were. Freddie got more and more manic, excitedly twisting and giggling as the girls got involved.

It sounds slightly mad, but it was a harmless game. I was watching them, laughing at the absurd ideas: 'This is a giraffe who's learning to swim in porridge,' Freddie said, giggling.

'It's okay if you're a bit different,' Emma said to him kindly, 'not normal.'

'Normal, normal, normal, normal,' Freddie kept repeating.

Which, of course, only made him appear more strange. And it became a bit of a joke, which he enjoyed: each time he did something weird, someone would shout, 'Normal!' and he would smile sheepishly, and join in: 'Normal, normal.' None of us knew what normal was any more.

But whilst it was fun allowing him to play, it was hard to get through to him about duties. He would chew his shoulder hard, turning his head away from us, as we tried to explain that he couldn't be a free spirit here – that he was being asked to work and come to meals and all the rest. Since he had been on a mission to prove that he was free, it was hard to take.

'Just . . .' he said.

We watched him. 'Just what?' Rachel said.

'Just want to play,' he whispered to his feet.

'What about responsibility?'

'That's for adults.'

'You're twenty-five.'

He looked up now, but we still had to strain to hear him. 'Responsibility means I'm getting old and am going to die.'

'Yep, I'm afraid so.'

It felt as if his fanatical expression of freedom was a tilt at mortality, and that the reason he wanted to avoid responsibility was to avoid ageing. But the fact that it was spoken, and out there, meant it could now be looked at. Freddie seemed to grow in the next few weeks. He did small things like lay the table. He was good at carpentry, and helped in the workshop.

His psychiatric nurse came to visit him after a month and couldn't believe the improvement. She, like us, could see that Freddie was emerging, like a butterfly from a chrysalis.

'What have you done?' she asked.

'Nothing,' Gav told her. 'We've just created a space for him.'

We were, I'm afraid, often surprised by the medical establishment's approach to mental illness. NHS staff referred us countless 'clients' going through schizophrenic or psychotic episodes for whom they felt they could do nothing. It often seemed that their only solution was to prescribe, and distribute, industrial quantities of neuroleptics. They were therefore amazed when they visited and saw their patients contentedly integrating into a community, having decided to stop their anti-psychotics. We frequently got the impression that rehabs and hospitals felt threatened by our community. 'You don't know what you're doing,' they kept implying. 'You're not professionals.' It was true: we weren't professionals. We were amateurs in the old-fashioned sense that we did it for love. Loren Mosher, the founder of the Soteria movement for people with mental illness, once described Soteria as a 'small, homelike, quiet, supportive, protective and tolerant social environment', with interventions by 'a non-professional staff'. That's exactly what we wanted to be, putting compassion, not pharmaceuticals, at the centre of any treatment.

One day Benny wanted to teach Freddie to dance. So she put on the beloved black leather jacket she had got for her ninth birthday and taught Freddie, Max and Jenny – who had come back for a respite week – some moves. As always, Benny was attracted to a mirror like a moth to a flame, so was looking at her reflection in the patio doors, seeing behind her the backing dancers: Jenny, holding her fat Jack Russell, Baxter; Max moving with the speed of a stoned snail; and Freddie. They were prancing around to Shania Twain's 'Man! I Feel Like a Woman'. What was funny was that they were all into it, concentrating on following Benny's choreography and ignoring our laughter. In some ways, it was a scene that epitomized this place: the children teaching the adults, showing them how to be children again. The adults were allowing the children to be teachers. Everyone was enjoying themselves and losing their self-consciousness. Leo was bouncing on the trampoline, shouting at the top of his voice, 'You're all in big chubble,' as he punched the air with his little fists. Emma was cycling around with one hand on the handlebars, the other scratching her nit-ridden head. Gav was playing table tennis with Callum, who had come back for Sunday lunch and for some reason had three pairs of glasses on his head. Brian was taping six inches of bubble wrap on to the saddle of my bike, as he said it hurt each time he rode it into town. Rachel was asking who wanted a cup of tea. It was a fairly typical Sunday afternoon.

Fra and I stood there, arm in arm, watching it all. The sun was out, and orange-tip butterflies were flitting amongst the corn-flowers. It was a cuckoo's nest, but it was our nest. It was our family. Someone had once told me that what we were doing was looking after life's 'offscourings'. It felt, now, as if the offscourings had become our offspring.

When our soldiers used to talk about the front line, I could understand what they were describing. Under fire and so close to death, they had felt truly alive. They experienced a rush they could get nowhere else, even if the cost was so high. It is, obviously, hyperbole to compare what we've been through with warfare. And I'm aware that I've probably dwelt too much on disputes and difficulties in this book – not just because I want to offer a corrective to the daydream of bucolic communalism but also because tension is an integral part of life here, and always the greatest teacher. It has, in fact, usually been a cheerful and harmonious place. But we've had plenty of battles. We've lived surrounded by stories of brothels and prisons, hospitals and so-called 'homes'. 'Abuse' is one of those words that trips off the tongue too readily. It's so easy to throw it like a hand grenade into modern conversation. But the long consequences of every type of abuse – substance abuse, verbal abuse, physical abuse, emotional abuse and sexual abuse – have always been present here.

We've been like a field hospital placed just behind the front line. Often, of course, warfare doesn't finish when a soldier retreats or retires: the battles become interiorized, continually replayed on a loop. Our field hospital has been full of emotional amputees, of patients with shellshock or PTSD. And inevitably, however much we've tried to make this place peaceful, there have been many flashbacks and flare-ups.

It's hard to know what difference we've made. We don't really know what we've done, which fires we've ignited or doused, which wounds we've staunched or drained. Some guests we never hear from again, as if they don't want to be reminded of a painful period in their lives. Most, though, keep coming back long after they've left, staying again for a few nights or a few weeks. A few people say they want to be buried here, laying down their bones in a place that changed their lives. And it has touched people: it's given them a centre, a place to which they return in all sorts of ways. Even those who resented the few rules when they were here now like being tethered, attached to a solid place from which they seem unwilling to depart. For the rootless it has offered a real home, a place where they – like a fruit tree – can be grafted on to a rootstock and be surprised by their fruits.

It has rooted us too. We know many of the hitchhikers we see by the side of the road. We meet many of the local schoolchil-dren, their parents and grandparents, thanks to Kath's wonderful forest school. Congregations and cavers, smallholders and stone-masons, carpenters and herbalists – all come up here for one reason or another. They feel a part of this community and we feel a part of theirs. It didn't take long for locals to realize that we were not a threatening commune, just an unorthodox community trying, as far as possible, to live off the land.

But despite all that, it's hard to measure what we've done. It's not possible to quantify self-esteem or belonging, self-respect or confidence. And by the usual yardsticks, we've often failed. Relapse has followed recovery; divorce has ensued despite reconciliation; depression and disorders have reappeared. Even the conservation work we've done is in jeopardy. We've planted hundreds of trees, but now the Chalara dieback of ash threatens the majority not only of what we've planted but of the established woodland too. There's no success in this game – and perhaps no failure either.

Considering that the fabled 'outcomes' are so uncertain, the toll of running this place has sometimes seemed absurdly high. We've done what we can to lessen it, but managing this project still feels, for Francesca and me, relentless. We're heavily laden. There are always crises, emergencies, phone calls, referrals, meetings, unexpected arrivals, paperwork and, most importantly, painful conversations. For five years I've had two full-time jobs, and – given the vagaries of being a freelance writer – less than half a decent salary. I love both jobs and they do, as I hoped they would, dovetail well. I relish swinging an axe and then swinging a pen; the one informs the other in mysterious ways. But the demands are incessant. There is never any downtime.

Which is why we always assumed that we weren't going to do this for ever. We imagined we would do it for, roughly, seven years and would then pass it on. A community can sometimes disintegrate when the founders don't know how to entrust it to someone else and so hang on to the bitter end, increasingly exhausted but always in command and resolutely resistant to change. We would rather leave it to people with new ideas and new energy, to pass it on while we, and it, are still in good shape. We're often talking about the importance of relinquishing, rather than acquiring, so one day we'll walk a different walk and relinquish this too. And when we do step away from it, I suspect it will take years to process quite what's happened. It already feels as if we've seen too much to take in. I catch myself sometimes staring into space, trying to get my head round what's gone on. 'The problem was,' as Michael Herr wrote in *Dispatches*, 'that you didn't always know what you were seeing until later, maybe years later, that a lot of it never made it in at all, it just stayed stored there in your eyes . . . The information isn't frozen, you are.' We want to get out before we're immobilized by sensory and emotional overload. We've set up a charity so that there's an organization prepared for a future without us.

We're also beginning to think about entrusting the project to other people because perhaps its work on us, as well as vice versa, is nearing an end. A wise communitarian I met recently said that you should stay in a community until its work of reconciliation within you is complete. For years I've relished the openness and the vulnerability here, and I think I've benefited as much as everyone else from the honesty of this environment. But I'm ready, perhaps, for the pendulum to swing back the other way now, towards strength and discretion, towards diplomacy and, even, emotional reticence. I've enjoyed relying on others, being interdependent. But lately I've felt weary of having always to ask favours, of having to borrow and blag things all the time because we're so hard up. I yearn to stand, or fall, by myself and am ready for, if not solitude, at least the stability and intimacy of the nuclear family about which I was once so dismissive.

And yet, despite contemplating withdrawal from this hothouse, I'm more convinced than ever of the advantages of communal living. It's like a spiritual greenhouse that accelerates growth. Every day feels adventurous and exciting. Unless you're an exceptional hermit, there's more chance of achieving maturity and wisdom in community than in solitude. And we, as a family, have grown together in this woodland. Francesca and I heeded the warnings about idealists who tried to save the world but inadvertently lost their spouses. We found that in many ways this sanctuary drew us together: we've been on a white-knuckle ride, sitting side by side with all the adrenaline, laughter and pain. To do something quite as challenging as this for so long, and emerge with exponentially more admiration for your spouse, is a great reward. In five years of extreme pressure, I've never seen Fra lose her temper or her cool (except for that time with Barry, the bonkers neighbour). She's like a mother to everyone, sitting at the head of the table, talking in Italian to the children and English to everyone else. I can't ever recall her being unkind, mean or unpleasant to, or angry with, any of our guests, which is a lot more than I can say for myself. She's said her piece often enough, but calmly and eloquently. And all this in what is, for her, a foreign language. Francesca's the real alchemist here, taking the base ingredients and turning them into stylish dishes: redcurrant *semifreddo*, *torta fritta*, elderflower sorbet. And when I show people round, hoping they might admire the orchard, the piglets or the polytunnel, all they normally say is, 'Your wife's incredible.'

We often wonder what long-term effect a place like this will have on our children. It's possible, given their hippie, agrarian upbringing, that they'll rebel by becoming urbane capitalists. Benny already berates me, as only she can, for being three months behind on her pocket money. 'I really don't want to charge interest,' she said a few weeks ago, 'but you leave me little choice.' If she's like that at nine, I doubt she'll be mucking out the pigs at nineteen. But the kids have absorbed the ethos of this place. They're completely unperturbed by the idea of sharing their food with people who have unusual behaviour, backgrounds or appearances. They seem to understand the importance of emotional openness but also of privacy and boundaries. They're so used to guests talking about their woes that they too talk about how they feel, sometimes with comic earnestness. Leo, having stubbed his toe, sat down at the table recently and told everyone, 'I'm worried about me.' Emma is learning to deal with her anger issues in the same way other guests do: by splitting logs, or meditating, or else just screaming very loudly. They've learned much about addiction and damaging, repetitive habits. This spring Benny, of her own volition, decided to give up TV for Lent. A few weeks in she called an emergency house meeting, telling everyone that she was powerless over TV's allure, that she wanted to get help and needed a sponsor. She was role-playing and laughing, but she knew how to diagnose, and deal with, her urges.

It's changed, I think, who I am. Running this community has made me hugely more empathetic towards others. I've yet to meet the person who is less sensitive than you think they are. Despite appearances, everyone is troubled. The prickliest person is usually more hurtful to themselves than to others. At the same time though it's made me more suspicious of and sceptical about people, about their motives and the way they present themselves. Almost everyone talks a better game than they play. Very few people tell us the whole story when they come here, perhaps because they themselves don't know their own narrative. Not many people are straight about how many units of alcohol they consume, or what they were inside for, or what happened in Helmand.

It's changed the way I deal with people. I don't pussyfoot around any more. I'm politely blunt. I've lost that awkward English way of desperately avoiding conflict or issues. I don't give out instant gratification. My knee-jerk position now is 'no' rather than 'yes'. I don't let things fester but bring them out into the open and talk about them, even when people are reluctant.

I've tried to tame my tongue, because words seem like a presumptuous interruption of stillness. That might sound a bit rich coming from a writer, but the lack of quiet and equilibrium is one of the things I've found hardest in this chaotic quarry of glossolalia. People are desperate to have their say. They want to keep moving. The noise and confusion is a reflection of a more general restlessness. 'Real silence,' Bonhoeffer wrote, 'real still-ness, really holding one's tongue comes only as the sober consequence of spiritual stillness.'

The trouble is that if you try to share your stability with the unstable, you often get pulled off balance yourself. You're centred until you try to help someone else centre themselves. Remaining stable or centred has taken epic amounts of energy and insight, and even then we've often found ourselves on the floor – with us resentful that we've been pulled to the ground, and guests upset that we haven't got them up on their feet. But it's precisely when that happens that we gain a real insight into what we're doing here. We had thought we were serving the poor but ended up realizing our own poverty. To keep this place going we lived way beyond our means, not just financially but emotionally. We were often absolutely wrecked. I thought we were giving rest to the weary, but ended up understanding how exhausted we were. I flattered myself that we were comforting mourners, only to find ourselves in mourning, grieving the loss of friends and relatives. As Michael Herr wrote, 'I went to cover the war and the war covered me.' We had been broken. I realized I wasn't a physician or a healer but one of the traumatized, exhausted patients. I wasn't stable or still or centred or whole. That was what we all had in common. It wasn't work, or our shared purse, or our table. It was the hard fall – suffering, sickness, poverty of spirit and all the rest. It was that which brought us together, and it turned us from a field hospital into a fellowship.

Henri Nouwen, the radical priest and writer, once suggested that 'Hospitality becomes community as it creates a unity based on the shared confession of our basic brokenness . . . a community not because wounds are cured and pains are alleviated, but because wounds and pains become openings or occasions for a new vision.' Windsor Hill Wood has, I hope, been a place of visions. It's somewhere people glimpse a future they thought they didn't have. Many, if not all, find a way forward, and taste – in the old line from the Psalms – 'honey from the rock'.

References

Preface

'I went to the woods...': Henry David Thoreau, *Walden, or, Life in the Woods* (Dover Thrift Editions, New York, 1995)

'All professions are conspiracies against the laity': George Bernard Shaw, 'The Doctor's Dilemma' (Penguin, London, 1957)

'so old that it looks like new': Peter Maurin, 'The CP and the CM' in *Easy Essays* at http://www.catholicworker.org/roundtable/easyessays.cfm <#<strong>The C.P. And C.M.

'success, like happiness cannot be pursued; it must ensue...': Viktor E. Frankl, *Man's Search for Meaning* (Random House, London, 2004)

Year One

'All good men love an axe': John Stewart Collis, *The Worm Forgives the Plough* (Vintage, London, 2008)

'the abandoned places of Empire': The Rutba House (ed.), *School(s) for Conversion: 12 Marks of a New Monasticism* (Cascade Books, Eugene, Oregon, 2005)

'Words scatter, silence gathers together': Pierre Lacout, *God is Silence* (Quaker Books, London, 1993)

'Resentment is like taking poison and waiting for the other person to die': The origin of this quotation is a source of debate. See: http://www. fakebuddhaquotes.com/holding-onto-anger-is-like-drinking-poison/

Year Two

'Let him who cannot be alone beware of community...': Dietrich Bonhoeffer, *Life Together* (SCM Press, London, 1954) 'we have to love our neighbour because he is there . . .': G. K. Chesterton, *Heresy* (House of Stratus, Thirsk, 2001)

'Think I'll pack it in, and buy a pick-up . . .': Neil Young, 'Out on the Weekend', from *Harvest* (Reprise Records)

'to help a patient become his or her own mother and father': Irvin Yalom, *Love's Executioner* (Penguin, London, 2013)

'the wood has no single minute of eclipse throughout the year . . .': H. E. Bates, *Through the Woods* (Little Toller Books, Wimborne Minster, 2011)

'it's a grave temptation to want to help people': Christine D. Pohl, *Making Room* (Eerdmans, Cambridge, 1999)

'. . . money is like sex . . .': James Baldwin, 'The Black Boy Looks at the White Boy', in *Esquire*, 1961

'we have always been too crowded up . . .': Richard Francis, *Fruitlands* (Yale University Press, London, 2011)

'Eat thy bread with joy': Ecclesiastes, 9:7

'You become addicted to a number of . . . effects . . .': Marya Hornbacher, *Wasted* (Flamingo, London, 1999)

'many poets are not poets . . .': Thomas Merton, *Seeds of Contemplation* (Hollis and Carter, London, 1949)

'the relationship that heals': Irvin Yalom, *Love's Executioner* (Penguin, London, 2013)

'For young men who have graduated from privileged colleges . . .': Robert Bly, *Iron John* (Rider, London, 2001)

Year Three

'People may come to our communities because they want to serve the poor . . .': Jean Vanier, *From Brokenness to Community* (Paulist Press, Mahwah, New Jersey, 1992)

'to put moral chains on their own appetites': Edmund Burke, 'Letter to a Member of the National Assembly', in *The Writings and Speeches of Edmund Burke*, vol. 4 (Cosimo Classics, New York, 2008)

'a sort of refuge for escapees from the moral law': Wendell Berry, *The Art of the Commonplace* (Counterpoint, Berkeley, 2004)

'It should tell us something that in healthy societies . . .': Wendell Berry, *The Art of the Commonplace* (Counterpoint, Berkeley, 2004)

'We will only stay in community...': Jean Vanier, *From Brokenness to Community* (Paulist Press, Mahwah, New Jersey, 1992)

'can remain loyal to the community, for all its faults...': Robert Van de Weyer, *The Little Gidding Way* (Darton, Longman and Todd, London, 1988)

'What happens to us in the depths of the wood...': Hilary Mantel, 'Wicked Parents in Fairytales', in *Guardian*, 10 October 2009

'...looks least like social services.': Christine D. Pohl, *Making Room* (Eerdmans, Cambridge, 1999)

' you have really gone through a gate...': John Stewart Collis, *The Worm Forgives the Plough* (Vintage, London, 2008)

'limits are imposed upon haste by nature': Wendell Berry, *The Art of the Commonplace* (Counterpoint, Berkeley, 2004)

Year Four

'Men are free when they belong to a living, organic, believing community...': D. H. Lawrence, *Studies in Classic American Literature* (Penguin, London, 1990)

'love and need... work is play': Robert Frost, 'Two Tramps in Mud Time', in *Collected Poems* (Vintage Classics, London, 2013)

'If you are to do the work of a prophet...': Richard Foster, *A Celebration of Discipline* (Hodder and Stoughton, London, 2008)

'in observing the behaviour of the slimmer and the anorexic...': Sheila MacLeod, *Art of Starvation* (Virago, London, 1981)

'general sense of superiority...': Sheila MacLeod, *Art of Starvation* (Virago, London, 1981)

'find the shortest, simplest way...': Mark Shepard, *The Community of the Ark* (Simple Productions, Friday Harbor, Washington, 2011)

'The soil is the great connector of lives...': Wendell Berry, *The Unsettling of America* (California University Press, Oakland, 2001)

'The ultimate goal of ...': Masanobu Fukuoka, *The One-Straw Revolution* (The New York Review of Books, New York, 2009)

Year Five

'Human beings will be happier...': William Rodney Allen (ed.), *Conversations with Kurt Vonnegut* (University Press of Mississippi, Jackson, 1988) 'the vernacular economy': Ivan Illich, *Shadow Work* (Marion Boyars, London, 1981)

'. . . pigs and hay/ filled a church oozing manure mud/from the porch': Ted Hughes, 'Nicholas Ferrar', in *Lupercal* (Faber, London, 1985)

'small, homelike, quiet, supportive, protective and tolerant social environment': Mosher L. R., 'Soteria and Other Alternatives to Acute Psychiatric Hospitalization: A Personal and Professional View', in *The Journal of Mental and Nervous Disease* (March 1999)

'The problem was that you didn't always know . . .': Michael Herr, *Dispatches* (Pan Books, London, 1978)

'Real silence, real stillness, really holding one's tongue . . .' Dietrich Bonhoeffer, *Life Together* (SCM Press, London, 1954)

'I went to cover the war and the war covered me': Michael Herr, *Dispatches* (Pan Books, London, 1978)

'Hospitality becomes community as it creates a unity . . .': Henri J. M. Nouwen, *The Wounded Healer* (Darton, Longman and Todd, London, 1994)

'honey from the rock': Psalm 81

Acknowledgements

Francesca and I are deeply indebted to all the guests who have spent time at Windsor Hill Wood. For obvious reasons, I haven't thanked them by name below, but their immense contribution to and connection with our community has made it what it is.

Tim Snowdon, Kirsteen Heselton, Jonathan Herbert, Dan and Waf Green, and Ed and Claire Davis have all offered wise counsel over many years and we're extremely grateful to them and their families.

Vicki Steward, Veronica Read, Naomi Glass, Pip Bromley, Donna McDowell, Robert Shaw, Polly Hancock and Karl and Kaye Watts have all been robust pillars of this place at one time or another. Thank you.

I'm very grateful to Michael Deegan and to everyone at the Pilsdon Community; and to Hilfield Friary and Downside Abbey for their continuing encouragement.

Carol and Stewart Henderson have repeatedly revolutionized WHW through their generosity.

For lending us trailers, boars and land, and for giving us heart, time, tools, advice and everything else, immense gratitude goes to: Shaun Wolff, Andrew Towner, Mike May, Scott and Catherine Iley, Bob and Jane Jones, Morag of the Marsh, Irish Gerry, Angus and Anne MacDonald, Richard and Sheena Brook, Hazel Rumsey,

Ian Mole, Fred Houwen, Dom Tetley and Lucy Brown, Julie and Peter Johnson, Sue and Lewis Morgan, John and Maddy Fleming, John and Sallie Vallins, Ian Brooks, Melissa and Rosie Meek, James and Paula Wilson, Jan and Peter Longden, David Hase, Kaaren Wallace, Kate and Andrew Lewis, Susan Tanner, Maia and Justin Wildridge, Sally Bamber, Jamie and Katharine Turnbull, Richard and Anna Joyce, Mark and Amanda Pickthall, Peter MacFadyen, Dawn Porter, Tony Martin, Paul Frampton, Richard Fenwick and Hazlegrove School, Peter Fanshawe, Steve Wharton, Tom Allerton, Diana Hand, the Somerset Community Foundation, the Mendip Hills Fund, Seedbed, Give It Up, Margaret Kelly and the Wincanton Methodists, Mo McManus and Fare Share, Andy Norris and everyone at Somerset Skills and Learning.

Many experts have helped us over the years. Sincere thanks to Tim Gatfield at the Cherry Wood Project, Pat Vincent at Green Mantle, Simon Nash at the Somerset Wildlife Trust, Charles Couzens at Ecos Maclean, Rupert Furneaux at Land Logic, Dave, Matt and all the team at Right Price DIY, Jay Abrahams at Biologic Design, and to Gabriel Ralls at Envirostoves. Alan Heeks, Mike Tait, Ros Baldwin, Bruno Healy, Yvette Alt-Reuss and Sarah Stansfield have all offered wisdom and strength.

For moral support and muscle over the years, we're indebted to: Jon Long, Andy Street, Richard and Sheena Brook, Branden Heselton, Andrew Buchanan, John Peppard, Jeremy Charlesworth, Kate Pawsey, Toby Guise, Claire Goodman, Sue Rice, Wendi and Martin Davis, David Trevena and Penny Walford, Merlin, Stephen Stokes, Emily Pitts, Mandy McKenna, Steve McGlen, Sue and Stephen Rye, Andrew and Valerie Hart, Kate Banks, Mark and Emma Boakes, Virginia Membrey, Nick and Barbie White, Paolo and Jeanne Mortarotti, David Bagott, Suzi Herbert,

Andrea Lewis and Russell Hartley, Emma and James Kendall, David and Pat Williamson, Vaughan and Rosalind Ives, Ollie Hibbert, Daniela Calebich, Paul and Maggie Massey, Lester Bennett, Rose and Ted Longman, Louise and Julian Tucker, Simon and Gibril Stanley, Gary and Ann Ralls, Robin Howell, Wayne Frapple, Lan and James Brown, Ian Lofthouse, Brid and James Fitzpatrick, Mervyn Lickfold, Christopher Somerville, Rupert and Polly Davis, Lo Zivo, Damion Greef, Eddie Wills, Julian Baggini and Antonia Macaro, Christopher Wakling, James McConnachie, Nell Lyshon, Richard Beecham and Ian Emerson, Lesley Chambers, Tom Stearn, Sukey Fenwick and Ryan Craig, Rob and Caroline Riley, Richard and Laura Pendlebury, and Gill and Jeremy Elston.

My generous brothers, and their wives, have always been there when we've needed them. Cheers to Paul, Marija, David and Vandana.

I'm very grateful to various editors who have, in publishing my work, kept this project afloat: to Andrew Holgate, John Mulholland, Marina Benjamin, Clare Margetson, Malik Meer, Clare Longrigg and Jonathan Shainin.

I'm indebted to Tim Lewis for originally commissioning my column in the *Observer*, and to Jon Riley at Quercus for having the courage to commission this book. I've benefited greatly from the advice of Josh Ireland, and from the professionalism of Rose Tomaszewska and Richard Arcus. Georgina Capel and her crew at Capel & Land have, as always, been exceptional, and Walter Donohue continues to be an amazing mentor.

Francesca's resolute open-heartedness has infused Windsor Hill Wood and, I hope, this book; and our children – Benedetta, Emma and Leonardo – have shared their home with graciousness and grit. I admire them for it.

Any foolishness or errors are, obviously, entirely mine.